I0439565

Nature Has the Cure

The First 100 Columns

Marie Lasater

Nature Has The Cure

ISBN: 1497526841
ISBN-13: 978-1497526846

DEDICATION

This book is dedicated to all the folks at the Missouri Native Plant Society, the patients who have taught me so much over the decades, and my grand-daughter Riley, who continues to give me inspiration.

Nature Has The Cure

CONTENTS

Nature Has The Cure

ACKNOWLEDGMENTS

I would like to acknowledge my editor at The Salem News for not only being the best boss ever, but allowing me latitude in the scope of my writing when this work was in column form.

I would also like to acknowledge the readers, who sent emails, asked great questions, and have given me terrific feedback.

Nature Has The Cure

1 INTRODUCTION

January 3, 2013

Welcome to a new weekly feature!

As a nursing student in the 1970's, I was intrigued that almost all of the medicines I studied came from plants – morphine from poppies, digitalis from foxglove, aspirin from the bark of a willow tree, to name a few.

It seemed to me that the medications with the most unusual side effects were those developed in the pharmaceutical laboratory. Morphine, for example, was superior for pain to the synthetic meperidine – that also caused seizures. Darvon is another synthetic pain medication. First marketed in 1957, Darvon has proven addicting, ineffective for pain, and causes cardiac complications. It has only been pulled from the market within the past year.

In 1989, I was in the health food store when I overheard a conversation. A customer was begging the clerk to check the back of store to see if there was an overlooked box of tryptophan. You see, tryptophan had been pulled from the shelves.

Hundreds of thousands of people had been taking Tryptophan for anxiety and depression – now it was not available. Why? There was reportedly one bad batch that was genetically engineered, from a factory in Japan. Because of this one incident, at one factory, the ONLY one that genetically engineered the product, it has disappeared forever. But something else happened that same year. Prozac came on to the US market. Of course, it was marketed for anxiety and depression, at a much higher cost, both financially and medically, than the effective, safe Tryptophan. And now it had no competitor.

As much as possible, this column is written for the person who wants to grow or gather their own natural cures. I am not a pharmacist, nor a doctor, and I am not licensed to diagnose or prescribe medicine. My articles reflect the knowledge I have gleaned over a nursing career spanning three decades. And of course, you should always check with your physician before taking any natural remedy.

ASPIRIN IN ITS PUREST FORM

Aspirin is one of the best drugs on the planet. It is an excellent analgesic, prevents strokes and heart attacks and reduces fever. The pharmaceutical industry would love to replace this practically free medication. I wouldn't be surprised if it were taken off the market in a similar manner to tryptophan. A number of laboratory produced, extremely expensive aspirin replacements are already on the market, and more are being developed.

If aspirin does disappear from the shelves, you need look no further than your backyard for a replacement. In 400 BC, Hippocrates, the Father of Modern Medicine, prescribed the first form of aspirin to for pain and fever. The source? The bark of the willow tree. The bark of white willow contains salacin, the active ingredient in salicylic acid (aspirin.) Purple and crack willow also contain salacin. Many sources say willow bark is actually more effective than aspirin in reducing pain and inflammation, but not fever, at a lower dose than aspirin. It takes somewhat longer to work, but the effects are longer lasting.

To make aspirin tea, simmer one to two teaspoons of dry bark in 8 ounces of water. You can drink this tea every 4 – 6 hours.

Caution: Aspirin can cause gastric irritation, ulcers and bleeding. For patients on Methotrexate or Dilantin, willow can increase blood levels of these drugs, causing toxicity.

Acetaminophen (Tylenol) was first marketed in the 1950's, with the purported benefit of not causing the gastric upset and bleeding tendencies caused by aspirin. Acetaminophen, however, is synthetic, and liver toxicity is a real concern with the use of this drug. 26,000 people are hospitalized, and 458 die each year from Tylenol overdose. Death is not immediate, but a few weeks later due to liver toxicity.

2 SWEET GUM TREE: THE NATIVE AMERICAN FLU MEDICINE

January 10, 2013

Remember all those worries about the shortage of Tamiflu with the outbreak of the bird flu? Besides being very expensive, and prescription only, the anti-viral drug Tamiflu is prone to shortages. Tamiflu works by stopping the replication of flu viruses.

There is good news though! The active ingredient in Tamiflu is shikimic acid – found in the seeds of the fruit on the sweet gum tree in the good ol' USA. Sweet Gum, a member of the witch hazel family, is plentiful here in Missouri. In fact, Saint James is known as the "Sweet Gum Capitol of Missouri" because of its many streets lined with the popular tree. Readers with the Sweet Gum tree on their property can attest to the tree's natural resistance to both insects and disease.

At first it was thought shikimic acid was only found in star anise fruit, a product of China. The shikimic acid in the Sweet Gum tree is present in nearly all parts of the tree, but is mostly found in the fruit seeds found in the mature tree. 4000 grams of sweet gum seeds are enough for 14 packages of Tamiflu – that is a lot of seed, but one tree can have up to a thousand seed pods. Native Americans recognized the benefits early on, and made tea from both the seeds and the bark of the tree.

Medicinal use of sweet gum dates back to 1651, and was used by early settlers and natives alike to treat colds and cure skin eruptions. Native Americans used to chew the hardened resin from the bark of Sweet Gum trees obtained by peeling the bark and scraping off the resin-like solid. This gum was used medicinally as well as for chewing gum. They also made various teas and medicines to treat dysentery and diarrhea from the bark and roots of sweet gum. Its effectiveness in healing wounds is well documented. The role of the Sweet Gum tree in treating hypertension is currently under investigation.

In addition to its medicinal properties, Sweet Gum is wildlife friendly, with birds and small rodents such as squirrels and chipmunks thriving on the seeds, so think twice before cutting down that messy tree!

3 TEA TREE OIL

January 17, 2013

Tea Tree Oil is an essential in my natural medicine cabinet. It is an antibacterial, antiviral, and antifungal. It clears up fungal infections on toenails in record time, and no matter how bad the infection was, you will end up with pristine nails.

When dabbed on a beginning fever blister, it will stop progression to a full lesion. When applied to a full lesion, it helps it to heal 50% faster.

Bad case of poison ivy? Tea Tree oil will dry it out, soothe the discomfort and hasten healing. It also reduces inflammation of many skin conditions, including eczema. It even works to decrease the pain of shingles, and promotes healing of the lesions.

Swabbing your external ear canal or the gum line with a drop of tea tree oil on a Q-tip will give instant relief to an earache or toothache. Dabbed on an insect bite or sting, it stops the pain and eliminates swelling.

For fungal infections of the nails, apply the oil on the nail and cuticle. Results are nearly instantaneous, as any new nail growth will not be affected by the fungus. Compare that with pharmaceutical preparations that can take months to work (and are a lot more expensive!)

Tea Tree Oil is also an outstanding treatment for athlete's foot. Dab it on the affected areas, or for worst cases, put one tablespoon in 2 quarts of warm water and soak feet for 10 minutes daily. Not just a temporary fix, several studies have confirmed that Tea Tree Oil actually eradicates the fungus causing athlete's foot. In addition, it has a nice, antiseptic smell, and also works as a mild anesthetic.

I used tea tree oil on a horse that had "warty ears." I applied tea tree oil directly to the warts, and they were gone within one week and never came back!

Other than swabbing the oil in small amounts in the ear canal or at the base of a sore tooth, never use tea tree oil internally.

So where to get Tea Tree Oil? It is readily purchased online for under $10 for half an ounce, a quantity that will last a LONG time. It is also found at most pharmacies. It only comes from a tree that grows in Australia, so unfortunately, you can't find it in your yard.

4 WHY I HATE STATINS

January 24, 2013

First of all, what is a "statin?" Answer: a drug that lowers cholesterol. There are several on the market, atorvastatin, simvastatin, and lovastatin are a few. They work in two ways, by blocking a substance your body needs to make cholesterol, and by causing your body to reabsorb cholesterol. Your body makes two kinds of cholesterol, LDL (the bad kind), and HDL (the good kind.) High LDL levels can lead to a build-up of plaque in your arteries, while HDL helps to prevent a build-up.

Side effects, serious ones, often occur. I have seen patients who actually died due to liver failure after taking statin medication. The first sign of toxicity are muscle aches, often in the leg muscles, and patients taking these drugs should have their liver enzymes tested every six months.

Rhabomyolysis is severe muscle damage caused by statins – some studies show that taking co-enzyme Q10 along with statin has a protective effect against the breakdown of muscle fibers that results in the release of muscle fiber contents into the bloodstream.

Do they work? It depends on how that is defined. They do, indeed, lower your serum cholesterol. On the other hand, a huge study in Cambridge, England with 65,000 subjects showed no decrease in the death rate in patients on statins from heart disease or other ailments.

There are many natural methods for lowering your cholesterol. 2 tablespoons of apple cider vinegar daily (divided doses) has shown remarkable results in many patients. This recipe also supports weight loss.

Foods with soluble fiber, such as oatmeal, decrease the absorption of cholesterol into your body. 5 to 10 grams of soluble fiber daily is recommended, and 1 ½ cups of oatmeal daily will meet that goal by providing 6 grams. I once had a stroke patient who had some swallowing difficulties, and he was eating oatmeal 3 times a day. His next cholesterol panel showed a dramatic decrease in both total and LDL cholesterol.

Red yeast rice is made by fermenting rice with red yeast and effectively lowers cholesterol. Once again, a natural remedy was pulled of the market because there was a pharmaceutical that mimicked it. In 2001, Red yeast rice was withdrawn by the FDA as it was too similar in structure to the prescription medication lovastatin. The nutritional supplement is still available on the internet, as it is only illegal in the US. Because it is structurally equivalent to lovastatin, it can cause all of the side effects seen with the prescription medication.

The results of several studies suggest fenugreek seeds may help lower cholesterol. In fact, fenugreek lowers both blood sugar and cholesterol. A member of the pea family, its seeds have been used medicinally for thousands of years. Put 2 teaspoons of Fenugreek seeds and one teaspoon of honey in one glass for water for a healthy drink. It is native to India, but seeds can be purchased from most seed companies, and will flourish in your home garden.

If you are seeking to try a natural cure to lower your cholesterol, please discuss this with your doctor. Many natural medications have undesirable interactions with pharmaceuticals, and it is very important that your health care provider has a full list, both prescribed and otherwise, of the medications and natural cures you are taking.

5 HIPPOCRATES MEDICINE CABINET: OIL OF OREGANO

January 31, 2013

This time of year everyone knows someone, often whole families, suffering with lingering upper respiratory symptoms like cough, sore throat, headache, sneezing and runny nose. Luckily, there is a safe, organic treatment that can either prevent the onset of symptoms, or greatly shorten the course of the disease. That help comes from the Oregano plant, in the form of Oil of Oregano.

I take Oil of Oregano at the first sign of sneezing, cough or a tickle in my throat. If I have been around someone with obvious upper respiratory symptoms, I will also take a preventative dose, and haven't been sick for years. Recently my horseshoer was working on my horse, and had been battling an upper respiratory infection for weeks. It is safe to say he was miserable! I gave him three drops of Oil of Oregano in a glass of water, and promised him he would feel better in a couple of hours, and much better in the morning. He gave me a dubious look, but drank the oregano. Later that evening he posted on Facebook that he thought I was crazy, but he felt better for the first time in weeks! He and his wife now keep Oil of Oregano in their medicine cabinet.

Not just any oregano will do. Most of us have *Origanum Marjoram* in our garden, while medicinal Oil of Oregano is derived from *Origanum Vulgare,* native to the Mediterranean, and a member of the mint family. The key compounds found in Origanum Vulgare are carvacrol and thymol. Carvacrol is a natural phenol that inhibits the growth of several bacterial strains. Thymol is an active ingredient in many mouthwashes and is a powerful fungicide. It has also been found to decrease bacterial resistance to antibiotics, working together with the antibiotic to make them more effective.

Oil of Oregano can be purchased in any health food store, or online. One preparation called "P-3" is particularly strong. If I have symptoms of a cold, I put 3 drops under my tongue, once or twice a day. This is strong stuff, and if you can't tolerate it, just put 3 drops in a small glass of water. You can also purchase the product in gelatin capsules, making it a little bit easier to ingest. Regardless, you will probably smell like an Italian dinner for a little while!

In 2005, the US Federal Trade commission brought legal action against a firm that promoted the beneficial effects of Oil of Oregano, claiming that "no representation as to any health benefit could be made without competent and reliable scientific evidence."

I've done some research of my own, and Pubmed.gov, the US National Library of Medicine database, lists 175 peer-reviewed publications that attest to the efficacy of Origanum Vulgare against a variety of diseases, including fungal, viral, bacterial, parasitic and even cancer.

Intrigued by low incidence of colon cancer in the Mediterranean diet, (which is heavily laced with oregano), researchers further studied the effect of *origanum vulgare* on colon adenocarcinoma cells and found evidence that the whole extract (not a specific component), selectively kills adenocarcinoma cells in the colon, sparing the normal tissue. Because of its effect on gram negative bacteria like e-coli, it has also been used as a treatment for food poisoning.

There are some contraindications to the use of concentrated Oil of Oregano. It can decrease the body's ability to absorb iron, so if you take it over time, an iron supplement is recommended. Pregnant women should NOT take Oil of Oregano as some animal studies have shown adverse effects on embryo development. Oil of Oregano should not been taken on a daily basis – it is metabolized in the liver, and taking too much can cause the liver to be overloaded. I advocate a "less is more" policy with this herbal preparation.

Oil of Oregano has strong active ingredients. Like other herbal medications, you should discuss its use with your health care provider.

6 YOUR OWN HERBAL APOTHECARY

February 7, 2013

In this week's column, I want to go over some basic tips on preparing your own medications from native plants. Rule number one is save all of your seeds! True, they may be hybrids, and won't grow, but you would be amazed how many heirloom seeds can be in the mix, even from produce bought at the supermarket. I have a motto "No seed left behind!" Testing my own policy, I planted the pits from 4 avocados I bought at Kroger. Three of them did nothing, but magically, the fourth pit took off growing like wildfire, and is now a beautiful 4 ½ foot tall, beautiful plant.

Likewise, I save my tomato, green pepper, apple, persimmon, soybean, and every other seed I can get my hands on. I have tomato seeds whose DNA goes back to the 1930's – and every year I get beautiful tomatoes, packed with those wonderful seeds that ensure that variety will live on for generations to come. Most plants you buy are labelled 'Heirloom," if indeed they are. Any cross-species are generally hybrids, guaranteeing that the seeds are sterile. Be sure to read the labels carefully when buying plants.

Even the smallest yard can yield bountiful ingredients for your herbal apothecary. Parsley is used in many preparations, and after you yield enough for pharmaceutical purposes, break off the parsley stems, and allow the leaves to dry on paper towels on the kitchen counter. Save the dried leaves in an empty spice bottle, and you will have delicious and nutritious fresh dried parsley on hand for cooking. Later in the season, when the parsley plant has turned brown, break the stalks and put them in a paper bag. Shake the bag, and the parsley seeds will fall to the bottom of the sack, ready to plant next year, or to barter with a friend.

Cilantro is as generous as parsley. After the cilantro is harvested, and the plant goes to seed, it is now called coriander. Harvest your coriander seeds in the same way as parsley. The ground seeds have medicinal uses (that will be discussed in a later column), and are also a key ingredient in chili powder and taco seasoning. Just put the seeds in your pepper grinder, and grind them when ready to use.

Other common Missouri garden plants that can be used in herbal preparations include basil, cayenne pepper, dill, fennel, garlic, mint, oregano (origanum vulgare variety!), rosemary, sage, and thyme,

When you prepare your dried herbs for medicinal uses, you can process them as tea ingredients, tinctures, infused oils or salves. I just lay my herbs on paper towels in a warm place in the kitchen to dry. If you are lucky enough to have a food dehydrator, that works great, and is much more efficient. In the summer, placing the plants on a screen in the direct sun is also an effective method. It is important to use only the best leaves for drying,

To make a concentrated tincture from dry herbs, you want to pick your plant when it is at its freshest, in order to capture the most active ingredients. You can put drops of tinctures under your tongue for quick absorption, or put them in a glass or water or tea to dilute them. Chop the herb or plant into small pieces, and place in a small jar, filling it only one third. Pour vinegar over your herbs, making sure there is at least 1" of liquid on top. Let the tincture sit for at least two weeks. Strain the tincture and store it in amber bottles.

For infused oils, chop into small pieces the part of the plant you are using. Fill a clean, dry glass jar with chopped pieces, and cover with olive oil. Use a butter knife to release any air bubbles. Cover the jar tightly. Put it in a warm space, and place a rag under the jar, as some of the oil may seep out. Let it sit for at least a month, shaking daily. Infused oils are used for wounds, bites, dry skin, massage oils for sore joints and as an ingredient in salves.

To make a salve, warm one cup of your infused oil over a low heat. Add 4 tablespoons of grated beeswax, and let it slowly melt. Dip a spoon in the mixture, and blow on it until it is cool, to check the texture. If too hard, add more oil, and if too soft, add more beeswax. When it reaches the right consistency, quickly pour it into clean, dry containers.

7 BLACK WALNUTS – SUPER FOOD IN YOUR BACKYARD!

February 14, 2013

Here in the Ozarks, we are blessed with a virtual smorgasbord of edible plants, and one of the most popular is the Black Walnut. 65% of the nation's annual wild walnut harvest comes from Missouri, with over a million dollars each year paid for the nuts.

Black Walnuts are high in protein and unsaturated fat (the healthy kind.) High in Omega-3 fatty acids, Tufts University researchers demonstrated that just one ounce of walnut meat contains 2.6 gram of fatty acids, more than is found in four ounces of mackerel. In 1994, the American Journal of Clinical Nutrition published a study that concluded those whose diets included nuts, either walnuts or almonds, were able to lower their LDL cholesterol by 9 to 10%.

Having trouble getting a good night's sleep? Eat a handful of Black Walnuts. Walnuts contain substances that influence the brain's seratonin levels, a chemical used to treat depression. Seratonin metabolizes into bio-available melatonin, which helps you fall asleep and stay asleep. Melatonin is produced from serotonin by the pineal gland, but natural production decreases as we age. Our native Black walnuts are a much richer source of serotonin-enhancing ingredients than English walnuts.

Worried about gaining weight? Several studies have shown that black walnuts actually work to prevent weight gain, and are a chief ingredient in the well-known Mediterranean diet. Walnuts are also a good dietary source of alpha-linoleic acid, (necessary for bone and heart health), magnesium, potassium, iron, copper, folate, and a wide range of B-complex vitamins. No wonder walnuts are often considered a super food!

Black walnut hulls contain Juglone, a chemical with antifungal, antiviral, antiparasitic and antibacterial properties. Black walnut hull extract, prepared from green hulls, can be used in a skin wash to treat ringworm and yeast infections of the skin. The extract was used internally for centuries by the Cherokee Indians to expel tapeworms and other intestinal parasites. Considered one of the most effective and safest natural worming methods, juglone can still be toxic, and should never be ingested long-term or by pregnant women.

Native Americans also chewed the inner bark of the Black Walnut tree to ease toothache pain. Black walnut hull tincture can strengthen and restore tooth enamel. Powderized black walnut shell is used as an abrasive in home-made toothpaste to remove plaque.

If you have walnut trees on your place, you likely have a ready supply of usable walnuts lying on the ground, even in February. A few tips on preparing Black Walnuts: Husk the nut prior to storage - I wear gloves and make a circumferential slit in the hull, sliding the nut out. I then wash the nut and place on a dry cloth to dry. Darker than usual nuts indicate insect damage, and you can assess the quality of the nut by dropping them in a clean bucket of water. Good nuts sink, and those that are too dry or have insects will float. Freeze the air-dried nuts in a Ziploc plastic bag – when it is time to crack the nut, the nutmeat will slide out easily.

8 THE BENEFITS OF GINGER

February 28, 2013

I spent my early years in Michigan, home to Vernor's Ginger Ale. For most folks in Michigan in the 1950's, Ginger Ale was practically a religion. My mother, also a Registered Nurse, treated just about every physical complaint with a bottle of ginger ale. I remember it having an almost instant effect on those childhood ailments. The active ingredient in Ginger Ale comes from the root of the perennial herb, *Zingiber officinale.* Ginger comes from the same plant family as Turmeric and Cardamom.

Ginger root has been around a long time, used in medicine for over 2000 years. In 2013, its use is mainly limited to upset stomach and intestinal problems. Short-term use safely helps alleviate nausea and vomiting experienced with pregnancy, and I know several patients undergoing chemotherapy who sip ginger ale during and after their treatment to ease the associated nausea. Ginger also eases car-sickness and motion-sickness in both children and adults.

Other less known uses of ginger include anti-inflammatory effects. A compound in the root called gingerol has been shown to decrease inflammation, with healing effects on rheumatoid arthritis, and other inflammatory diseases.Ginger root may help prevent heart disease by lowering LDL cholesterol and keeping blood platelets from sticking together, according to the University of Maryland Medical Center.

In an exciting development for Type II diabetics, researchers at the University of Sydney published a study last November using data from several sources and clinical trials that demonstrated the anti-hyperglycemic effect of ginger, stating "The mechanisms underlying these actions are associated with insulin release and action, and improved carbohydrate and lipid metabolism."

Although there are no definitive studies on the use of ginger in treating cancer per se, the medical literature is replete with pharmaceutical studies evaluating the use of gingerol in chemotherapeutic agents, with one stated benefit being fewer side effects. In February, 2011, researchers at Georgia State University in Atlanta published a study entitled "Benefits of Whole Ginger Extract in Prostate Cancer." They found that ginger extract significantly reduced prostate cancer cells, with no toxicity to the normal, surrounding cells.

So how to make use of this great herb that possesses virtually no side effects? Although not a native plant, you can easily grow ginger in Missouri. First, purchase a nice bulb of fresh ginger. Look for a fresh, moist root with growth buds (they look like the eyes on a potato.) Each of those growth buds can be cut off to start a ginger plant. You can also plant the whole root, with the growing buds facing up. Ginger is a tropical plant, and likes warm, moist soil. If planting outdoors, make sure it is after the frost, and don't plant in the direct sun, making sure the plant gets plenty of water. A 14-inch diameter pot can easily support 3 growth buds if growing indoors. Ginger grows to about 2 or 3 feet in height with beautiful green leaves. At the end of summer when the leaves begin to turn brown, cut the water back to force rhizomes. When the leaves die, your ginger is ready to harvest. The entire process takes about 8 – 10 months. You can replant the growth buds, after saving the bulk of the root.

After harvesting the root, it can be processed in two ways: use fresh ginger to make your own ginger ale, and dry and process a portion of the root for use in cooking.

To save ginger spice for later use in recipes, such as ginger dressing or as an ingredient in stir-fry, first peel and slice the root. Sun dry the pieces, or use your dehydrator. You can then hand chop the pieces and store them in a clean, reused spice bottle. I run my dried ginger through my coffee grinder, providing me with nice small flakes. Your fresh dried ginger will last for years on the shelf, and it only takes a fraction of the amount needed for store-bought ginger in your recipes.

You can also easily make your own Ginger Ale! I recently bought of case of Vernor's Ginger Ale for old times' sake. Nowhere on the ingredients did I see "ginger" listed. What I did see was high-fructose corn syrup (HFCS). For those that don't already know, HFCS has no nutritional value, and is essentially a fattening agent. Time to home brew!

Ginger Ale recipe (makes two 2 quart bottles)

Ingredients

- 3 Oz. Chopped fresh ginger root
- 6 3/4 cup sugar
- 4 ½ quarts water
- 1/4 teaspoon yeast (bread yeast will work, but ale yeast is better)
- 3 Tbs orange juice
- 3 Tbs.lemon juice

Directions

Place the ginger, sugar, and juices and 1 ½ quart of the water into a 2-quart pot and simmer over medium high heat until sugar is dissolved (at least 30 minutes), stirring frequently. Remove from the heat, cover and allow to steep for 1 hour.

Pour the syrup through a kitchen strainer, taking care to extract all the juice from the mixture. Mix the brew with the remaining 3 quarts of water. Cool to at least room temperature, placing in the refrigerator if necessary.

Using a funnel, pour the syrup into clean 2-liter plastic bottles, adding 1/8 tsp yeast to each bottle. Place the cap on the bottle, gently shake to combine and leave the bottle at room temperature for 48 hours. You can squeeze the bottle to check carbonation progress. When the bottle is hard to squeeze, carbonation is complete, and it is time to refrigerate the ginger ale, which will keep up to 2 weeks. You may have to uncap the bottle to let some carbonation escape.

If you want to skip the fermentation process, delete the yeast, and substitute 2 quarts of club soda when adding water to the prepared syrup. The ginger ale can then be promptly refrigerated.

9 VITAMIN D – 20 MINUTES TO MAKE YOUR OWN SUNSHINE VITAMIN

March 7, 2013

When my son was born, I was living and working at a hospital in Panama, Central America. With a husband on long deployments, and working 12 hour shifts in the Intensive Care Unit, I employed a Panamanian woman as a caregiver for my infant son. Every day she would put him in his stroller, and take him to the park for his "Vitamin D." Since virtually every other nanny in the country did the same thing, I thought it was a plot to get out of the house. I was wrong. Sunlight exposure is a primary source of Vitamin D in Latin American countries, and many other regions of the world. Today researchers are finding that neither adults nor children receive adequate Vitamin D from their diets or supplements.

Besides bone diseases like osteoporosis and rickets, Vitamin D deficiency is linked to diabetes, heart disease and depression. I have seen firsthand the effect of Vitamin D from sunshine on mood and overall health while working with critically ill patients. One woman in particular comes to mind. On life support in the ICU, she was not expected to live more than a few days, but desperately wanted to see her dog. I couldn't figure out a way to sneak the dog in, so the respiratory therapist and I placed her on a portable respirator, and wheeled her bed outside the hospital, into the sunshine, where she was reunited with her pet. To everyone's surprise, the next day she was breathing well enough to remove the respirator, and was discharged home the following week. Of course, "pet therapy" played a role, but I've always made it a point since that time to get patients outdoors whenever possible.

Vitamin D may protect from the common cold. In the winter, when we get our lowest sunlight exposure, is when we are most susceptible to colds and flu. A recent study in the Archives of Internal Medicine that included 19,000 people showed the link between lack of sunlight exposure and respiratory tract infections.

Obesity is strongly linked with low vitamin D levels, with one recent study stating "Vitamin D Deficiency Is the Cause of Obesity." The theory is that low Vitamin D levels create metabolic syndrome, which triggers your body to store fat.

Older adults are at higher risk of Vitamin D deficiency, as they tend to spend more time indoors, while their requirements are increasing. Vitamin D deficiency is a large risk factor in osteoporosis, and its most serious complication, a hip fracture. Most health care providers routinely check vitamin D levels in older adults, and prescribe supplements when needed.

Vitamin D is not naturally present in most foods, with the flesh of fatty fish and fish liver oil being the best sources. The good news is that you can produce your own by going out into the sunlight. When the ultraviolet rays hit your skin, it triggers the production of Vitamin D. Vitamin D from sun exposure, food or supplements is not available to the body until it undergoes transformation in the liver and kidneys. Vitamin D is a fat-soluble vitamin, which means you CAN get too much. (The other fat-soluble vitamins are A, E and K.) There have been reports of young women with severe Vitamin D toxicity due to overuse of tanning beds, for example.

A lot of factors affect the amount of ultraviolet exposure needed to create the optimal amount of Vitamin D. Sun exposure through glass does not trigger Vitamin D, and sunscreens with SPF greater than 8 also block its synthesis, as does pollution. Some Vitamin D researchers suggest 5-30 minutes of sun exposure between 10 am and 3 pm at least twice weekly to the face, arms, legs or back to allow adequate vitamin D synthesis. Moderate use of commercial tanning beds is also effective. On the other hand, those who avoid the sun should include good dietary sources of Vitamin D in their diet, or take supplements to get their recommended intake.

In summary, sunlight is necessary for health, even 5 minutes twice weekly has beneficial effects. It is always wise to shield cancer-prone areas such as the face, neck and forearms.

10 TURMERIC – A SPICY APPROACH TO YOUR HEALTH

March 14, 2013

Little known Turmeric possibly has more health benefits than any other herb. Used for over 2500 years mainly for its anti-inflammatory properties, it is now known to have over twenty uses. Turmeric is a perennial plant in the ginger family that comes from the rhizomes (underground stems) of the plant Curcuma longa.

Curcumin, the active ingredient in Turmeric, has protective effects on the liver, and also inhibits the cox-II enzyme (providing pain relief), while maintaining cox-1 enzymes (protecting the stomach), making it superior in the treatment of many forms of arthritis and fibromyalgia.

It is also a powerful anti-oxidant, and has shown useful effects in several cancers, especially breast and prostate, and may prevent metastases in many different kinds of cancer. Although there is some concern about the bio-availability of turmeric due its low solubility and rapid metabolism in the body, the medical literature is full of studies showing its beneficial effects. In a study from Emory University released earlier this month, researchers Park et al found "Curcumin fulfills the characteristics for an ideal chemopreventive agent with its low toxicity, affordability, and easy accessibility." Other studies have shown that in addition to preventing cancer, Turmeric can also cause cancer cells to die.

With several affected family members, I've incorporated turmeric into my daily diet because of its promise in the prevention of Alzheimer's Disease. The way it works is by preventing amyloid buildup. Amyloid is a type of protein plaque found in the brains of Alzheimer's patients.

Other health benefits of Turmeric range from the treatment of psoriasis and other skin conditions to slowing the progression of Multiple Sclerosis. It normalizes blood sugar levels in patients with Type 2 diabetes by blocking key enzymes associated with the disease.

Turmeric also works well in animals with joint problems, such as dogs and horses, and is credited with helping the famous racehorse Seabiscuit in his recovery. In the case of Seabiscuit, turmeric was used in a poultice applied to his affected leg. A turmeric poultice also works as a drawing salve.

At normal dosages, turmeric is very safe. Some people are allergic, usually resulting in a skin rash. There have been some non-medical reports of increased gall stones in patients taking turmeric, and pregnant women should always use caution during their pregnancy.

How much to take? 250 to 500 mg. daily is recommended. ¼ teaspoon a day of dry powder provides about 500 mg. It can also be purchased in 250 mg – 500 mg capsules, and is very inexpensive in bulk. Turmeric is used in virtually all mustard condiments, giving them the yellow color, and boosting the flavor.

I make a delicious honey mustard dressing with turmeric, coarse grain mustard, honey and vinegar. For an Asian taste, leave out the honey and vinegar, adding sesame oil and ginger. Not just for salads, this makes a great pretzel dipping sauce for a healthy, low calorie afternoon snack.

11 HAWTHORN – MISSOURI'S OWN HEART MEDICINE

March 21, 2013

"And every shepherd tells his tale under the hawthorn in the dale."
John Milton (1608-1674)

I continue to be astounded at the wealth of medicinal plants in Missouri. In 1923, the white Hawthorn blossom was named the Missouri State Flower by then Governor Arthur M. Hyde. The legislation does not name a specific variety of the plant, and Missouri has over 100 varieties of hawthorn, also known as the Crataegus species. Excellent honey plants, they are heavily cross-pollinated by bees. Hawthorn is a woody plant that can grow to 20 feet in height, and is found throughout Missouri in low, wet woods and wooded valleys. In late September or early October, the tree produces red, apple-shaped fruits that can be used to make jams and jellies.

Hawthorn has a long history of use in Europe and China for food, and in traditional medicine. Widely used for fences in England, many varieties have been used in landscaping. Wild hawthorn berries are commonly called "haws," derived from the root word for hedge. Natural health products containing hawthorn have been used in North America since the 1800's for the treatment of heart problems such as hypertension, angina, arrhythmia, and congestive heart failure. Traditionally, Native American tribes used hawthorn to treat gastrointestinal ailments and heart problems, and consumed the fruit as food.

I have a friend in England, and hawthorn jelly is very popular there. Its cranberry color makes it a popular Christmas gift. Keeping in mind that the English palate is somewhat different than our own, Missourians may want to try adding haws to their blackberry jam and jelly recipes for a richer flavor and added nutrition.

Hawthorn extract has been used for cardiovascular diseases for centuries in several countries. Most homeopathic medications dedicated to lowering blood pressure contain hawthorn. Recent trials have demonstrated its efficacy for the treatment of heart failure, and the results of several small trials suggest it may lower blood pressure. It appears to work by strengthening and slowing the heart, an effect similar to digitalis, and should not be taken in addition to digitalis due to the additive effect in the body, resulting in dangerously low blood pressure.

Not just for your heart, there are many other medicinal uses of hawthorn currently being investigated, including stimulated hair growth, treatment of anxiety, and decreasing airway inflammation in asthma.

It usually takes 6 weeks to achieve the benefit of hawthorn supplementation. Dosage recommendations cite 1 teaspoon of hawthorn syrup daily (see recipe). As hawthorn is an active cardiac medication, you should discuss its use with your health care provider prior to use.

Hawthorn Syrup

Boil 1 cup of ripe hawthorn berries in 3 cups of water for 2 minutes, then simmer for an additional 5 minutes. Remove from heat, and thoroughly mash the berries in the water. Strain the liquid into a bowl, adding one cup of honey. Mix well, then pour the syrup into a clean, recycled amber bottle. Store in the refrigerator.

12 DANDELIONS – ONE MAN'S WEED, ANOTHER MAN'S MEDICINE

March 28, 2013

When I grew up, dandelions *(Taraxacum officinale)* were the enemy. My father had a perfect yard, and I was taxed with digging up all the pretty yellow plants, being sure to get the roots. While many, if not most, people would be happy if they never saw another dandelion, the plants are actually valuable herbs useful as both medicine and food.

As a source of nutrition, dandelion is almost a perfect food. All parts of the dandelion are routinely consumed as food in several areas of the world. In addition to providing essential minerals like iron, potassium and zinc, the plant is also rich in Vitamins A, B, C and D.

In Korean herbal medicine dandelion has been used to improve energy levels and health. While there are no published human studies, in 2012 researchers looked at the anti-fatigue and immune-enhancing effects on dandelion on mice. In forced-swimming test, mice fed dandelion could swim longer, and had stronger immune systems.

Throughout history, dandelion roots and leaves have been used to treat liver problems. A natural diuretic, Native Americans boiled dandelion leaves, making a tonic to treat kidney disease, swelling, skin problems, heartburn, and upset stomach.

For centuries, dandelion has been used in traditional Chinese medicine to treat stomach problems, appendicitis, and breast inflammation. In Europe, it was used in remedies for fever, boils, eye problems, diabetes, and diarrhea.

All parts of the Dandelion are useful. The leaves act as a diuretic, stimulate the appetite and help digestion. The leaves also add nutrition and flavor to salads, sandwiches, and teas.

The Dandelion flower has antioxidant properties, and a few petals sprinkled on a salad add both color and flavor. The flowers have long been used to make dandelion wine.

Many herbalists recommend dandelion root to detoxify the liver and gallbladder. The roots are used in some coffee substitutes, with an anti-fatigue effect similar to that of caffeine.

Some preliminary animal studies also suggest that dandelion may help normalize blood sugar levels and lower total cholesterol and triglycerides while raising HDL, "good," cholesterol in diabetic mice. Dandelions are in a group of anti-diabetic plants that inhibit alpha glucosidase. Alpha glucosidase breaks down starches into glucose, causing blood sugar levels to rise, so blocking the enzyme is a good thing for Type 2 diabetics.

Always talk with your health care provider before adding any natural medicine to your health care regime. Plants DO have active properties, and can interact with other medications. Some traditional doses include:

- Dried leaf infusion: 1 - 2 teaspoonfuls, 3 times daily. Pour hot water onto dried leaf and steep for 5 - 10 minutes. Drink as directed.
- Dried root decoction: 1/2 - 2 teaspoonfuls, 3 times daily. Place root into boiling water for 5 - 10 minutes. Strain and drink as directed.

And don't forget to sprinkle a few dandelion leaves and petals on your next salad!

13 OH, MY ACHING HEAD! FEVERFEW FOR MIGRAINE

April 4, 2013

Feverfew, also known as Bachelor Buttons, was originally native to the Balkan mountains of Eastern Europe. It now grows throughout North America, and thrives in the Missouri climate. A member of the genus Tanacetum parthenium, feverfew is a perennial herb that has daisy-like flowers, and blooms over the summer, preferring the full sun.

For centuries, feverfew has been used in medicine. As its name indicates, it has been primarily used for fevers. It has also been shown to relieve the pain of headache and toothache. As the herb has been studied in recent years, more applications have found including migraine headaches, psoriasis and tinnitus (ringing in the ears).

For those fortunate to have never experienced a migraine, they are not your normal headache. Migraines can last for weeks, and can incapacitate the sufferer. The pain of a migraine is throbbing, on one side of the head, and can cause vision changes and nausea. Unfortunately, traditional pain medications tend to cause rebound migraines, creating a vicious cycle. There is a new category of drugs to prevent migraines, but these can only be taken a few times a month, and can have many side effects. They are also very expensive, approximately $13 per tablet.

In a 2012 Dartmouth study, they found "Butterbur and feverfew are the 2 herbal oral preparations best studied, and they seem to have real potential to help many patients with migraine and perhaps other headache types." (Butterbur will be discussed in a future column.) Several studies recommend feverfew for migraine, including a 2009 study by the New York Headache Center.

In 2011, the American Headache Society published a study showing "Sublingual feverfew/ginger appears safe and effective as a first-line preventive treatment for a population of migraine sufferers who frequently experience mild headache prior to the onset of moderate to severe headache." This combination of feverfew and ginger is now marketed as LipiGesic-M, and is available in pharmacies. Of course, *Nature Has the Cure* readers have all the ingredients in their backyard!

The dried leaves—and sometimes flowers and stems—of feverfew are used to make supplements, including capsules, tablets, and liquid extracts. The leaves are sometimes eaten fresh. In the study mentioned above, dried feverfew leaves and dried ginger were taken sublingually (under the tongue) at the start of a migraine...

Side effects for feverfew are rare. Sublingual use, or chewing the leaves, can cause canker sores, and swelling of the lips and tongue. If feverfew is overused, stopping it can *cause* headaches and nervousness. Pregnant women should not take feverfew. It can cause miscarriage by making the uterus contract. People who are allergic to plants in the daisy family, including ragweed and chrysanthemums should avoid feverfew. Feverfew may interact with blood thinners, so should not be taken by persons taking these medications without the knowledge of your health care provider.

It is extremely important to tell your health care provider about any natural medicines you use. Even if you are not asked, give them a full picture of what you do to manage your health. Years ago while working in the ICU, I admitted a young woman who came in with profuse bleeding. Her platelets, components that help blood clot, were practically nonexistent. Her husband said she took no medications, but when I asked about natural cures, I found out she was taking huge doses of red currant, a natural blood thinner. She had not told her doctor, so he never tested her blood to see if she was on the right dosage. Unfortunately, she did not make it, a tragic death that could have been prevented by good communication with her health care practitioner.

14 MEDICINAL PROPERTIES OF GARLIC

April 11, 2013

In the earliest days, when antibiotics and other pharmacy products did not exist, a bulb of garlic itself represented a whole pharmacy inventory due to its many uses.

Today, garlic is greatly beneficial in the treatment of hypertension and as a cancer preventative. It has also shown promise in slowing the processes of atherosclerosis, or hardening of the arteries. It is well regarded as a natural antibiotic. In previous columns, we have talked about the use of apple cider vinegar and hawthorn for high blood pressure. Many herbalists combine these ingredients with garlic for a synergistic, or additive effect.

Not only is garlic one of the most potent antihypertensive (blood pressure lowering) plants around, it also boosts the effects of pharmaceuticals, such as propranolol, enabling a lower dose. Interestingly enough, there is evidence that garlic seems to lower systolic blood pressure only in patients in whom it is elevated, not those with normal or low blood pressure.

Native to Europe, wild garlic (*Allium vineale L.)* is plentiful in Missouri. Not too popular with wheat farmers, as it can taint the taste of flour, or with dairy farmers, as folks aren't too fond of garlic-flavored milk, wild garlic is still an herb-gatherer's dream. Wild onion and wild garlic are easy to confuse, and sometimes wild onion smells like garlic, and vice-versa. Unlike onion, wild garlic has 2 -4 green hollow leaves that look like chives, and a membrane covered bulb. Wild onion has flat leaves, and a reticulated bulb without a membrane. When in full bloom, the leaves of the wild garlic plant are topped with white flowers.

The best time to harvest wild garlic in Missouri is in the months of May and June. Abundant in fields and roadsides, wild garlic thrives well in rocky soils. Always dig your garlic, don't pull it. Brush off any dirt, and leave the roots and leaves on while the bulb dries for 3 -4 weeks, preferably inside. After drying, store your garlic in a cool, dark place with some air circulation, and your bulbs can last up to 6 months.

For high blood pressure, 4 grams of fresh garlic (approximately one clove) once daily is recommended. For prevention of colon, rectal, and stomach cancer, include 1 – 7 cloves of fresh or cooked garlic weekly to your diet.

Garlic can decrease the effects of some medications, especially anti-rejection medications like cyclosporine taken by transplant patients, so always check with your doctor if you plan to take higher doses of garlic than what you would normally get from your diet.

15 TREATING ALLERGIES – NATURALLY!

April 18, 2013

This week's column is written by Tamara Glascock, owner of Tamera's Herbes in Edgar Springs. Tamera is an expert at "Herb Walks," i.e. walking through the pasture and gleaning medicinal plants. She also formulates a wide range of natural health and beauty products, hypo-allergenic, of course!

Pet dander, pollen and ragweed are just a few of the things that trigger allergic reactions, and here in the Ozarks we have plenty of each. When we encounter one of these triggers, our immune-system responds by producing an over-abundance of the chemical that causes inflammation in an attempt to fend off the invader. The results are fits of sneezing, runny nose, watery eyes and maybe a skin rash.

Fortunately, Mother Nature has provided us with some awesome natural treatments that can help ease the symptoms of allergies and provide much-needed relief.

Many allergies, especially those that come from the environment, can be controlled and treated by eating a diet rich in fresh, raw fruits and vegetables. They provide the vitamins and minerals that are crucial for developing a strong, healthy immune system. Plenty of fresh water will help keep the system hydrated and the organs of the body functioning smoothly. In particular, quercetin, a flavonoid that is found in many dark fruits and vegetables like cherries, apples, red grapes and blueberries, will help defend your body against allergens. It is also found in bee pollen, which doubles as a natural histamine that alleviates inflammation.

Neti pots are my first choice when I need quick relief from a sinus infection. They work by clearing the nasal passages of irritants and organisms that cause pain and inflammation. To help prevent sinus infections and fend off symptoms of allergies, use 1 teaspoon of sea salt in 2 cups of distilled water warmed to body temperature. Adding 1/8 teaspoon of goldenseal will help clear up any infection that may be present, and it will soothe and protect the delicate membranes of the nasal cavity.

Garlic (allium sativum) has been used for centuries because of its exceptional ability to regulate and strengthen the immune system. Studies have shown that 3-4 average-sized cloves of garlic have the antibiotic equivalency of one dose of penicillin. Garlic is especially useful if your attack of allergies has transformed itself into a sinus infection.

Numerous studies have shown that stinging nettle (Urticadioica) has a high rate of effectiveness against allergies because of its anti-inflammatory properties. It is believed to work by blocking histamine receptors, prostaglandin production and the release of enzymes from mast cells. A tea made from 1-2 teaspoons of nettle leaves is a soothing addition to the neti pot.

If your allergies have produced a skin rash, there are many natural alternatives for helping sooth the pain and inflammation. Chickweed, calendula, comfrey, burdock and plantain are just of few herbs that can be found in almost any lawn, pasture or health food store in the Midwest. Alone or used together, all of them can be made into a wash or a salve. To make a soothing skin wash, add 1-2 Tbsp of dried herb to 4 cups of distilled water. Let steep in hot, but not boiling, water for 10-15 minutes, or until water cools to a comfortable temperature. Strain and use a soft cloth to apply the wash to irritated skin. For a little extra punch, add 1/8 cup of raw apple cider vinegar. This mixture can be kept in the refrigerator for up to a week.

To learn more about Tamera's approach to natural medicine, visit her blog at http://tamarasherbes.wordpress.com.

16 BEST NATURAL REMEDIES FOR VISION

April 25, 2013

I've struggled with my vision all of my life. Born with essentially "Swiss cheese" corneas, I remember being told as a young child I would need corneal transplants. When I was four years old, my mother found me in the garden, where I had pulled up and eaten all of the carrots. My mother took me to the pediatrician; because I ate so many carrots, I actually turned orange from the carotene! With the benefit of 20/20 hindsight, I realize even as a child my body knew what it was lacking.

The main eyesight problems we struggle with are cataracts, glaucoma, and macular degeneration.

Cataracts

There have been many long-term studies of the effect of nutrition on eyesight. The Harvard Nurses' Health Study has tracked 120,000 nurses for over 40 years. One finding shows that the nurses who consumed foods high in Vitamin C, Vitamin E and carotenoids, like spinach and carrots, were 40% less likely to develop cataracts. One cup of raw spinach offers 18% of your Vitamin E requirement and 14% of your Vitamin C requirement, two vitamins essential for your eyes.

The major cause of cataracts is free-radicals. Free radicals are atoms with unpaired electrons that cause damage to the tissues in the body by altering their chemical structure. They can develop inside the body or be caused by exposure to toxins in the environment. Free radicals are the enemy! Healthy eating can neutralize them. Curcumin is able to neutralize free-radicals, and is a well-established anti-cataract herb. Readers will remember from a previous column that curcumin is a principle component of turmeric, found in prepared mustard and curry.

Macular Degeneration

Age related macular degeneration (AMD) is the leading cause of blindness for people aged 50 and older. The macula of the eye is responsible for our central, high-resolution vision, allowing us to read, see detail and recognize faces. Risk factors include older age, genetic factors, smoking, white race, high intake of vegetable fat, and low intake of dietary antioxidants and zinc.

Excellent antioxidants for the eyes include lutein and zeaxanthin. These compounds are carotenoid pigments that give yellow or orange color to various common foods such as cantaloupe, pasta, corn, carrots, orange/yellow peppers, fish, salmon and eggs. They have also been strongly linked with reduced risk of AMD and cataracts.

Glaucoma

Glaucoma is known at "the sneak thief of sight." Caused by fluid pressure build-up inside the eyes due to slowed fluid drainage, glaucoma can cause damage to the optic nerve and other parts other parts of the eye leading to vision loss and blindness. There are no symptoms in the early stage, which is why a regular eye examination is important.

Natural medicines for glaucoma include cod liver oil or other fish oil to increase the fluid outflow from the eye. A compound called forskolin, derived from the Coleus plant, (a member of the mint family) decreases the production of extra fluid in the eye. (You cannot take forskolin if you are taking calcium channel blockers or nitrates.) Gingko and Vitamin C have also been found "possibly effective" in the treatment of glaucoma. A 2012 study by the Ophthalmology Dept. at the University of California found that a higher intake of fruits and vegetables high in vitamins A and C and carotenoids may be associated with a decreased likelihood of glaucoma in older, high-risk women.

No eye disease should be taken lightly. The eye is a major sensory organ that requires special care for a healthy and productive lifestyle. Some eye diseases, such as glaucoma, can require surgical treatment. Of all the eye diseases, macular degeneration appears to benefit most from a healthy diet. Things can change rather rapidly with our eyes, making a yearly eye examination very important.

Here's a recipe rich in lutein, antioxidants, and vitamins. Your eyes will thank you for it!

Vision Salad

At least 3 greens from this list:

Spinach greens, turnip greens, mustard greens, collards, kale, arugula, broccoli.

Shredded carrots.

Diced tomatoes.

Blueberries or red grapes

Honey/mustard salad dressing (mix 1 Tbs. Honey with 1 Tbs. Mustard, ½ Tbs. Vinegar, and a pinch of ginger per serving.)

17 A NATURAL APPROACH TO WEIGHT LOSS

May 2, 2013

I get email from readers, lots of emails. I love hearing your feedback and questions, so keep them coming!

This column is dedicated to folks who are trying to control food cravings, increase their metabolism, and drop some unwanted pounds. Our bodies have a natural rhythm, and we are not designed to be fat. This plan is based on my personal experience, and what has worked for my patients over the years. When making positive changes, it is always best to think about what you CAN do, not what you can't do.

We've all heard that we need to exercise for 20 minutes, at least 3 times a week. The timing of your exercise routine really matters! Exercising late at night can impair your sleep (more about that later.) The best time to exercise is in the first half hour after you wake up. It can be a short routine; even 5 minutes will make a difference. Before you are even fully awake, do as many sit-ups as you can in 2 minutes. Don't worry how many that is. If you stay with it on a daily basis, you will be amazed how many sit-ups you can do. Next, walk for 3 minutes. You can walk in place, walk up and down stairs, or walk around your yard – just for 3 minutes. Then you are done! This 5 minute a day routine will start a change in your body, with increased metabolism and alertness.

(Those of us who have attained a certain age will remember former Miss America Phyllis George losing 50 pounds after working up to 100 sit-ups per day. Second to running, I think sit-ups are the best all-around exercise. They have the added benefit of taking the workload off your back by toning your stomach muscles.)

When you eat breakfast, make sure you have a little protein, otherwise you will be ravenous in a few hours. If you don't have time to cook eggs, foods like yogurt, peanut butter, even bacon or sausage will provide protein to keep your blood sugar stable.

I make a large 32 oz glass of "lemonade" with 2 Tbs. Apple cider vinegar, 1 Tbs. lemon, and 2 Tbs. honey. I put this on ice in a sports bottle to sip throughout the day, especially if I get hungry in between meals. Apple cider vinegar promotes weight loss, and we discussed in a previous article the beneficial effects it has on blood pressure. Drinking coffee is fine, it promotes mental alertness, and increases metabolism, but keep it to 2 cups a day, and never drink it after 3:30 pm, in order to not interrupt your sleep cycle. I like to put a little cinnamon in my coffee – it adds a nice flavor, and also stabilizes blood sugar.

When eating lunch, prepare or order half of what you would usually eat. Save the other half for a late afternoon snack, or for lunch tomorrow. This is a great time to get out in the sun! Exposure to sunlight for just 5-10 minutes elevates mood and triggers Vitamin D production, a hormone/vitamin that promotes weight loss.

In the late afternoon or early evening, it is time to do 5 minutes of strength training. With your knees bent or straight, do as many push-ups as you can do in 2 1/2 minutes. Rest a few minutes, then do another set – no longer than 2 ½ minutes. When you first get started, you may only be able to do one push-up, but the more you weigh, the better workout you will get. This is easy to forget, so work it in to your regular routine. If you watch the news, do your push-ups during the first and second commercial break.

Eat dinner between 5 – 7 pm. In order to jumpstart your weight loss, add fish to your menu at least 2 times a week. Avoid foods containing high fructose corn syrup. HFCS is a fattening agent that has found its way into many foods you wouldn't suspect, like ketchup, bread, pasta, etc. Read the labels! Many times the only way to avoid HFCS is by purchasing the more expensive "gourmet" products. You are worth it!

If you want to lose weight, it is very important to get enough sleep. Make getting at least 6 – 8 hours of sleep per night a priority. If you are hungry at bedtime, eat a snack with tryptophan, a natural sleep aid. A glass of milk, a bowl of frozen yogurt or ice cream will work! Another tip for hungry cravings just before sleep is to take 1 or 2 Tums. Tums are a good source of calcium, and they lower stomach acid that can make you feel hungry.

18 RED CLOVER: NATURE'S HELP WITH MENOPAUSE

May 9, 2013

The Red Clover (***Trifolium pratense***) that grows in pastures and yards throughout Missouri, is actually native to Europe, Western Asia and Africa. It was introduced to the British Isles from Germany in the 1600's, and the English colonists brought it to North America 100 years later.

Unlike many introduced plants, Red Clover is a welcome plant that produces high-quality forage. It is highly valued for its ability to increase soil fertility through nitrogen fixation.

Red Clover been used for many medicinal purposes, including the treatment of bronchitis, asthma, certain cancers, and as an aid to stop smoking. There are many anecdotal reports that drinking two cups of Red Clover tea daily stops nicotine craving.

Red Clover contains estrogen-like compounds called isoflavones that mimic the effect of natural estrogen. The use of the plant to relieve menopausal symptoms has been well-researched, and the active ingredients in Red Clover have been formulated in a drug (Promensil) to combat hot flashes and night sweats. In pre-menopausal women, Red Clover has been administered to promote normal menstrual cycles and to balance the acid-alkaline level of the vagina to promote conception.

Red Clover can also have a noticeable effect on the development of osteoporosis associated with menopause. Significant bone loss can occur when estrogen levels drop, and by keeping estrogen levels stable, the plant slows bone loss and maintains the density of the bones.

The isoflavones in Red Clover increase your body's HDL (the good cholesterol). It also helps your heart and blood vessels by increasing the elasticity of your arteries, and having blood-thinning effects that can prevent the development of clots.

In a study at the University of Maryland Medical Center, it was found that Red Clover can prevent the growth of new cancer cells in your body, and may even kill existing ones, mainly affecting endometrial and prostate cancers.

Nutritionally, Red Clover is rich in calcium, selenium, chromium, magnesium, niacin, phosphorus, potassium, thiamine and Vitamin C. It's no wonder our local honey has so many wonderful nutritional and medicinal properties, as bees love to visit the plant!

Due to Red Clover's activity on estrogen receptors, it should be avoided in women with a history of breast cancer, endometriosis, ovarian cancer, uterine cancer, uterine fibroids, or other estrogen-sensitive conditions, but others have suggested the high isoflavone content counteracts this, and even provides benefits in these conditions. A family history of these cancers is *not* a contraindication to its use. Due to its blood-thinning properties, Red Clover should not be used by persons who are taking anticoagulants, like coumadin.

To make a medicinal tea, use either fresh or dried flower heads, harvesting at first flowering, as late blooms may have fungal infections. Add 1 – 2 teaspoons of flower per cup of boiled water and steep for 10 minutes. Strain the tea before drinking. For an extra boost, sweeten to taste with a teaspoon of local honey.

19 ROSEMARY - THE MEMORY HERB

May 16, 2013

Best known as a cooking herb, rosemary (Rosmarinus officinalis) is the subject of many recent studies. I recently became interested in rosemary when I used the plant in a class for at risk youth. While talking about the wonders of our senses, I passed around several aromatic herbs, rosemary being one of them. The young teens in the class had never smelt rosemary, but were captivated by the smell, and I witnessed a definite increase in their level of alertness. When I researched this effect, I found that a tea made from rosemary leaves has long been known as an antidote to mental fatigue. Crushing the leaves and inhaling the vapors instantly clears the mind and improves focus.

In 2010, the effects of rosemary on speed of memory were examined in three separate studies. One extremely interesting study looked at "environmental context-dependent memory effects" of the herb on memory. Simply stated, just having the smell of rosemary in the air enhanced learning and memory.

In 2012, a study involving elderly subjects over 75 years of age examined the effect of dried rosemary leaf powder on mental performance. The lowest dose of Rosemary (750 mg) was found to have a beneficial effect on speed of memory (how quickly we can access facts.)

Rosemary and its distillates (carnosic acid and carnosol) are known to possess anti-oxidant activity that may be beneficial for cancer, especially prostate cancer. Rosemary enhances the anti-tumor effect of the cancer drug 5-fluorouracil. Rosemarinic acid, also found in sage, thyme, oregano, lemon balm, and peppermint has antiviral, antibacterial, anti-inflammatory and antioxidant properties. It is useful in the treatment of Alzheimer's disease, as it remains in the bloodstream long enough to reach the brain, unlike many other substances, and decreases certain brain activities thought to contribute to Alzheimer's.

Rosemary oil is a rubefacient – that means it brings blood to the surface of the skin. This effect may explain its effect on hair growth. There are many shampoos and conditioners on the market that contain rosemary, as it prevents dandruff and stimulates hair growth. You can easily make your own hair rinse by simmering rosemary branches with the leaves for 30 minutes, cooling the solution, and using it after shampooing. Rosemary is particularly effective to reverse the hair loss in male pattern baldness.

We've discussed only a few of the medicinal properties of Rosemary. Unlike many herbs, it is well-absorbed from both the intestinal tract and through the skin. It relaxes the smooth muscles of the trachea and the intestines. Its effect on the trachea and bronchioles make it useful in the treatment of bronchial asthma. It has also been used to treat renal colic, menstrual cramps peptic ulcer, inflammatory diseases, liver toxicity, atherosclerosis, heart disease, cataracts, cancer and poor sperm motility.

Steam extraction is the best method to release the essential oils from the leaves of the rosemary plant. This is best accomplished with a steam distiller that can be purchased at your local natural foods store. If you don't have access to a steam distiller, here is a simple crock pot method that will yield a less powerful product.

1. Allow rosemary leaves to dry fully, and strip the leaves from the stalks.

2. In your crock-pot, combine 2 – 3 ounces of rosemary leaves with 2 cups of grape seed oil. Add two cups of water.
3. Heat on the lowest setting for three hours.
4. Strain oil into a clean, sterilized dark glass jar. Store in a cool, dark place.

If you have never had the opportunity to inhale the fragrance of fresh rosemary, give it a try. You can expect a memorable experience!

20 BLACKBERRIES – NATURE'S GIFT

May 23, 2013

It is only fitting with the blackberry bushes already full of unripened fruit that this week's column be dedicated to this extremely nutritious and delicious plant with multiple medicinal uses. A member of the rose family, and also the brambleberry family as blackberries are sometimes called, the berries have a unique design, which contributes to their nutritional value. The multiple droplets on each berry contribute extra skin and seeds, adding to the fiber content, making blackberries a plant with one of the highest fiber contents.

As every Missourian knows, the fruit is edible either raw or used in jellies, jams and many recipes. You may be less familiar with the use of the early spring shoots of the bush that can be peeled and used in salads. Both the leaves and root of the plant also have medicinal uses.

The root is the most astringent part of the plant, used to treat sore throat, mouth ulcers and inflammation of the gums. Leaves and roots should be gathered from first year plants, and then dried for later use. The berries themselves usually ripen in late June. They can be either canned or quick frozen. Freezing requires minimal prep by merely washing the berries and placing them in storage containers or bags for freezing. The flash freezing method actually traps the nutrients in the berry, losing little of the nutritional value. There is nothing like a summer-fresh blackberry cobbler in the middle of winter to chase away the cold weather blues!

Medicinal properties of blackberry leaf tea have described for centuries. In early Rome, soldiers would chew the leaves for increased stamina. It is likely the vitamins and minerals present in blackberry leaves provided this benefit. Blackberry leaf tea can be used as a gargle for treating thrush (a yeast infection in the oral cavity that often occurs after a course of antibiotics, marked by a white plaque over the tongue.) The tea also makes a pleasant, effective mouthwash. To make blackberry tea, add two tablespoons of dried leaves and root back to one pint of boiling water, allow to steep for ten minutes. For a sweeter and more flavorful tea, simply add the fruit of 4-5 berries to the basic tea mixture. Despite the tea's medicinal properties, it is safe, and even beneficial to drink it daily, as it is high in antioxidants and vitamins A and C, potassium and calcium.

Some readers of a certain age may well remember blackberry tea as an effective cure for diarrhea, and its effectiveness for this condition has been well documented. My grandmother made a cough remedy by cooking the berries over a low heat with enough water to cover until the juice was extracted from the berries. She was careful not to boil them. She then strained the mixture and added ½ cup of honey to each cup of blackberry juice, and reheated until the honey was dissolved. She then poured the mixture into a small clean bottle. I saw her take a sip of this cough mixture frequently, and she remained healthy into her late 90's, when she died of old age in her home. She was never sick, and never hospitalized.

2013 looks certain to be a bumper crop year, so I challenge my readers to go out and pick at least a quart of berries this summer. They are free for the picking, and are all along the roadside, along crop fields, beside creeks and streams, and at the edge of the woods.

21 LEAF OF THREE, LET IT BE. NOT THAT EASY

May 30, 2013

It's not the poison ivy that gets you, it's the contact dermatitis!

If you have never been exposed to urushiol, the chemical in poison oak and ivy, you can consider yourself lucky. 15% of the population is immune to poison ivy. For the rest of us, after exposure to the oily resin produced by the plant, at least 50% can look forward to 2 to 3 weeks of misery. Adding insult to injury, most cases occur between July and August, making it hard to cover up with bulky clothing.

Poison Ivy is NOT contagious in the usual sense. Once you have washed the oils from your skin, you can't affect another person, no matter how bad a rash you develop. Years ago, one of my neighbors was working in poison ivy. Afterwards, he came in the house, took a shower, and never developed a rash. Unfortunately, he left his towel on the towel rack, and his daughter used it to dry her face, ending up with a severe contact dermatitis. In the same way, poison ivy can be transmitted by our pets, on their fur.

Caution! It is very dangerous to burn poison ivy as the oils become aerosolized, and breathing them in can seriously affect your lungs.

Prevention

Washing the oily resin from your skin with cool water within 30 minutes will usually prevent a rash. The best soaps to use are lye soap or Fels-naphtha as they dissolve the oil and prevent it from penetrating the skin.

While there are protective lotions to ward off poison ivy (they act by slowing the absorption of urushiol into your skin by about 30 – 45 minutes) the best defense is a good offense, i.e. wearing long sleeve shirts and long pants and gloves if necessary for protection.

Symptoms

12 to 24 hours after coming in contact with urushiol oil from poison ivy, sufferers develop contact dermatitis, an immune response to urushiol that causes a skin condition with redness and itching. It generally progresses to swelling and fluid filled vesicles. Chronic cases can develop, causing patches of the skin to resemble lichen (moss), with cracks and fissures.

Scratching or popping the fluid filled lesion does not spread the rash. New lesions may show up a few days after the initial lesion, but these are less sensitive areas of the skin that took longer to react.

Treatment

A case of poison ivy usually lasts 3 weeks with no treatment. There are some things you can do to speed up the process, however.

Don't scratch! Scratching leads to breaks in the skin that can lead to a secondary bacterial infection, and also delays healing of the lesions. There is a great alternative to scratching – In the shower, or under the kitchen faucet, run the hottest water you can tolerate over the affected area. You will have instant relief that lasts for several hours.

Dry out the lesions by dabbing them with a cotton ball soaked with vinegar. You can also bathe the lesions with lye soap, or Fels-Naptha.

After the lesions have begun to dry out, promote healing by applying a wet to dry saline dressing. Soak a gauze square in a saline solution made with 1 cup of water to which 1 teaspoon of salt has been added. Wring the extra moisture out of the gauze, and place it directly over the lesions. Secure the dressing with an Ace bandage, This is an excellent dressing to apply at bedtime, and you will be amazed at the healing effects of a simple salt water solution.

If all else fails, see your health care provider for a one-time steroid injection. You will have relief in 12 – 24 hours. In severe cases, your doctor may prescribe oral prednisone. Be sure to taper off oral steroids as prescribed, because if you stop them all at once, you can have a rebound of the symptoms. Aspirin works like a very mild steroid, and also provides some relief.

22 THE TRUTH ABOUT ARTIFICIAL SWEETENERS

June 6, 2013

Chances are you know someone with bladder cancer. I know several, and the one thing they have in common is that they are all diabetic. I blame artificial sweeteners. Artificial sweeteners are also linked to obesity, headaches, seizures, birth defects, worsened diabetes, and behavioral problems.

Five non-nutritive sweeteners with intense sweetening power have FDA approval (aspartame, acesulfame-K, neotame, saccharin, and sucralose). FDA approval does not mean the sweetener is safe, especially in the case of aspartame. In fact, 85 percent of all complaints registered with the FDA are for adverse reactions to the chemical.

Aspartame

Also known as Equal or NutraSweet, the blue packaged sweetener is a well-known neurotoxin. Discovered by Searle Pharmaceuticals in the 1960's while working with wood alcohol, Aspartame is composed of three ingredients: methanol, phenylalanine and aspartic acid. Methanol is used to make formaldehyde, paint strippers, carburetor cleaners, etc. If people drink Methanol, it causes them to become blind. The second component is phenylalanine, and the third ingredient is aspartic acid. Aspartic acid is a neurotoxin that crosses the blood-brain barrier, causing cell death in the nervous system.

It is no surprise that it was difficult to get the toxic Aspartame approved for public use. Multiple early studies showed that the chemical caused brain damage in mice, severe obesity, and even death. Longer term studies showed tumors in test animals.

In 1969, cyclamates were banned, opening the door for Aspartame. (Cyclamates were unbanned in1984 after Aspartame's approval.) Searle fought an uphill battle to get Aspartame approved, as many scientists from several countries documented the poisonous effects of the chemical. That changed in 1977 when Donald Rumsfeld was briefly made president of Searle, in order to handle "aspartame approval studies." Aspartame was subsequently approved, with the caveat it should only be used in cold beverages, as heating caused the methanol it contained to degenerate into methyl alcohol. Since the body temperature is 98.6, it is obvious that this toxic chemical while be released when ingested, no matter what the initial temperature may be. After Aspartame's initial approval in 1981, Monsanto purchased G.D. Searle and Co. in 1985 and created a subsidiary called "The Nutrasweet Company." (Funny that a non-nutritive sweetener could legally be called "Nutrasweet.")

Today Aspartame is ubiquitous. It is in virtually every chewing gum, even "sugary" brands like big Red and Juicy Fruit. Read the labels! Keep in mind that chewing gum is essentially a drug-delivery device, as chemicals are readily absorbed through the tissues of the mouth into the underlying blood vessels, with a direct path to the brain. (I have found one gum that doesn't contain Aspartame, and that is Fruit Stripe.)

Neotame

If there is anything more toxic than Aspartame, it is Neotame, FDA approved in 2002. Another chemical produced by Monsanto, Neotame is 7,000 – 13,000 times as sweet as table sugar, Neotame is chemically related to Aspartame, but can be used in smaller quantities, making it attractive to food manufacturers. Even Monsanto's own pre-approval studies of Neotame revealed adverse reactions. Unfortunately, Monsanto only conducted a few one-day studies rather than looking at long-term effects. It will be hard to know if you are ingesting Neotame, as the USDA doesn't require labeling of this chemical sweetener, with the exception of organic foods, where it must be labeled. Like Aspartame, Neotame metabolizes to formaldehyde when consumed.

Acesulfame-K

Approved for use in 1988, potassium salt acesulfame-K (Sunette or Sweet One) stimulates insulin release in a dose-dependent fashion, causing low blood sugar attacks that can lead to overeating. (The word is out that diet sodas don't help you lose weight; if anything, they make you gain weight.) Although less toxic than alternatives, Acesulfame-K is usually used in conjunction with another non-nutritive sweeteners. In animal studies, acesulfame-K was found to produce tumors primarily in males. The chemical affects prenatal development by affecting the offspring's sweet preference.

This article is Part 1 of a three-part series – next week we will look at the remaining non-nutritive sweeteners, and begin to look at healthier choices.

23 THE TRUTH ABOUT ARTIFICIAL SWEETENERS – PART 2

June 13, 2013

Last week we discussed the most toxic artificial sweeteners available: aspartame, acesulfame-K, and neotame. There are two reasonable alternatives available that can be safely used in small amounts, saccharin and sucralose.

Saccharin

"Anyone who thinks saccharin is dangerous is an idiot" *Teddy Roosevelt*

The oldest artificial sweetener, and the least expensive, Saccharin (the pink one) was discovered by a student researcher at Johns Hopkins University in 1879. The basic substance, benzoic sulfilimaine, is a synthetic compound derived from coal tar.

Extremely safe for diabetics, Saccharin has zero effect on the glycemic index; a measure of how quickly blood sugars rise after eating a particular food.

With the help of the sugar industry, the use of saccharin was restricted in food during the early 1900's, but due to the sugar shortages of WWI and WWII, restrictions were later lifted. In 1958, saccharin was grandfathered in by the FDA and classified as "generally considered as safe" (GRAS). In 1972, the FDA removed saccharin from the GRAS substances, and issued a regulation limiting the use of saccharin. In a follow-up study in 1977, one Canadian researcher did rat studies, and found an increase in bladder tumors, primarily in male rats. In 1991, The National Academy of Science reviewed the studies, and found that saccharin was not causing bladder tumors in rats, rather there were impurities in the saccharin used, and problems with the studies. The FDA then removed its proposal to ban saccharin, and the National Toxicology Program removed saccharin from its list of cancer causing substances in 2000.

Later studies performed in Europe on humans showed NO association between saccharin and bladder cancer. Looking back, we can see that saccharin went through a lot of regulatory grief while aspartame was gaining a foothold.

I have to say that I agree with Teddy Roosevelt. At 300 times the sweetness of sugar, and zero glycemic index, I feel pretty safe with a pinch of saccharin to sweeten my coffee.

Sucralose

Also known as Splenda (the yellow one) sucralose is touted as 600 times as sweet as table sugar and twice as sweet as saccharin. It is stable at any temperature, and can be used in baking. Discovered in 1976 in England where it was patented, Sucralose was later approved in Canada in 1991, and in the U.S. in 1998.

Sucralose is derived from table sugar through a complex chemical process. Its use doesn't promote cavities, and it is safe for use by diabetics, as it does not increase the glycemic index. In the US, however, Splenda is mixed with maltodextrin or dextrose (both made from corn) as "bulking agents." These additives add about 2 – 4 calories per packet. Maltodextrin has an extremely high glycemic index (double that of table sugar), necessitating caution in diabetic users.

For years, Splenda was manufactured at a plant in MacIntosh, Alabama, but production moved to Singapore in 2009, and the Alabama plant was closed. In good news for both Tate and Lyle, the makers of Splenda, and the citizens of MacIntosh, Splenda sales boomed in 2011, and the Alabama plant reopened in 2012.

There are some new cautions regarding the use of sucralose. In a 2006 study, a link between sucralose and migraine was found, and many neurologists list the sweetener as a migraine trigger. Earlier this week, sucralose was downgraded from "safe" to "use with caution" by the CSPI (Center for Science in the Public Interest.) after an Italian study found that sucralose, like aspartame, caused leukemia in mice. Sucralose has also been suggested as contributing to inflammatory bowel disease when used in high doses.

Since sucralose replaces table sugar in a 1:1 volume, larger amounts of the sweetener must be used to get the desired taste.

Next week we will look at nutritive sugar replacements, including natural sweeteners that can be grown at home!

24 NATURAL SWEETNERS

June 20, 2014

Over the last two weeks, we've reviewed the major artificial sweeteners that are on the market. In what results in a "pick your poison" scenario, some artificial sweeteners are less harmful than others, but all have a degree of toxicity.

Now for the good news! There are excellent natural sweeteners that are not only delicious, they actually provide nutrition and health benefits as they sweeten.

Stevia

An herb from the Chrysanthemum family, Stevia Rebaudiana is native to Paraguay and Brazil, but grows well in Missouri. This particular species of Stevia yields a very sweet natural sweetener called Stevioside in its leaves. Stevia has become well-known for its intense sweetness (250-300 times sweeter than sucrose). Stevia is safe for diabetics, and does not promote tooth decay.

Stevia provides many health benefits, including anti-hyperglycemic, anti-hypertensive, anti-inflammatory, anti-tumor, anti-diarrheal, diuretic, and immunomodulatory actions. Researchers have found that these effects are only evident when the baseline measures are higher than normal. In other words, Stevia will not lower a normal blood sugar or a normal blood pressure.

Stevia was not FDA approved in the US until 2011, and then only as a "refined sweetener." Pure Stevia is hard to find, as it is commercially mixed with either maltodextrin or erythritol. You can find it on the store shelves as *Truvia* or *Stevia in the Raw.*

Stevia in the Raw, is not in the raw. It is stevia mixed with maltodextrin. Used as a bulking agent, Maltodextrin has an extremely high glycemic index (double that of table sugar), necessitating caution in diabetic users.

Truvia is mixed with Erythritol. Erythritol (the chemical formally known as anhydride) is a sugar alcohol. Like its relative Xylitol, it can cause abdominal gas, cramping and pain, largely because this nondigestible compound passes through the intestinal tract unabsorbed. What is Erythritol? Erythritol is used to make biobutanediols. Butadiene is used to make synthetic rubber, and has DNA altering effects.

Even though pure Stevia is not FDA approved as a food additive, you can easily make your own Stevia sweetener.

Start your seeds inside, and you should have seedlings in 2 weeks. You can then transplant them outside, or keep them in pots. Although perennials, they don't winter well, so you will have to bring them inside when it gets cold.

You can make stevia liquid sweetener from fresh or dried leaves, but the fresh leaves are sweeter. The stems are usually discarded.

Stevia Extract

Chop up stevia leaves and put them in a glass jar, cover them with alcohol (the kind you drink!). The alcohol will be removed later in the process. Vodka, brandy and cognac work well. Put in a cool spot for 48 hours, mixing gently by inverting the jar several times a day. Strain your leaves and liquid through a coffee filter into a pot and simmer gently for 25 minutes. This will burn off the alcohol and concentrate the sweetener. Strain through another coffee filter into a dark glass bottle. Store in the refrigerator for 3 months of sweetener. A few drops will suffice to sweeten anything, and your homemade sweetener is not destroyed in the baking process.

For those who prefer not to use alcohol,, Stevia sweetener can be prepared by adding ½ cup of tightly packed chopped leaves to 1 cup of simmering water. Don't boil, but remove from heat and steep or 45 minutes, as you would tea. Strain with a coffee filter into a clean, dark glass jar, and store in the refrigerator. This method works well, but the alcohol method leaches more of the stevioside from the leaves.

Dried Stevia

You can also crush dried stevia leaves in your coffee grinder, and use 2 - 3 Tbs. of ground Stevia in place of 1 cup of sugar.

Honey

A discussion on natural sweeteners would not be complete without mentioning honey. Did you know that much of the store-bought honey has the beneficial pollen removed? We have some wonderful beekeepers here in the Ozarks, and the slightly higher price for pure, organic, LOCAL honey is well worth it. With a glycemic index of 30, honey has approximately 1/3 the effect on glucose levels as table sugar.

In addition, natural honey reduces blood lipids, homocysteine, and CRP in normal and hyperlipidemic subjects. Many studies have found NATURAL honey to be a reasonable sugar substitute in Type 1 diabetics, with less effect on blood glucose than a slice of bread.

Emails from readers are always welcome. An upcoming article entitled "Things My Mother Forgot To Tell Me' is in the works, and I'd love to include anecdotes from my readers on natural cures you have discovered, that your mother may or may not have passed on! Email calhorselover@yahoo.com, and you may see your suggestion in an upcoming article.

25 PARSLEY – EASY TO GROW AND EASY TO LOVE

June 27, 2014

Many of us think of parsley (Petroselinum crispum) as merely a garnish. Not just any garnish, but one that serves as a breath freshener and digestive aid after a meal.

Not only does a bright green sprig of parsley make a meal look more appetizing, butchers have long tucked a spring of parsley in with fresh meat to add visual appeal and retard bacterial growth.

Tumor Fighting

Parsley is one of the most abundant sources of Apigenin, This flavonoid is absorbed into the intestinal tract, and hinders the ability of gastrointestinal cancers to progress and spread by several different mechanisms, including interrupting blood supply to a tumor, and reducing the ability of the tumor to absorb glucose in order to grow. It has been shown to be more effective than some drugs in preventing metastasis, the spread of cancer.

Parsley has also be shown to inhibit prostate, breast, and endometrial cancer.

Treatment for Gout

Long used in Mediterranean medicine, parsley is a must for gout sufferers, as it reduces uric acid levels that cause gout. In a 2011 study at the University of Leipzig in Germany, it was found that the Apigenin found in parsley worked in much the same way as the synthetic drug Allopurinol in blocking xanthine oxidase, an enzyme well known to contribute significantly to the pathological process that causes gout.

Metabolic Syndrome

Another medicinal property of parsley is its role in treating metabolic syndrome. Studies have shown parsley improves both glucose and lipid metabolism, and it has been called a "potent anti-hypoglycemic."

Antibacterial Properties

One of the reasons parsley is so good for bad breath is its antibacterial properties. Many studies have shown the effectiveness of parsley on bacteria, such as E. coli, in the gastrointestinal tract. Parsley also boosts the activity of some antibiotics, such as Doxycycline.

Chelation for Heavy Metals

Parsley has been found to remove heavy metal deposits in the body. A sort of chelation therapy, parsley binds with both mercury and lead, and helps to excrete them from the body. (Cilantro works well for this also.) If you are concerned about heavy metals, a baseline test costs about $20 for each metal tested. One half cup of fresh parsley thrown into the blender daily with your favorite juice has been shown to increase the elimination of heavy metals through your urine within weeks.

Precautions

Pregnant women shouldn't eat a lot of parsley, as it can cause uterine contractions.

Grow Your Own

It is incredibly easy to grow parsley in Missouri. A perennial plant, it goes to seed in its second year, and in my garden, it has self-propagated. When harvesting the leaves and stems, pick them early in the morning. They readily dry on the counter top, or in a commercial dehydrator. The dried leaves will keep for years in the cabinet.

Colcannon

My Irish mother routinely made a classic dish with parsley and potatoes called colcannon. As a kid, I called it "grass potatoes." Whatever you call it, this Irish staple is delicious.

2Lbs. Potatoes
½ c. sliced onion
¼ c. butter
2 tsp. dried parsley

Wash and peel potatoes. Cut in bite-sized pieces and with onion and water. Boil until soft. Drain potatoes. Melt butter in pot; add parsley, cooked potatoes and onion. Stir to mix.

Leftovers: Cook with milk to make potato soup, adding a little bacon and shredded cheddar cheese if desired.

26 TAKING A FRESH LOOK AT SALT

July 4, 2013

Salt is nature's oldest cure. A chemical compound made from sodium and chloride, salt is extremely important, and has many uses. The ability of salt to preserve foods was discovered thousands of years ago, and it is so valuable that even the word salt comes from the word salary, as salt was a welcome currency in years gone by.

Somewhere along the line, salt has gotten a bad reputation. Salt is a major component of our internal system, making up 0.9% of our body fluids. While we only need about 500 mg of salt daily (1/4 teaspoon!) in our diet under normal conditions, our salt requirement changes in hot weather and with exercise.

Hyponatremia = not enough salt

I've admitted many patients over the years that refuse to eat ANY salt, and they end up very ill with low sodium levels, a serious condition called hyponatremia. They may get by in the winter, but in the summer, a huge amount of (sodium) salt is lost through the skin. In Panama, where the weather was always hot and humid, many bathroom facilities had salt tablets in them for the taking.

We normally lose about 5 mmol of sodium a day, but with exercise and sweating, the amount of sodium lost through the skin can be 20 times higher. Drinking just water when you are sweating excessively can actually worsen a decreased blood sodium level. Symptoms of low sodium are headache, confusion, nausea, seizures, weakness, restlessness, and muscle spasms. These symptoms can progress to seizures and coma. A glass of lemonade has about 30 mg of sodium, and is a good replacement drink when you are sweating.

That being said, some folks are salt sensitive. Eating too much salt can raise their blood pressure. We should never cook with salt, as a few grains of salt sprinkled on *after* cooking does much more to enhance the flavor of food.

Medicinal Uses of Salt

When used in medicine, a salt solution is referred to as *saline.* Saline solution is a good thing to keep on hand, and costs virtually pennies to make. A warm saline gargle will decrease sore throat pain and promote healing.

When working in home health, many of my patients had non-healing wounds of various natures, often diabetic ulcers. Sometimes expensive solutions and treatments were ordered to treat the wounds, but the best treatment was a wet –to-dry saline dressing, applied twice daily. Wounds that hadn't improved in months often looked better after just a couple days with this simple, inexpensive method.

To apply a wet to dry dressing, you need clean hospital gloves, gauze squares, saline, and a gauze wrap. Open the package of the gauze dressing, and pour saline on the gauze while it is still in the wrapper, With gloved hands, gently open the gauze square, and crinkle it up, wringing out 90% of the saline. Pack the gauze loosely into the wound. Wrap the wound with dry gauze, or tape a dry gauze pad over it. When the next dressing change is due 12 hours later, the gauze should have dried, and will pull off dead skin with it, and you will see new buds of healthy pink granulation tissue in the base of the wound.

Make your own saline

8 oz. tap water

¼ oz. salt

(multiply ingredients for larger quantities)

Heat water until warm but not boiling. Mix salt in with spoon until it fully dissolved and pour into a clean, reused plastic container. Date the container, and store in refrigerator. The solution stays fresh in the refrigerator for several months.

Iodized Salt

When buying salt, be sure to purchase the iodized version. Adequate iodine is needed for a healthy thyroid gland, and this is an easy way to get your daily requirement, especially if you do not like to eat fish.

27 COCONUT OIL, FACT AND FICTION

July 11, 2013

Coconut oil is getting lots of good press these days, with even Dr. Oz touting the benefits. I'm a little skeptical, and decided to research it for myself. As a product high in saturated fats, most of us have avoided coconut oil for many years. Now there are claims that coconut oil helps memory loss in Alzheimer's, increases good cholesterol, and decreases belly fat, among other amazing "cures."

In order to get a feel for the sudden surge in coconut oil popularity, I took a close look at newspapers in the coconut producing countries. A May, 2013 article in Hindu Business Line entitled 'Supply Glut Puts Pressure on Vegoil Prices,' warns "due to an increase in production of major oilseeds and tree-based oils (palm oil, coconut oil), world vegetable oil production is likely to witness a big jump of six million tons to reach a new high of 166 million tons in 2013-14. " That's a lot of excess coconut oil.

A 2008 government document from the Philippines laments the fall in coconut oil prices to a record low. The Philippine government estimates that they supply 760 million dollars in product to the US annually with more than 20 million Filipinos depending on the product, and introduced a bill to provide to promote the use of coconut products.

There are many more articles on coconut futures, but it is clear that there is an over-supply of coconut oil on the market, and many countries are dependent on coconut oil exports.

Effect on Obesity

Coconut oil is a staple of the diet in Sri Lanka, where the coconut tree and its products are a major export product. The relationship between coconut fats and health has been the subject of much debate and misinformation. Since coconut fats account for 80% of the fat intake among Sri Lankans, it makes sense to look at the obesity rates and health of this population.

The National Library of Medicine cites a 2010 study that documents a relatively high prevalence of overweight and obesity (particularly abdominal obesity) among adults in Sri Lanka, calling for "urgent public health interventions to needed to control the problem."

Many, many internet sites promote sales of coconut oil to "dissolve belly fat." Even if coconut oil does help people lose weight, keep in mind that coconut oil is loaded with saturated fat: 12 grams in 1 tablespoon versus 7 grams in a tablespoon of butter. It also has 120 calories per tablespoon.

Effect on cholesterol and metabolism

The top 5 coconut producing countries are Indonesia, Philippines, India, Brazil and Sri Lanka, so it is not surprising that most of the recent positive studies on the effects of coconut oil come from these countries. While there are anecdotal accounts of the beneficial effect of coconut oil on HDL (good cholesterol) the scientific evidence is lacking.

In general, unsaturated fats, (those that are liquid at room temperature), are better for you than saturated fats. Although coconut oil is 92% saturated fatty acids, there is some evidence that coconut oil may be better for you than corn oil. Coconut oil is unique because it is composed predominately of medium chain triglycerides.

Medium chain triglycerides (MCTs) are easily absorbed and directly used in the body to produce energy, unlike long-chain fatty acids. MCTs don't need bile salts for absorption into the body, so they are good for people with malnutrition or problems digesting food. In a presumably reliable 1967 US Army study, blood cholesterol levels were found to be unaffected by coconut oil, unlike corn oil. Of course, almost all corn oil today comes from GMO (genetically modified) corn, unlike coconut oil that has yet to be genetically modified, although there are registered patents to do so.

Eating some fats are important, because when you ingest fat, it stimulates the release of the hormone cholecystokinin, a natural appetite suppressant. Fat in food also helps you absorb vitamins A, D, E and K. While the long-term studies on coconut oil are not yet available, coconut oil is certainly no worse than other fats, and may actually convey some benefits.

(To be continued next week.)

28 COCONUT OIL, FACT AND FICTION (PART 2)

July 18, 2013

We talked last week about some of the dramatic claims made about coconut oil, claims that have not been fully vetted by scientific studies. Coconut Oil does have many proven benefits, and is a great ingredient in both cooking and natural hygiene products.

Uses in Cooking

Coconut oil is very stable oil at room temperatures because it is resistant to rancidity. It does make excellent cooking oil, one that is stable at high temperatures, with the added benefit of enhancing food flavors. Coconut oil is a better choice than the commonly used poly-unsaturated fats, such as soybean and other vegetable oils. These oils can become rancid during cooking, causing harmful effects on body cells.

Effect on Hair Damage

Coconut Oil is unsurpassed for preventing hair damage. In several studies looking at various oils used in hair care products, coconut oil was the only oil found to significantly reduce the protein loss for both undamaged and damaged hair when used as a pre-wash and post-wash grooming product. Both commonly used sunflower and mineral oils do not help at all in reducing the protein loss from hair. Coconut oil has a high affinity for hair proteins and is able to penetrate inside the hair shaft

Effect on Memory

Studies performed in the 1980's did not show any beneficial effects on memory. Recently, these early studies have been discredited, because they used nutritionally depleted coconut oil; not the pure, 100% oil available on the market today. A newer 2004 study by the University of British Columbia performed on rats showed that coconut oil helped reduce memory impairment by decreasing inflammation and improving nerve transmission in the brain. The jury is still out on the effects of coconut oil on memory, at least until some long-term studies in humans are completed.

There is one way coconut oil can help prevent Alzheimer's - by making your own aluminum-free deodorant!

Aluminum is a neurotoxin, and has long been suspected of contributing to Alzheimer's. Approximately 90% of deodorants and antiperspirant contain aluminum, and this is important because deodorant can be readily absorbed through the skin, and absorption is especially rapid through little nicks due to underarm shaving. (Keep in mind the risk for Alzheimer's is approximately double in women.)

Fortunately, it is easy to make your own chemical free, aluminum free deodorant, and coconut oil is an integral part.

Chemical Free Deodorant

Ingredients:

6-8 Tbs. of coconut oil in its solid state*
1/4 cup baking soda
1/4 cup arrowroot powder or cornstarch (arrowroot is preferred)
Essential oils if desired (peppermint, orange, pine work well).

Directions:

1. Combine equal portions of baking soda & arrowroot powder/cornstarch.

2. Slowly add coconut oil and work it in with a spoon or hand blender until it maintains a firm but pliable texture. It should be about the same texture as commercial deodorant, solid but able to be applied easily. If it is too wet, add further arrowroot powder/cornstarch to thicken.

3. You can either scoop this recipe into your old deodorant dispensers or place in a small container with lid and apply with fingers with each use. Makes about 1 cup. This recipe lasts about 3 months for two people with regular daily use.

4. *Store below 75 degrees to keep deodorant in solid form. Above that temperature, coconut oil liquefies.

If you want to add coconut oil to your diet, generally 3 tsp. daily are recommended. It can be added to coffee, giving it a pleasant coconut flavor.

29 PRICKLY PEAR CACTUS – A PLANT TO TREASURE

July 25, 2013

If you have a rocky field on your place, chances are you have some scattered cactus plants. Considered a nuisance, Prickly Pear Cactus (*Opuntia humifusa*) is a native plant that thrives in Missouri, and grows all the way from southern Canada to Argentina.

What you may be surprised to know is the fact that the prickly pear cactus is considered a gourmet food item, and even a staple in many areas of the world. Found in abundance in Mexico, prickly pear has been used for centuries as a food source. It has also been used in traditional medicine in American Indian, Mexican, and Korean cultures.

A perennial plant, the prickly pear has several usable parts: the flesh of the round stem pad segments known as nopales, flowers and fruits. The flowers of the prickly pear are extremely important for bees, and areas with many of these plants are found to have the most bees.

Prickly Pear in Medicine

Medicinal uses of prickly pear cactus include boosting insulin sensitivity in type 2 diabetics, lowering high cholesterol, treating obesity, and relieving the symptoms of an enlarged prostate. It is also used to fight viral infections.

The active ingredients in prickly pear cactus also protect the joints, improve bone density, and help prevent colon cancer. Cells in the colon are very susceptible to the anti-cancer properties of *Opuntia*, the variety of prickly pear that is native to Missouri.

In a recently published 2013 study from Berlin, Germany, prickly pear was found to reduce body weight by blocking dietary fat absorption by at least 28%.

Heated poultices have been used to treat rheumatic disorders, erythema, and chronic skin conditions. Prickly pear poultices can be applied to breasts to promote milk flow in nursing mothers.

Powdered prickly pear cactus flowers can decrease the symptoms of an enlarged prostate, such as frequent strong urges to urinate.

Precautions

Prickly pear interacts with diabetic medications as it can lower blood sugar, so these should not be taken together.

Although generally well-tolerated, prickly pear can cause increased stool volume and frequency, similar to prescription weight loss medications (such as Orlistat) that reduce fat absorption.

Prickly Pear As a Food

One cup of raw prickly pear contains 61 calories, which are composed of about 5 percent protein, 10 percent fat and 85 percent carbohydrate. A *very* nutritious food, Prickly pear is high in fiber, magnesium, calcium, potassium, vitamin C, riboflavin and niacin.

When selecting plants for cooking, keep in mind that only the young plant is eaten, as older plants are too tough.

The juice can be used to make jellies and candies, and a wonderful recipe for prickly pear marmalade can be found in the Ball Blue Book for Canning.

Prickly Pear Candy

4 cups prickly pear cactus
3 cups granulated sugar
1 cup water
2 tablespoons orange juice

Select prickly pear cactus. Remove spines and outside layer (skin) with a knife. Cut pulp across in slices one-inch thick.

Soak overnight in cold water. Remove from water, cut in 1" cubes and cook in boiling water until tender. Drain.

Heat the sugar and water until sugar is dissolved. Then add cactus. Cook slowly in the syrup until nearly all the syrup is absorbed. Do not scorch! Remove cactus from syrup, drain and roll in granulated or powdered sugar. For colored cactus candy, any vegetable food coloring may be added to the syrup.

Stuffed Prickly Pear Cactus

6 large prickly pear cactus pads, (cleaned of spines and barbs)
1/4 medium white onion
1 large garlic clove, peeled and halved
Salt
6 slices Monterey Jack cheese or 6 slices Gouda cheese
1/4-1/2 cup flour
3 eggs, separated, at room temperature
Corn oil (for frying)

Place the whole cactus pads, onion and garlic in a large pot with water to cover and salt to taste. Bring to a boil and cook for 15 minutes, or until the pads are tender but still firm. Drain and rinse.

Starting at the wide, curved end, carefully slice each paddle horizontally, as if butterflying a chop for stuffing. Do not cut all the way through to the narrow end (the thicker part where the pad is attached to the main plant) but leave approximately 1 1/2" uncut.

Place a slice of cheese between the two sections and press flat. Dredge the pads in flour.

Beat egg whites until they form stiff peaks, and fold in the lightly beaten egg yolks.

Pour enough oil into large skillet so that it comes up at least 1/2 inch. Heat the oil until sizzling hot. Dip the stuffed cactus in the egg batter to coat and fry in the hot oil until golden brown on each side.

The pads of the prickly pear are called nopales, and are very tasty when properly prepared.

30 WHATEVER HAPPENED TO SASSAFRAS?

August 1, 2013

Sassafras leaves, roots and bark have been used in medicine for centuries. Found only from Canada to Mexico (and Brazil), the plant was one of the first exports from the Jamestown Colony back to England. Sassafras was so valuable to the early colonies it was known as a "secret commodity" in Virginia, and guarded accordingly. In fact, Sir Walter Raleigh held a monopoly on all quantities of sassafras shipped from Virginia, which made him an astoundingly wealthy man, since the going rate was 1000 to 2000 British Pounds per ton back in 1602. Its value in Europe was understandable, as it proved to be a cure for gonorrhea and syphilis, diseases that were rampant at the time.

Although no longer approved for medicinal use, sassafras was once a cure for almost everything, The oil, roots and bark of the sassafras tree contain the chemical safrole, an ingredient used to treat a multitude of illnesses, such as skin sores, kidney problems, toothaches, rheumatism, swelling, menstrual disorders, sexually transmitted diseases, bronchitis, high blood pressure, and dysentery.

Sassafras Banned

In 1960, the FDA banned the use of sassafras oil and safrole in commercially mass-produced foods and drugs, after laboratory tests determined that safrole was toxic to the liver and could cause cancer in rats and mice. In 1976, sassafras tea was banned in any form, a ban that lasted until the passage of the Dietary Supplement Health and

Education Act in 1994. At that time, sassafras root extracts from which the safrole has been removed were deemed permissible, and are still widely used commercially in teas and root beers, but obviously have no medicinal value.

More recent studies by the U.S. National Toxicology Program, however, found that it took a dose of 2,350 mg to reach a "toxic endpoint" (that is, where 50 percent of the animals died) in mice, which puts safrole in the "slightly toxic" category. Since there have been no human studies, nobody really knows what levels might be dangerous to people

An exhaustive review of the research provides only two examples where sassafras was found to be harmful in people: an 80 year old woman who was drinking 10 glasses of sassafras tea daily, and complained of hot flashes and palpitations; and a gentleman who experienced profuse sweating after drinking sassafras tea.

Interestingly, in a research study published last year, safrole was found to kill squamous cell cancer cells on the human tongue. In addition, alcohol ingestion has been found to be much more likely to predispose to cancer than safrole.

As further proof that sassafras has limited toxicity, its leaves and twigs are an important food source for white tail deer, groundhogs, rabbits, black bears, beavers, wild turkeys, and a multitude of other birds and small mammals that don't appear to be suffering any ill effects.

In next week's article we will discuss the many medicinal uses of Sassafras.

31 WHATEVER HAPPENED TO SASSAFRAS? (Part 2)

August 8, 2013

In last week's article, we talked about the somewhat infamous history of sassafras. Despite the bad press, sassafras continues to be a staple in Ozarks, and no one seems to be suffering as a result.

Use in Medicine

Bark

The mild aromatic safrole oil from the bark can be made into a tea, or 5 to 10 drops can be placed on a sugar cube to treat kidney diseases, gastrointestinal problems, scurvy, colds, rheumatism and skin inflammation. This dose can be taken up to three times daily.

Sassafras tea can also be taken as an anticoagulant (blood thinner), so its use should be avoided in persons with bleeding disorders, or those on commercial blood thinning medications.

Leaves

Filé powder, used in making gumbo, is a spicy herb made from the dried and ground leaves of the sassafras tree. It is widely used in the Creole cuisine found in Louisiana.

Roots

The roots of the sassafras tree can also be steeped to make teas, and were used in the flavoring of traditional root beer until banned by the FDA.

Steam distillation of dried root bark produces an essential oil consisting mostly of safrole which can be used as a fragrance in perfumes and soups, and for aromatherapy.

Topical Application

Although you will find sassafras oil, tincture, and root bark available for sale, they are "legally" intended for external use only. Some people apply sassafras directly to the skin to treat skin problems, achy joints (rheumatism), swollen eyes, sprains, and insect bites or stings. Sassafras oil is also applied to the skin to kill germs and head lice.

Precautions

Sassafras can cause sweating and hot flashes. High amounts can cause vomiting, high blood pressure, hallucinations, and more severe side effects. It can cause skin rashes when used on the skin.

The old-timers wisely only used sassafras in the springtime, thereby limiting the amount of safrole, and avoiding side-effects.

Although Safrole fed to mice and rats in tremendous amounts has been shown to cause cancer in these animals, there is likely a more pressing reason for the ban on the extract. Safrole is a precursor for the manufacture of the illegal_drug MDMA, which is, in turn, the most common active ingredient in Ecstasy tablets. It's probably not a good idea to sell sassafras in any form as its transport is monitored internationally by the United Nations.

Of course banning consumption of sassafras and stopping it are two different things. The USDA has an excellent document on sassafras that neglects to mention the "hazards." You can check out their informational brochure on sassafras here: http://plants.usda.gov/plantguide/pdf/cs_saal5.pdf.

Sassafras Tea

Cut and wash a root from your sassafras tree, taking care not to greatly disturb the root system. After washing, cut root into small pieces, 3 inches long.

Allow roots to dry in a cool, dark place, (Not in the sun, as that will cause them to lose flavor.)

Boil 2- 4 ounces of dried root bark in a quart of water for 20 minutes, and then allow roots to steep until the water cools. The water should be a deep, brownish-red (root beer color!) Strain through a coffee filter if you don't want any sediment. Add sugar or honey to taste.

You would likely have to drink gallons of Sassafras tea to get enough safrole to cause any health problems, but it is usually best to be safer than sorry and watch the intake of this fantastic tasting tea.

32 CINNAMON – TRUE OR IMPOSTER?

Part 1 of 2 parts

August 15, 2013

Last week we discussed the wonderful medicinal properties of safrole, the active ingredient in sassafras. In addition to components like cinnamaldehyde, safrole is also found in cinnamon. Cinnamon doesn't have the restrictions and bans currently placed on the sassafras plant, likely because the only place true cinnamon grows is in Sri Lanka (formerly known as Ceylon.) As one of the substances comprising the holy paste the priests used to spread on the altar before the sacrifices as described in Exodus, cinnamon has been used by man for thousands of centuries. In Roman times, a pound of cinnamon cost the equivalent of 10 months of labor. The Emperor Nero is reputed to have honored his deceased wife by burning a year's supply at the funeral for his wife in 65 AD. Cinnamon continues to be widely used, both as a spice and as a traditional medicine.

What is true cinnamon? *Cinnamom verum or Cinnamonum zeylanicum* contains the active safrole oil. What is sold in grocery stores as cinnamon is actually cassis, a completely different plant. The term "cassia" never refers to true Ceylon cinnamon but rather to other species often called "Chinese cinnamon" or "Vietnamese cinnamon," and this is what you will find in your local grocery store.

Real Ceylon cinnamon is more expensive than any of the cassia versions, but it is also the cinnamon that provides health benefits such as blood sugar regulation. What true cinnamon and cassia do not have in common is their coumarin content. Coumarin is a blood thinner, and may account for ant-killing properties of the "false cinnamon." Coumarin is also used in rat poison. The level of naturally occurring coumarins in Ceylon cinnamon appears to be very small and lower than the amount that could cause health risks, but the level of naturally occurring coumarins in the cassia cinnamons appears to be higher and may pose a risk to people if consumed in large amounts. Ceylon Cinnamon has between 2-5 ppm of coumarin compared to Cassia (2000-5000 ppm). **This means 1 teaspoon of cassia cinnamon powder contains 5.8 to 12.1 mg of coumarin, which may be above the Tolerable Daily Intake for smaller individuals.** Coumarin is also moderately toxic to the liver and kidneys. In other words, use the false cinnamon you likely have in your kitchen for ant killer, and purchase true cinnamon for your own use.

There is no way to tell the difference between cinnamon powders made from Ceylon/true cinnamon vs. cassia/false cinnamon unless the country of origin is identified on the label. Expect to pay more for true cinnamon. With stick cinnamon, it is easy to tell the difference between true and false cinnamon. Real cinnamon is a tan color, whereas cinnamon cassia is a reddish brown to dark brown. Rolled cassia sticks have thicker bark, and curl inward from both sides toward the center as they dry. Real cinnamon sticks curl from one side only and roll up like a newspaper. The surface of cinnamon cassia is rough and uneven, whereas real Ceylon cinnamon bark is smooth. With true cinnamon sticks you can use a coffee grinder to easily grind the sticks into a powder, trying to grind Cassia will likely burn up the motor!

Cinnamon is cultivated by growing the tree for two years, then coppicing it. This forces the growth of about a dozen branches from the roots. These branches are then harvested by scraping off the outer bark, then beating the branch evenly with a hammer to loosen the inner bark. The inner bark is then pried out in long rolls. Only the inner bark is used, and these paper-like strips curl into rolls, called quills, when they are dried. The quills are then cut into 2- 4 inch lengths for sale.

Next week we will discuss the many health benefits true cinnamon provides.

33 CINNAMON – TRUE OR IMPOSTER?   Part 2

August 22, 2013

Now that we know the difference between true Cinnamon and the cassia substitute sold in most stores, let's discuss the medicinal uses.

Cinnamon and Alzheimer's Disease

A recently published study from Tel Aviv, Israel found that a ground powder from cinnamon sticks not only prevented the progression of Alzheimer's disease in mice, but broke up the amyloid fibers in the brain that are characteristic of the disease, giving some hope it might even offer a cure. Results became apparent within only four months. One of the primary researchers who now drinks cinnamon tea daily states "It not only prevents Alzheimer's but other viral diseases, like the flu." The effect of cinnamon on Alzheimer's disease progression was replicated in a 2013 study at the University of California in Santa Barbara.

Cinnamon and Blood Sugar

One of the most widely touted benefits of cinnamon is its effect on blood sugar, and it is widely used in the traditional system of medicine to treat diabetes in India. If you have tried cinnamon as a supplement here in the United States, you have likely not noticed any effect, as the cassis version of cinnamon does not offer any benefit on lowering blood sugar. True cinnamon protects the pancreas, and helps it to secrete insulin. Cinnamon has been found to reduce fasting blood sugar levels, normalize Hg A1C, lower LDL and increase HDL cholesterol and increase circulating insulin levels. Cinnamon significantly improved metabolic derangements associated with insulin resistance, and also shows beneficial effects against diabetic neuropathy and nephropathy, with no significant toxic effects on the liver and kidney.

Cinnamon and blood pressure

In one study, cinnamon was found to lowers blood pressure in patients with pre-diabetes and Type 2 diabetes. In an animal study, cinnamon extract was given intravenously, and provoked a long-lasting decrease in blood pressure. Average blood pressure readings decreased by up to 30%, depending on the dose. The effect of cinnamon on blood pressure is thought to work by dilating blood vessels, which in turn decreases the workload of the heart.

Cinnamon and alertness

One study found that cinnamon may increase alertness by increasing blood flow to the brain. Just smelling cinnamon has been found to keep drivers more alert.

Cautions

Cinnamon is one of the best tolerated natural cures. There is one case report of a 68-year-old Caucasian female with type 2 diabetes mellitus who experienced an acute exacerbation of her rosacea 2 weeks after self-initiating cinnamon oil pills to lower her blood sugar levels. No other cases have been reported.

One researcher does warn that over-consumption of cinnamon could harm liver functions, due to a component called cinnamaldehyde. The recommendation is not to exceed 10 grams of cinnamon a day, (slightly less than one tablespoon.)

If you are diabetic, and want to try cinnamon to see how it affects your blood sugar levels, let your doctor know, and keep track of your cinnamon consumption. I've found a good way to take cinnamon is by stirring one teaspoon into my morning coffee.

Cinnamon is also an excellent additive to most teas, and you can even make cinnamon tea from the raw cinnamon sticks.

True cinnamon is light tan in color, has smooth bark, is thin and

crumbles easily.

Cassia "cinnamon" is reddish to dark brown, has thick, hard bark, and

rolls inward from the sides.

34 WATERMELON ~ WHAT THE ANGELS EAT

August 29, 2013

"It is chief of this world's luxuries….when one has tasted it, he knows what Angels eat. It was not a Southern watermelon that Eve took, we know it because she repented."

Mark Twain

Chances are you have a 10 pound watermelon sitting on your kitchen counter right now, ready to serve at your Labor Day feast. If not, you might want to pick one up, as watermelon truly has something for everyone, not just a heavenly taste.

Arginine

Watermelon is a rich source of citrulline, an amino acid that metabolizes to arginine, a truly amazing essential amino acid for humans. Arginine boosts the immune system, protecting us from viruses. Arginine plays an important role in healing of wounds, removes ammonia from the body, and stimulates the release of beneficial hormones. It reduces healing time of injuries (especially bone), quickens repair time of damaged tissue (as in burn victims), and helps decrease blood pressure in hypertensive persons.

Recently, a study using a combination of arginine and antioxidant vitamins showed that this combination may help to combat abnormally high blood pressure during high risk pregnancies, a condition known as pre-eclampsia.

Nitric Oxide

The citrullin in watermelon also generates nitric oxide. Nitric oxide improves blood flow by relaxing blood vessels. It's through nitric oxide production that drugs like Viagra, Cialis, and Levitra work. Enough said on that topic!

Lycopene

Watermelon contains more lycopene than tomatoes. In fact, one cup of watermelon contains 6889 mcg.of Lycophene, compared with one cup of tomatoes that offer 4631 mcg. Lycophene is extremely important to men, because it has been repeatedly shown to decrease the risk of prostate cancer up to one third. According to the National Cancer Institute, one out of every six American men develops prostate cancer in his lifetime.

Don't Forget the Seeds!

Not only is the fruit of the watermelon nutritious, the seeds have remarkable qualities all on their own. Watermelon seeds contain a chemical that increases the permeability of capillaries in the kidneys, allowing a greater output of urine which in turn decreases swelling, and flushes toxins and deposits from the urinary system. The seeds can also be ground to make a nutritious flour, containing phosphorus, potassium, magnesium, manganese and calcium.

Precautions

Watermelon and all its components, including seeds and rind, contain nutrients which have never been shown to be harmful.

Watermelon Seed Tea

This recipe is from Edgar Cayce – take the seeds from a watermelon and allow them to dry. Grind them up with a nut or coffee grinder, and pour one pint of boiling water over 2 tablespoons of ground seeds. Drink the tea three times weekly. This tea promotes urination, and prevents formation of kidney stones. There is also some evidence that watermelon seed also lowers blood pressure, and prevents prostate dysfunction.

35 PERSIMMONS FOR HEALTH AND DIET

September 5, 2013

The American Persimmon (Diospyros virginiana) is a wonderful, versatile plant. The fruit of the persimmon is rich in vitamin C, calcium and potassium.

My friend Penny Frazier says Persimmon tea has changed her life. Penny lives in the woods, and makes her living by harvesting native plants. (Check out her website *Goods From the Woods* at www.pinenut.com) Her allergies were severe until she discovered that tea made from dried Persimmon leaves cured her allergies!

To make tea, pick the young leaves, or the calyx of the fruit (the part that attaches the fruit to the branch.) Dry overnight – add one teaspoon of dried leaves/calyx to one cup of hot water for tea.

Medical researchers studying the fruit of the persimmon have found the relatively high contents of fibers, phenolics, minerals and trace elements make persimmon a good addition to an anti-atherosclerotic diet. The lipid-lowering effects of the persimmon have been replicated in several studies and recently published research shows that that fruit of the persimmon significantly lowers cholesterol over a 12 week period when taken before meals.

The Catawba Indians boiled persimmon tree bark in water and made a mouth rinse that was used to treat thrush, otherwise known as Candida, a fungal disease of the mouth. Recent university studies verify the effect of persimmon fruit against several pathogenic viruses.

Confederate soldiers roasted the seeds and used them as a coffee substitute. Persimmon seed tea has a rich, coffee-like flavor, but alas, no caffeine! Naturally sweet persimmons are delicious in pies and cookies, and make a unique dessert to take to any function, that will definitely get attention!

Warning: eating the unripened fruit of the persimmon tree can cause phytobezoars (a conglomerate of undigested matter in the stomach.) Native Americans taught the early settlers that the fruit should be left on the tree and not eaten until the first frost to prevent complications of eating the unripened fruit.

In the Ozarks, we predict the severity of the upcoming winter by slicing a persimmon and observing the silverware-shaped formation inside of the fruit. The folklore about the seed says that a spoon means snow while a fork is a milder winter and a knife is a cold biting winter.

The wood of the persimmon tree is very hard, and is used to make golf-club heads. There is pretty much nothing this tree can't do!

Fortunately, this is going to be a GREAT year for persimmons. My trees are already loaded with fruit. To buy inexpensive persimmon seedlings for planting, contact the George O. White nursery here in Licking at 573-674-3229. If you have extra persimmons after harvest, the nursery will also purchase them from you by the pound.

Missouri persimmon tree, ready for harvest!

36 The Many Uses of Celery

September 12, 2013

Celery (Apium graveolens) is not as boring as it may seem. In addition to being one of the key vegetables used by "juicers," both the seed and juice of celery have multiple medicinal uses, including treatment of joint pain, insomnia, menstrual discomfort, intestinal gas, urine retention, high blood pressure and peptic ulcers.

The use of celery in medicine was described in the writings of Hippocrates, where he prescribed a diuretic composed of a vinegar solution of celery, water and honey. The ancient Greeks also used celery to make wine, which was served as an award at athletic games. As an all-purpose vegetable, celery leaves were also worn as crowns to prevent hangovers.

Considered an aphrodisiac in the 17th century, love potions made from celery were quite popular in Europe during that era.

In many countries, celery is grown for its seeds. Actually very small fruit, these "seeds" yield a valuable volatile oil used for perfumes and medications. The seeds also contain an organic compound called *apiol*, and can be used in cooking as either whole seeds or ground.

Pain Relieving Properties

In the year 30 AD, Aulus Cornelius Celsus wrote about the use of celery seed in pills for relieving pain. In a more recent study at the University of Queensland in Australia published in 1999, herbal formulations containing celery seed were as found to be effective as ibuprofen in treating arthritis, without causing gastric bleeding that can be a side-effect of many arthritis medications. Celery appears to be most effective in treating joint pain associated with arthritis, likely due to its anti-inflammatory properties. For menstrual discomfort, celery seed can be taken three times a day for the first three days of the menstrual cycle.

Lowering Blood Pressure

Celery seeds contain a compound, 3-*n*-butylphthalide, that has been demonstrated to lower blood pressure. Many homeopathic solutions used to treat high blood pressure contain celery as a major ingredient. In fact, the National Library of Medicine lists study after study showing the BP lowering capabilities of celery, with one researcher going as far as saying, "It can be concluded that celery seed extracts have antihypertensive properties, and can be considered as an antihypertensive agent in chronic treatment of elevated BP."

Peptic Ulcer

In other recent developments, celery oil was found to be potent agent for treating H. pylori infections (the causative organism in peptic ulcers). It also reduces intestinal gas, likely by destroying destructive bacteria in the gut.

Antioxidants

Celery seeds contain lutein, a substance that has the potential to prevent cancer and tumor growth. Fiber, flavonoids, coumarins, linoleic acid and certain essential oils are also contained in celery seed. Scientists have now identified at least a dozen other types of antioxidant nutrients in celery. The antioxidant support we get from celery has been shown to help protect us against unwanted oxygen damage to our cells, blood vessels, and organ systems.

Insect Repellent

Celery oil combined with 5% Vanilla is found to provide strong repellent action against a wide range of mosquito species, with no skin irritation or other side effects. It compares well to commercial insect repellents.

New Research

Probably most exciting is the effect of 3-*n*-butylphthalide on Lewy bodies in the brain. Lewy bodies are abnormal clumps of protein that develop inside nerve cells in the brain, and are found in Parkinson's Disease (PD) and some forms of dementia. This chemical found in celery reduces the formation of Lewy bodies associated with Parkinson's, and studies imply that it may be a potential effective therapeutic agent for the treatment of PD.

Maintaining Nutrients

Steaming is the preferred method of cooking whole celery in order to preserve from 83 – 99% of its nutrients. 5 -7 days is recommended as the window of time for consuming fresh celery. You should wait to chop fresh celery just prior to cooking or serving in order to maintain maximum benefit.

Precautions

Celery oil and celery seeds may be unsafe when used during pregnancy, as large amounts may act as a uterine stimulant. Bergapten in the seeds can increase photosensitivity, so the use of essential oil externally in bright sunshine should be avoided.

Celery can cause allergic reactions in people who are sensitive to certain other plants and spices including wild carrot, mugwort, birch, and dandelion. This has been called the "celery-carrot-mugwort-spice syndrome."

In addition, celery is among a small group of foods (headed by peanuts) that appear to provoke the most severe allergic reactions; for people with celery allergy, exposure can cause potentially fatal anaphylactic shock

Dosage

The typical recommendation for making celery seed tea is steeping 1 to 3 g or 1 tsp. of crushed celery seeds in 1 cup of boiling water for about 15 minutes, says the University of Maryland Medical Center. You can drink up to 3 cups of celery seed tea daily.

37 PURSLANE, MARTHA WASHINGTON AND WALDEN POND

(Part 1 of 2)

September 19, 2013

During a visit last month with my good friend and fellow nurse Tara Bukowsky, she introduced me to a delicious outdoor snack – Purslane (**Portulaca oleraca).**Growing wild throughout Missouri, Purslane, also known by the slanderous nickname "Pigweed," has bite sized pluckable leaves that are tasty and nutritious. Purslane easily grows in poor, compacted soils under drought conditions, and likely arrived in North America via Canada from Africa and the Middle East prior to the days of Columbus. Despite being with us a very long time, Purslane is now considered a "noxious" weed, and its usage as a nutritive and medicinal source hasn't really caught on in the USA. As the eighth most common plant in the world, you are certain to have Purslane growing somewhere on your property, sometimes in the most unusual places.

Purslane throughout history

As a popular food in past centuries, dozens of recipes have been handed down for this nutritional powerhouse. George Washington's wife Martha even recorded a recipe for Pickled Purslane in 1749:

> *"Gather ye pursland when it stalkie & will snap when you break it.*
> *Boyle it in a kettle of fayre water without any salt, & when it is tender,*
> *make a pickle of salt & water, as you doe for other pickles.*
> *& when it is cold, make it pretty sharp with vinegar*
> *& cover it as you did ye other prementioned pickles."*

While engaging in a quest to live simply and independently at Walden Pond in 1854, Henry David Thoreau dined on Purslane and wrote: *"I have made a satisfactory dinner off a dish of purslane which I gathered and boiled. Yet men have come to such a pass that they frequently starve, not from want of necessaries, but for want of luxuries."*

Nutritional Benefits

While purslane has largely been forgotten since the time of our great-grandparents, it may be making a comeback, especially in regards to nutrition. The Department of Plant Science at the University of Connecticut, reports "Purslane is receiving much attention for cultivation by the United States Department of Agriculture as part of their effort to bring about a modification in the western diet with increased intake of fresh fruits and vegetables."

Michael Pollan, a noted writer on topics involving food and the environment, has labeled Purslane, "One of the two most nutritious plants on the planet." This is likely true, as purslane provides more Omega-3 fatty acids than any other leafy green plant. It contains an extraordinary amount of one of the Omega-3's mostly found in fish, so if you don't like seafood, you might want to consider adding Purslane to your diet. It contains vitamins A, C, B and E, and minerals magnesium, potassium, calcium and iron. One cup of cooked leaves contains 90 mg of calcium, 561 mg of potassium, and more than 2,000 IUs of vitamin A.

Although I think the leaves are the tastiest, the entire plant is edible, and is used much as you would use spinach - in salads, pasta dishes and soups.

Next week we will explore the many medicinal uses of this amazing plant.

38 PURSLANE (part 2)

September 26, 2013

Last week we talked about the tremendous nutritional benefits of purslane, (Portulaca oleracea), including the fact that it contains seven times higher levels of Vitamin E, ascorbic acid and glutathione (antioxidants) than spinach leaves, and is also the richest known source of omega-3 fatty acids of any vegetable. The plant is also unparalleled in the treatment of several medical conditions, and has specialized protective effects on the body.

Medicinal uses

Purslane has been found to reduce infection, reduce fever, speed wound healing, act as a bronchodilator and cough suppressant, and work as an anti-fungal medication. In addition to these generalized applications, purslane has proven superlative in the treatment of several other conditions.

Oral Lichen Planus

Purslane is a clinically effective treatment for oral lichen planus, a chronic, inflammatory condition affecting the mucous membranes in the mouth that can lead to cancer. In a recent study, approximately 83% of the oral lichen planus patients showed partial to complete clinical improvement after ingesting the plant. Its leaves can also be used to treat insect or snake bites, boils, diarrhea, hemorrhoids and internal bleeding.

Cancer

Rich in anti-oxidants, purslane has been found to inhibit cervical cancer cell growth, and is likely beneficial in preventing other cancers.

Type 2 Diabetes

In a 2011 study, diabetic subjects were divided into 2 groups. Half of them received 5 grams of purslane seeds daily, and the other half received Metformin 1500 mg a day. The purslane subjects showed similar blood glucose control to those taking Metformin, with a corresponding increase in HDL (the "good" cholesterol)

Removal of Bisphenol A

Portulaca oleracea efficiently removes <u>bisphenol A (BPA)</u>, an endocrine-disrupting chemical, which is found in plastic bottles. BPA mimics estrogen, and is thought to contribute in infertility in men, and also alters glucose and lipid metabolism, causing weight gain in some cases. Increased levels of BPA also lead to Type-2 diabetes and hypertension. BPA is so harmful to infants that recent laws dictate that plastic baby bottles be made BPA-free. Our humble friend purslane breaks bisphenol A down into smaller metabolites which are then excreted from the body before they can cause damage.

Parkinson's Disease

Even more impressive than celery, purslane has protective properties against developing brain damage and Parkinson's disease. The flowers of purslane contain a form of dopamine, a chemical used by brain cells to help control body movement. Parkinson's disease happens when the brain cells that make dopamine are destroyed. Purslane not only protects these brain cells, but provides an external source of dopamine. A July, 2013 study from Helwan University in Cairo, Egypt, concluded that "purslane may be considered as a potential neuroprotective agent against environmental factors affecting the function of the dopaminergic system in the brain."

Liver Fibrosis

Purslane has been found to a have a protective and curative effect on the liver with liver fibrosis, especially after ligation of bile ducts, so it should be included in the diet after gallbladder removal.

Where to find Purslane

As the eighth most common plant in the world, purslane is easy to forage. It likes to grow in impossible areas, like between the cracks of sidewalks, in the bottom of old planters, and other areas close to the earth. You can readily spot it by its pinkish/red stems.

Precautions:

Uncooked purslane leaves contain a high amount of oxalate, a compound found in some types of kidney stones. (Cooking purslane decreases the oxalate content by one third, however, and its levels are about the same as spinach.) People with kidney stones that are known to be composed of oxalate are advised to avoid eating purslane.

(Portulaca oleracea), grows everywhere throughout Missouri, and is a low-lying plant that grows close to the earth. You can recognize it by the pinkish/red stems.

39 HICKORY NUTS

October 3, 2013

When I was growing up in the 1970's, I clearly remember naturalist Euell Gibbons on television promoting a breakfast cereal that tasted "like roast hickory nuts." I never had the opportunity to actually taste roast hickory nuts until I became an adult. Now I am hooked!

While Missouri has some of the most delicious black walnuts in the world (there is even a new ice cream flavor featuring Missouri Black Walnuts!), hickory nuts have a more subtle flavor, and can be used for a greater variety of foods, and are used to make kanuchi, a food staple of the Cherokee Nation.

The art of making kanuchi balls is an ancient Cherokee tradition that dates back to 2000 BC. In a laborious process, seasoned hickory nuts are cracked open with a rock or hammer, with the larger shell pieces removed. The remaining nut meat and small shell fragment are pounded and pulverized until they stick together. The poultice is then shaped into a ball which is later used in hickory nut soup.

Harvesting

Taking a tip from the Cherokee experts, after gathering hickory nuts, the green husks should be immediately removed and the nut seasoned by placing it near a heat source for further hardening to prevent bug infestation. Hickory nuts should be seasoned for at least one month before use to ensure that the taste is mature and not green. Once seasoned, hickory nuts may be stored for up to a year. My neighbor Carolyn Wilson offers a valuable time-saving tip: Store the seasoned nuts in the freezer before cracking – this helps the nut meat to pop easily out of the shell.

Varieties

There are 17 species of Hickory worldwide, with 8 of those found in Missouri. Hickories are further divided into 2 groups: pecan hickories and true hickories. In Missouri, pecan, bitternut and water hickory are members of the pecan hickory group. Shagbark, shellbark, mockernut, pignut and black hickory are members of the true hickories. (The only nut considered bitter and inedible comes from the pignut hickory.)

Value

As an option for a home-based industry, the going rate for shelled Hickory nuts sold online is $25.00 - $30.00 per pound. It takes skill and patience to remove the nutmeats without shattering them into tiny pieces, that's why you won't find hickory nuts in grocery stores. They are farmers' market treasures typically sold only by those who gather and shell them.

Nutrition

Loaded with essential amino acids, one ounce of hickory nuts has 180 calories, 3.6 gm of protein, and 18.2 gm of fat (only 2 gm of which are "bad" fats.) Hickory nuts also provide vitamins B1, B6 and magnesium and phosphorus.

Excellent roasted, hickory nuts are a great substitute for pecans in pecan pie, and I've used them in place of pine nuts when making pesto.

Medicinal uses

Very little has been written the medicinal uses of hickory nuts. There is some research on the use of hickory nut oil for the common cough, and an extract from the nut is being evaluated in the treatment of some forms of cancer, specifically colon and lung. The Chippewa Indians used smoke from smoldering hickory roots to treat convulsions. Speaking of smoke, when cooking outdoors, taking the time to gather some hickory branches for the fire greatly improves the taste of grilled and smoked meat.

Precautions

Unlike walnuts that are toxic to dogs and horses, hickory nuts are non-toxic to all animals, and are an important food for many species of wildlife. Squirrels, turkeys and ducks all feed on the nuts, even preferring them to acorns.

Of course, folks with an allergy to other tree nuts can be allergic to hickory nuts.

Wild Turkey Stuffing

1¼ cups dry Wild Rice
2 cups Hickory Nuts
8 oz ground sausage (optional)
1 Tbsp butter
2 large celery ribs, diced
1 medium onion, minced
1 tsp salt
½ tsp black pepper

1. Cook Wild Rice in 3½ cups water until very tender. Wild Rice takes up to an hour to cook, add more water if needed.
2. Cook sausage until well-done in a skillet. Add to the rice.
3. Add the butter, onion, and celery to the sausage drippings and sauté until tender.
4. Add sauté to the rice and sausage mixture along with salt and pepper and Hickory Nuts.
5. Mix together well. Stuff your wild turkey with this mixture.

Shagbark Hickory is common in Texas County, and yields the largest nuts with great flavor.

40 APPLE SEASON – DON'T THROW AWAY THOSE PEELS!

October 10, 2013

The fall harvest is here, and many of us will be making applesauce and apple preserves. Don't throw away those apple peels and cores; you can use them to make your own organic, non-pasteurized apple cider vinegar!! With prices averaging around 50 cents an ounce, you will see quite a cost-savings.

Some of the medicinal uses for apple cider vinegar (ACV) include: lowering blood sugar levels after eating, aiding slow digestion, supporting weight loss, relieving leg cramps, treating sore throats and sinus problems, lowering cholesterol and blood pressure, helping prevent kidney stones, and treating dandruff and vaginal infections.

Acetic Acid

Next to water, acetic acid is the main component of vinegar. In fact, the name acetic acid derives from acetum, the Latin word for vinegar. Vinegar is widely used as a table condiment, and also to pickle foods.

Acetic acid dissolves inorganic salts like calcium, making it an excellent cleaning product that removes calcium buildup.

Medical Uses

Weight Loss

One of the most publicized benefits of apple cider vinegar is weight loss. One of the ways it helps out in this department is with control of hunger cravings. In a 2005 study, vinegar supplementation was found to lower glucose and insulin responses and improve feelings of satiety lasting up to two hours after the subjects ate a meal consisting of a portion of white bread. Other studies have found that natural pectin contained in ACV mixes with water after ingestion, causing it to expand in the stomach, creating a feeling of fullness. For this purpose, 1 to 2 tsp. of apple cider vinegar should be taken with water right before a meal.

Anemia

When acetic acid comes in contact with food, it promotes the body's absorption and utilization of iron. Iron is essential in developing healthy red blood cells, which in turn carry life giving oxygen throughout the body. This mechanism also increases body metabolism, and may contribute to the weight loss many people experience when adding ACV to their diet.

Diabetes

The benefits of ACV in controlling both blood sugar and cholesterol levels are subject of ongoing research. In a 2013 study, normal and diabetic animals were fed with standard animal food containing 6% apple cider vinegar for 4 weeks. Fasting blood glucose did not change, while HbA1c significantly decreased in the diabetic group. In normal rats fed with vinegar, significant reduction of LDL (bad) cholesterol and significant increase of HDL (good) cholesterol levels were observed. Apple cider vinegar also reduced serum triglyceride levels and increased HDL in diabetic animals. The study authors concluded that apple cider vinegar may be of great value in managing complications of diabetes.

Polycystic ovary syndrome

Polycystic ovary syndrome (PCOS) is marked by Infrequent or prolonged menstrual periods, excess hair growth, acne and obesity. In adult women, difficulty becoming pregnant or unexplained weight gain may be the first sign. In a study published in January, 2013, Women suffering from polycystic ovary syndrome took 1 tablespoon of ACV daily for 3 months with their meals. Ovulatory menstruation was observed within

40 days in four of seven patients. Insulin resistance and hormone levels improved, suggesting the possibility of vinegar to restore ovulatory function through improving insulin sensitivity in PCOS patients, avoiding pharmacological treatment. The researchers concluded: "Intake of vinegar might reduce medical cost and treatment time for insulin resistance, anovulation, and infertility in patients with PCOS."

Kidney stones

Anyone who has passed a kidney stone know how excruciatingly painful they are. If you passed one kidney stone, your chance of having another attack is as high as 80%. For unknown reasons, the southeastern US is known as the "kidney stone belt." There are four kinds of kidney stones: calcium oxalate, struvite, uric acid and cysteine, but calcium oxalate stones are by far the most common. Apple cider vinegar has been found to prevent the formation of calcium oxalate stones by alkalinizing the urine. Yes, vinegar's main component is acetic acid, but through a series of metabolic processes in the body, ACV decreases the acidity of the urine, making it difficult for stones to form.

Precautions

As an acid, ACV can cause erosion of tooth enamel. You should drink ACV quickly, and rinse your mouth afterward to avoid damaging tooth enamel.

Home Made Apple Cider Vinegar

Save cores and apple peels from apples. (Separate the seeds from the cores and save for planting!) Place the peels and cores in a large, clean glass container. Cover completely with water. Place a clean towel or paper napkin over the top of the glass container, and secure with a rubber band.

Place the container in a cool, dark place. You will know it is ready when you begin to smell vinegar! Strain the solution into a clean glass or plastic container with a lid, using a metal strainer or coffee filter.

No refrigeration necessary. Enjoy your fresh, organic, non-pasteurized ACV! It also makes a great gift for friends who love to cook and can.

41 BASIL

October 17, 2013

I currently work with a group of at-risk teens, and provide weekly health groups. One of my groups is aromatherapy, where the teens are introduced to the restorative powers of plants containing essential oils. A recurring favorite of the groups is sweet basil. Many of the teens exclaim "where on earth can you find this!?" Basil evokes fond memories of family gatherings, and seems to have a calming effect.

Many essential oils derived from a variety of plants have been traditionally used as alternative treatments for headaches, migraines, allergies, fatigue, and stress; also, they have long been used as antibacterial agents due to their antimicrobial properties, and oil of basil is no exception.

In addition to its restorative and rejuvenating uses in aromatherapy, Basil is a wonderful food source, and has many medicinal properties. The parts of the plant that grow above the ground are used to make medicine.Basil is a good source of calcium, Vitamin C, potassium, magnesium and iron.

Medicinal Uses

Fungal Infections

The most widely touted medicinal use of basil is treatment of intestinal worms, and some fungal infections. It has been used successfully to treat ringworm when the oil is applied to the skin. There is a fungal infection of the hair shaft called Piedra that causes damage to the hair shaft. Essential oils from Basil have proven effective against this fungus, and it is applied like a shampoo. Oil of Basil has also been used effectively on warts. There is no real scientific evidence regarding the use of basil as a wormer, but as noted under precautions, basil does contain a chemical called estragole that is toxic in high doses.

Stroke

A 2011 study used basil (Ocimum basilicum) extract in an animal study looking at the effect on stroke. It was found to greatly decrease brain infarct size after occlusion of the carotid artery, leading researchers to conclude that "the results of the study suggest that Ocimum basilicum could be useful clinically in the prevention of stroke."

Effect on Blood Glucose

Research studies dating back decades have shown the blood sugar lowering effects of basil. A landmark 1996 study in humans found that basil leaves caused fasting blood sugar to fall by 21 mg/dl, and postprandial (after eating) blood sugar to fall by 15.8, concluding that "basil leaves may be prescribed as adjunct to dietary therapy and drug treatment in mild to moderate non-insulin dependent diabetes."

Seizure Control

A "hot off the presses" study just uploaded to the National Library of Medicine demonstrates the antiepileptic function of several essential oils, including basil. Oil of basil does cross the blood/brain barrier and was found to decrease both the frequency and severity of seizures in laboratory animals. With these findings, there are sure to be more research studies looking into the development of seizure medications of a more natural origin than those currently available.

Precautions

Basil also contains many chemicals, including estragole, a chemical that increases the risk of liver cancer in laboratory animals. Excessive use of the concentrated oil of basil is not recommended for consumption.

Basil is safe in food amounts, and it seems to be safe in medicinal amounts when used by adults short-term. In some people basil can cause low blood sugar.

Basil/Hickory Nut Pesto

1 cup packed fresh basil leaves

¼ cup grated Parmesan or Romano cheese

¼ cup extra virgin olive oil

1/8 cup hickory nuts

1 medium garlic clove

Salt and pepper to taste

Combine basil and hickory nuts, pulse in a blender. Add garlic and cheese and pulse until blended. Turn blender on low, and slowly pour the olive oil in a steady stream into the mixture, stirring as necessary to ensure the pesto is fully mixed.

Serve warm with fresh pasta, or cold over toasted French bread slices.

42 Acorns

October 24, 2013

I've received several emails about the use of acorns for either food or medicine. This comes as no surprise, as they are ankle deep in some places – more than the squirrels and deer can consume.

The answer is yes, acorns are a valuable food source, and have indirect implications for health. One caution should be noted due to the level of tannins in most Missouri acorns; there is a purifying process involved before humans can safely consume them. Without removing the tannins, acorns are quite bitter, and can leave painful sores in your mouth and esophagus.

Oak trees don't begin to produce acorns until they are about 20 years old, but usually the first full crop won't happen until the tree is about 50. The average 100-year old oak produces about 2,200 acorns per season. Only one in 10,000 will actually become a tree, leaving the rest as a food source.

And what a great food source acorns are! The average nutritional breakdown of acorns from the white oak is as follows: 50.4% carbohydrates, 34.7% water, 4.7% fat, 4.4.% protein, 4.2% fiber, 1.6% ash. Acorns are rich in B vitamins and trace minerals, and provide 4% of the RDA of calcium and iron. A pound of shelled acorns provide 1,265 calories, and 100 grams (3.5 ounces) has 500 calories and 30 grams of oil.

Masting and Leaching

Over the centuries, acorns have supported a large population of Native Americans in California, and the grinding stones used to grind acorns into flour are still scattered over the western countryside. White settlers never really learned to tap the nutrients available in acorns (it involves a fair amount of work), and as a result using acorns for human nutrition went out of style in the U.S. around the turn of the century. But acorn flour is making a comeback – naturally gluten-free, it has a hearty, nutty flavor only found in gourmet and artisan breads.

The seed crop from an oak, the acorns, is called a "mast," and gathering a crop of acorns is called masting. The best Missouri trees from which to harvest acorns are white oak and pin oak. These trees produce the sweetest acorns, lowest in tannins. Acorns from black and red oak are best left to the squirrels. When gathering acorns, keep in mind that the bigger the cap on the acorn, the more bitter it will be.

Tannins can be removed by soaking chopped acorns in several changes of water, until water no longer turns brown. Being rich in fat, acorn flour can spoil easily, so generally it should be refrigerated until use.

To leach the tannins from the nut, shuck the acorns into cold water (important to prevent oxidation and discoloration), and use enough of them to fill a blender up about 1/3 of the way. Add water to fill the blender to half way, and blenderize until milkshake consistency. Put the mix in a large glass jar with 50% water, and 50% acorn mix. Each morning, pour off the water, being careful to not lose too much of your acorn flour. Refill the jar, cap it and shake vigorously, turning it upside down to make sure all the acorn flour is suspended in the water. Repeat as necessary. The acorn flour is ready when it is bland to the taste, with no bitterness. Strain the wet flour through a strainer and cheese cloth to remove as much water as possible. Spread the flour on an oven tray or solid dehydrator tray, and dry at about 100 degrees. Turn the flour often so that it dries evenly. When dry, run it through a coffee grinder to get a coarse flour consistency.

Interesting Acorn Facts

During World War II Japanese school children collected over one million tons of acorns to help feed the nation as rice and flour supplies dwindled.

The Norse legend that Thor sheltered from a thunderstorm under an oak tree has led to the belief that having an acorn on a windowsill will prevent a house from being struck by lightning, hence the popularity of window blind pulls decorated as acorns

Acorn flour alone is gluten free, so it does not rise.

An easy way to harvest a lot of acorns is with a shop-vac (with a long cord)!

Many folks find that hitting acorns with a hammer on the pointy end makes them easier to shell.

Acorn Bread

2 cups acorn flour

2 cups white flour

3 teaspoons baking powder

1/3 cup maple syrup or sugar

1 egg

1/2 cup milk

3 tablespoons olive oil

Mix ingredients and bake in pan at 400 degrees for 30 minutes or until done.

43 CATTAILS – PROVIDER OF THE POND

October 31, 2013

Some folks get dismayed with the arrival of cattails to their pond banks. Not me! Every part of the cattail (typha latifolia) is edible, with the exception of the leaves. The pollen can be used essentially "as-is" for a flour expander, and the roots can also be ground into flour. The sticky sap between the leaves is high in starch and makes an excellent thickener for soups and gravies. The inner white parts of the shoots at the base of the leaves can be pulled out and then steamed or eaten raw like asparagus.

A 3 ounce serving of cattail roots contains 25 calories. They are a good source of Iron and Phosphorus, and a _very_ good source of dietary fiber, Vitamin K, Vitamin B6, Calcium, Magnesium, Potassium and Manganese.

Cattail Flour

In last week's column we discussed making flour from acorns. Another excellent gluten-free flour can be made from cattails, and is much easier than making acorn flour. In the Spring, watch for the yellow pollen to develop on the skinny tip on top of the brown velvety cattail part. If you catch it at the right time, it is easy to harvest a good amount in 30 minutes. One method is to bend the top of the cattail over a bread bag, and shake the stem until the pollen falls off into the bag. In a pinch, the pure pollen can be used like flour, although it is best mixed with regular flour. You can substitute up to 30-50% of regular flour in a recipe with cattail pollen, with excellent results. The pollen flour is similar to saffron, giving foods an enhanced flavor and an appetizing yellow color to baked goods.

Medicinal Uses

Most of the pharmacological properties of cattails are found in the pollen. The pollen can be used as a hemostat, or "bleeding stopper." We use a similar (expensive!) item in the hospital called Surgicel, and it is placed directly on cuts to control bleeding, acting almost as an artificial scab.

Fresh, pulverized root of the cattails can be used as a poultice on infections and stings. The mashed root can also be used as a tooth polish.

The sticky sap at the base of the green leaf provides disinfection, stops bleeding, and also acts as a numbing agent.

The leaves can be boiled to make an external skin wash.

The young flowers of the cattail plant (May through July) can be ingested to treat diarrhea.

Other Health Benefits

Cattails filter out toxins in murky streams, and help to stop river bank erosion. The roots have been shown to filter large amounts of lead out of polluted reservoirs. This will ultimately result in purer water, but ingestion of cattails from a polluted pond should obviously be avoided.

Precautions

Cattails are known to be an emmaogogue (menstruation inducing), so they should be avoided by pregnant women.

Although cattails are safe and edible for people, they may be toxic to some grazing animals.

Other Uses

The Chippewa made floating toys out of the cattail leaves, and used fluff from the pods to insulate footwear in the winter.

Cattail pollen pancakes

1/2 C cattail pollen

1/2 C all purpose flour

2 tsp baking powder

1 C milk (for buttermilk, add 2 Tbsp white vinegar to ¾ C milk)

1 egg

1/4 tsp salt

1 Tbsp sugar

2 Tbsp oil

Mix dry ingredients, then add milk and oil. Mix only until moistened. Heat griddle or pan until water drops sizzle. Pour batter on the hot griddle. Turn pancakes when they are full of bubbles, just before they break. Serve hot. Makes 10 four inch pancakes.

44 ELDERBERRIES – WHAT WE CAN LEARN FROM THE WALKING DEAD

November 7, 2013

Fans of the Walking Dead surely took note two weeks ago when Herschel, the aging veterinarian, went to the woods to gather herbs to save members of his colony from the flu.

The berries he picked were from the American Elderberry bush (Sambucus Canadensis), long reputed to be effective against the flu virus. Juice from elderberries is used to treat many conditions, including arthritic pains, colds, headaches, constipation, neuralgia, urinary tract conditions, and intestinal infections.

Intestinal Parasites

In a recent study, elderberry fruit was found to have excellent action (78% effective), against a parasite called giardia that causes an infection of the intestinal tract. Traditional treatment has unpleasant side effects like severe nausea. You can contract giardia by swallowing stream or lake water, with resulting watery, foul-smelling diarrhea, lasting 2 – 4 weeks – not a good thing!

Anti-Viral Activity

In 2013, researchers investigated the antiviral effect of concentrated juice of elderberry (CJ-E) on the human influenza A virus, and found "a relatively strong defense against infection." They concluded that concentrated elderberry juice had a beneficial effect by stimulating the body's immune response and preventing viral infection.

Other research studies this year looked at over the counter medications touted to prevent respiratory infections, including Sinupret and Theramax, both of which contain elderberry extract. They found that these preparations showed a broad spectrum of antiviral activity against viruses commonly known to cause respiratory infections, including adenovirus, RSV, and several forms of influenza. These medicines are thought to help by blocking virus absorption into the body.

When elderberry juice was compared with Tamiflu in blocking H1N1 infection, a study published in Phytochemistry in 2009 concluded, "H1N1 inhibition activities of the elderberry flavonoids compare favorably to the known anti-influenza activities of Oseltamivir (Tamiflu)." They further found that flavonoids from the elderberry extract bind to the H1N1 virus and, when bound, block the ability of the viruses to infect host cells.

Topical Applications

Water made with flowers from the Elderberry plant is used in lotions as a mild astringent. When applied externally, elderberry helps decrease inflammation, bruising and sprains.

When used in sunscreen products, formulations made from elderberries "fulfill the official requirements for sunscreen products due to their broad spectrum of UV protection combined with their high photostability and remarkable antioxidant properties."

Packed With Nutrition

In addition to cancer-fighting natural antioxidants and antiviral phenolic compounds believed to be antiviral and of use in treating the common cold, elderberries are naturally high in Vitamin C, with one cup supplying 87% of the recommended daily requirement. They are also high in Vitamin A, calcium, iron, and dietary fiber. Low calorie, too!

Other Uses

For those with a little bit of land, looking for a home-based business idea, look no further. The demand for elderberry products is exploding, as the public recognizes the distinctive health benefits. Sales of elderberry seeds, extract, dried flowers, jelly, jams, juice and dyes are brisk on the internet. To start your elderberry orchard, now is the time to purchase your seedlings from the George O. White State Forest Nursery in Licking.

Dosing

Elderberries can be made into a syrup, or prepared as a tea, wine, infusion, decoction, or tincture. The berries are bitter, so they always require a sweetener of some sort. During flu season, 1 Tbs. daily of elderberry syrup will keep your immune system strong.

ELDERBERRY SYRUP RECIPE:

- 1/2 cup fresh or dried elderberries
- 3 cups water
- cinnamon stick (or ground cinnamon)
- cloves (if desired)
- 1/2 to 1 cup **local honey**

Bring the elderberries, water and spices to a boil. Allow to simmer for 20-30 minutes. Remove from heat and strain and discard the solids. Let cool just a bit and then add honey and stir until well mixed. Store in a cool place in a dark-colored glass jar.

Precautions

Uncooked or unripe elderberries can cause nausea and vomiting.

The American Elderberry loves Missouri soil and climate.

45 TIME TO TALK ABOUT TOOTHPASTE

Part 1

November 14, 2013

For most of my life, I have gagged horribly when brushing my teeth, a feeling that only subsided after rinsing my mouth thoroughly, and removing any vestige of toothpaste. Like everyone else, I grew up bombarded by TV dentists telling me that fluoride would prevent cavities.

The word is now out on fluoride. City and local governments are quietly removing it from their water supplies, or not so quietly, due to public demand.

What is fluoride? All of my columns begin at the National Library of Medicine. That is where is research and verify, searching through the old "landmark" studies, and recently published research, looking for the facts.

The Dirty Truth

Fluoride is a by-product of aluminum smelting. Early cases of fluorosis (fluoride poisoning) were reported in the early 1900's due to fluoride being dumped into the waterways. In 1932, skeletal fluorosis was discovered as an occupational disease in aluminum smelter workers. With the industrial output necessitated by WWII, contamination of drinking water supplies with the byproduct fluoride increased.

In the 1940's, William Gafafer, senior statistician of the U.S. Public Health Service, identified the problem and wrote " *The dumping of industrial wastes into our rivers and streams is an unjustifiable although time-honored practice which should be discontinued. But, we must face the fact that the practice will not and probably cannot be eliminated at this time".*

The folks at Alcoa came up with a solution – they could sell fluoride to the government to add to the drinking water supply to prevent cavities! Now the problem of eliminating hazardous material was gone, and they even got paid for it.

When the argument was raised that ALCOA´s sodium fluoride is a waste product of their aluminum production, the Journal of the American Dental Association was quick to publish a denial in the form of a classic disinformation piece presented by ALCOA´s Chemical Sales Manager H. P. Bonebrake in 1955:

"DENIES SODIUM FLUORIDE IS INDUSTRY´S WASTE PRODUCT

The Aluminum Company of America last month denied that sodium fluoride is a waste product of aluminum manufacture. ... ´We make no direct sales of sodium fluoride, all of our production being handled through chemical distributors´. ... The letter pointed out also that a high percentage of sodium fluoride is obtained from phosphate rock. ´We have no operations involving phosphate rock."

The Facts

There is scientific evidence that fluoride can kill cavity-causing bacteria, after all, it IS a poison, but do the risks outweigh the benefits? Let's look at some of the well-known effects of fluoride:

Effect on Intestinal Tract

Fluoride has several mechanisms of toxicity. Ingested fluoride initially acts locally on the intestinal mucosa. It can form hydrofluoric acid in the stomach, which leads to GI irritation or corrosive effects. Following ingestion, the GI tract is the earliest and most commonly affected organ system. In a 2011 analysis from the Medical College of Georgia that looked at fluoride toxicity, they found that around 30,000 calls to US poison control centers concerning acute exposures in children are made each year, most of which involve temporary gastrointestinal effects, but others require medical treatment.

To be continued next week

46 TIME TO TALK ABOUT TOOTHPASTE

Part 2

November 21, 2013

Last week we began discussing the toxic effects of fluoride. Poison Control Centers receive approximately 30,000 calls each year due to acute fluoride exposures in children. Dental products are the most common cause of fluoride toxicity because of their relatively high fluoride concentrations, pleasant flavors, and their presence in non-secure locations in most homes. For example, ingestion of only 1.8 ounces of a standard fluoridated toothpaste by a 22 pound child delivers enough fluoride to reach a toxic dose.

Effect on IQ

A 2012 study from Harvard University showed evidence of fluoride's possible effect on neurological development in children, including IQ scores, concluding "children in high-fluoride areas had significantly lower IQ scores than those who lived in low-fluoride areas."

Dental fluorosis

Among the potential hazards of fluoridation in children, the best established is dental fluorosis, a mottling of the teeth caused by excessive ingestion of fluoride when they are forming in the jaw. The effects are cosmetic rather than functional and cause problems only when the disorder is severe.

Fractures

Other possible adverse effects that have been proposed include cancer, arthritis, and fractures. About half of ingested fluoride is taken up by bone, where once absorbed, fluoride binds with calcium ions leading to hypocalcemia with weakening of the bone structure. Several recent studies have examined the relation of fluoride toothpaste to hip fractures.

Thyroid

One of the most controversial issues is the impact of fluoride on the thyroid gland. Many people are not aware that in the first half of the 20th century, fluoride was used medically as an anti-thyroid drug, to slow down the thyroid function in hyperthyroid patients. Fluoride was found to be effective at suppressing or reducing thyroid function, according to research, and the dose needed to reduce thyroid function was low -- 2 to 5 mg per day over a period of months, about the same amount folks receive in fluoridated drinking water. Could our water and toothpaste be making us fat?

From the FDA website

FDA regulations require the following warning must be placed on all fluoride-containing products: "**Keep out of reach of children under 6 years of age.** If more than used for brushing is accidentally swallowed, get medical help or contact a Poison Control Center right away." Further FDA precautions include "Instruct children under 12 years of age in good brushing and rinsing habits (to minimize swallowing). Supervise children as necessary until capable of using without supervision." When was the last time you read your toothpaste label? No wonder all European countries now ban fluoride in the drinking water. It is truly a poison.

The word is definitely out regarding fluoride, and toothpaste recipes abound on the internet. Here is my favorite recipe:

Home Made Toothpaste

1/2 Cup Virgin Coconut Oil

2-3 Tablespoons baking soda

15-20 drops peppermint oil

2-3 drops tea tree oil (optional – for oral antiseptic)

Heat coconut oil until liquid form, add ingredients and mix well. Place in a glass jar and allow to cool. (I actually save old toothpaste tubes, rinse them out, and refill them with my homemade toothpaste while it is still warm – did you know you can recrimp the opened end of a toothpaste tube with regular pliers?)

47 MAGNESIUM – CAN'T LIVE WITHOUT IT!

Part 1

November 28, 2013

I've been a professional nurse since the 1970's, and I clearly remember the day Dr. Durkin burst through the door to the ICU, shouting "Check the magnesium level!" He had just been to an international conference, and had attended days of classes on the role of magnesium in health.

Decades ago, checking magnesium levels was rarely included in laboratory testing. In today's world, magnesium levels are checked at least daily on critically ill patients, and for good reason. My brilliant critical care instructor, Vee Rice, used to compare the effects of magnesium to valium, due to its ability to calm the nervous system, an effect that prevents many heart and nervous system problems.

Magnesium is the fourth most abundant mineral in the body, and assists with over 300 metabolic processes. Magnesium plays a critical role in nerve transmission, cardiac rhythm, neuromuscular conduction, muscular contraction, blood vessel tone, blood pressure, and glucose and insulin metabolism. Magnesium clearly plays a major role in disease prevention and overall health. Low levels of magnesium have been associated with a number of chronic diseases including migraine headaches, Alzheimer's disease, cerebrovascular accident (stroke), hypertension, cardiovascular disease, seizures and type 2 diabetes.

Magnesium is an essential mineral for optimal metabolic function. Research has shown that the mineral content of magnesium in processed food sources is steadily declining. Experts say that many people in the U.S. aren't eating enough foods with magnesium, leading to magnesium depletion. Hundreds of studies have shown the effectiveness of magnesium in eclampsia and preeclampsia (high blood pressure and seizures associated with pregnancy), heart arrhythmias, severe asthma, and migraine. Other areas that have shown promising results include lowering the risk of metabolic syndrome, improving glucose and insulin metabolism, relieving symptoms of dysmenorrhea, and alleviating leg cramps in women who are pregnant. Magnesium is also the main ingredient in many antacids and laxatives.

Adults who consume less than the recommended amount of magnesium are more likely to have elevated inflammation markers. Inflammation, in turn, has been associated with major health conditions such as heart disease, diabetes, and certain cancers. Also, low magnesium appears to be a risk factor for osteoporosis. There's some evidence that eating foods high in magnesium can help prevent high blood pressure.

Magnesium and seizures

Magnesium sulfate has been used for over 100 years to prevent and treat eclamptic seizures, and continues to be used extensively. Magnesium decreases the seizure threshold by acting as a central nervous system depressant and may also block transmission of neuromuscular signals by reducing acetylcholine release. Since acetylcholine transmits nerve impulses, this action can reduce seizure activity. Magnesium sulfate also acts as a calcium antagonist, decreasing the amount of calcium found in cells. Decreased calcium in the cells can cause blood vessels to relax. Relaxing blood vessels may also decrease seizure activity, as otherwise blood vessels can spasm, causing reduced blood flow to the brain – a process that can trigger a seizure.

Basic research studies have shown the presence of a so-called magnesium block in the mature brain. The "magnesium block" blocks impulses from the N-methyl-d-aspartate (NMDA)receptor that sends current through the brain causing seizures in susceptible patients. Infants don't have this magnesium block, therefore they can have seizures that are later outgrown. The mature brain shows little response to NMDA unless magnesium ions are removed from the cerebrospinal fluid.

Recently, there have been several cases of new-onset seizures in patients taking ulcer medications, such as Omeprazole (Prilosec). It is thought that these medications impair magnesium absorption from the stomach, significantly lowering the body's magnesium level. Several patients taking the proton-pump inhibitors for peptlc ulcers reported headaches, dizziness, muscle cramps, heart arrhythmias and hand numbness as early symptoms before progressing to seizures. Symptoms were resolved by discontinuing the offending medication and replacing the patient's magnesium.

To be continued next week...

48 MAGNESIUM – CAN'T LIVE WITHOUT IT!

Part 2

December 5, 2013

Last week we talked about the role of magnesium in the treatment of seizures. Magnesium has been proven effective in the treatment of several other conditions.

Magnesium and blood pressure

If you have high blood pressure, chances are you have been prescribed a calcium channel blocker. Magnesium is nature's natural calcium blocker, and is unique as it can act on most types of calcium channels in vascular smooth muscle. One major effect of decreased calcium in the cell is arterial relaxation that may subsequently lower peripheral and cerebral vascular resistance, relieve vasospasm, and decrease arterial blood pressure.

Magnesium and Migraine

There is a great deal of evidence that most migraine patients should be treated with magnesium. It is estimated that up to half of migraine sufferers have much lower magnesium levels than healthy controls. The fact that magnesium helps prevent spasm of the blood vessels leading to the brain may partially explain its role in migraine prevention. Many migraine protocols used in neurology utilize magnesium supplementation as a first-line approach to treatment.

Magnesium and metabolic syndrome

The importance of magnesium intake in relation to the metabolic syndrome has been increasingly recognized. Magnesium is an essential mineral, critical for a number of metabolic functions in the human body. Animal studies indicate a pivotal role of magnesium in glucose homeostasis and insulin secretion and action. Experimental and clinical studies suggest that magnesium intake may be inversely related to the risk of hypertension and type 2 diabetes mellitus, and may decrease blood triglyceride and increase HDL (good) cholesterol levels.

Magnesium and depression

In 1921, the American Journal of Psychiatry published the first article looking at the effect of magnesium on depression. Sixty percent of cases of clinical depression are considered to be treatment-resistant depression (TRD). Magnesium-deficiency causes N-methyl-d-aspartate (NMDA) coupled calcium channels to remain open, causing nerve damage and neurological dysfunction, which may appear to humans as major depression. In animal studies, ingesting magnesium led to anti-depressant-like effects that were comparable to those of strong anti-depressant drugs. Low magnesium levels have been found in patients that have attempted suicide. Although that circa 1921 report of magnesium treatment for agitated depression showed success in 220 out of 250 cases, and there are modern case reports showing rapid termination of TRD with magnesium, only a few modern clinical trials can be found. A 2008 randomized clinical trial showed that magnesium was as effective as the tricyclic anti-depressant imipramine in treating depression in diabetics - without any of the side effects.

Food Sources

It's safe to get large amounts of magnesium from food. But excessive use of magnesium supplements can be toxic. Adults should limit their magnesium intake to 350 mg/day. Although magnesium is safe in most people at appropriate dosages, magnesium may cause adverse effects or death at high dosages. Because magnesium is excreted by the kidneys, it should be used with caution in patients with kidney disease.

Food sources of magnesium include green leafy vegetables, nuts, beans, peas, soybeans, whole grains, and even white potatoes. Magnesium has been largely removed from processed foods. The foods highest in magnesium are raw spinach, squash and pumpkin seeds, mackerel, soybeans, brown rice, avocados, plain non-fat yogurt, bananas, figs and dark chocolate.

Epson salts

There is some evidence that Magnesium can be absorbed through the skin in small amounts, as in soaking in a bath with 2 cups of Epsom salts added. (Epsom salts are magnesium sulfate.) A dose of Epsom salts is also a very efficient laxative.

Precautions

Magnesium supplements can cause nausea, cramps, and diarrhea. Magnesium supplements often cause softening of stool. People with diabetes, intestinal disease, heart disease or kidney disease should not take magnesium before speaking with their health care provider. Signs of a magnesium overdose can include nausea, diarrhea, low blood pressure, muscle weakness, confusion and fatigue. At very high doses, magnesium can be *fatal*.

49 THE DECISION TO VACCINATE

Part 1

By: Tamara Glascock

December 12, 2013

(Over the next 2 weeks, *Nature Has the Cure* will feature guest author Tamara Glascock, certified herbalist from Edgar Springs.)

The decision to vaccinate is becoming more difficult and inspires a wealth of questions. Are they safe? Which ones do we really need? Aren't they mandatory? Finding the answers can be difficult, especially as more studies reveal the dangers of many of the commonly available vaccines.

Let's start simple. Vaccines are not mandatory in Missouri. Should you forego giving your child vaccines, you only need to obtain a waiver form from your physician, or online from the Department of Health (health.mo.gov/immunizations/orderform2.php).

The rest of the questions are more volatile and have no easy answers. Understanding the basic operation of the immune system can help, though. Vaccines work by exposing the person to a tiny amount of the actual disease. The immune system reacts by fighting off that disease, then remembering it when it encounters it again in the future, then stops it before it can take hold in the system. *In theory.*

This is where things get complicated. The immune system develops over the first months of life by being exposed to germs, bacteria and viruses. It learns a little bit at a time as you come into contact with these bugs by being out in the real world. Over time, your immune system knows what belongs in your body, and what doesn't. It will automatically react to the bad bugs by burning them off via built-in control mechanisms within the body, while leaving the good ones alone. If there are a lot of these bad bugs, the body will produce a fever that will cook those little fellas to death and then flush them out of the system via the elimination channels (intestines, skin, urinary tract).

However, by introducing diseases through artificial means (vaccinations), you are, in essence, tricking the immune system. It goes a little wonky fighting off all of the germs, bacteria and viruses, including the good ones. It leaves behind a vague memory of the actual disease and it may, or may not, recognize it later on. Hence, the need for vaccine boosters. Unfortunately, the vaccine can backfire, ending in contracting the disease from the vaccine itself.

One must also consider the questionable ingredients added to many vaccines. Thimerosal (a mercury-containing compound), animal organ tissue, aluminum and formaldehyde are just a few of the dangerous ingredients found in vaccines. Each dose of the current flu vaccine contains 5 mcg. of mercury, for example. Trying to read the ingredient list on most vaccines requires a fluent scientific vocabulary and a large dictionary, and the only 'natural' ingredient most of them contain is the disease itself.

Are vaccines really necessary? In a perfect world, the answer would be an unequivocal "No!" If only we lived in a perfect world. So many factors play into this issue that making a decision can be difficult.

In my opinion, there are some vaccines that should be avoided at all costs, by all people of all ages, ethnicities and locations. Vaccines for Chicken Pox and Influenza are two of these. Not only are they unnecessary, they are often dangerous.

Chicken Pox and Shingles

Until 1995 when the Chicken Pox vaccine was first made available in the US, the traditional school of thought on this 'disease' was that it was best to expose your child while they were young. Sounds a little crazy, but there is a bit of logic behind this thought. Even the CDC admits that the chance of developing Chicken Pox more than once is very rare. Chicken Pox IS highly contagious, and approximately 98% of the population tests positive for exposure. In many ways, Chicken Pox is its own natural vaccine and is far more effective and less dangerous than those being pushed by the big Pharmaceutical companies. Shingles (Herpes Zoster) can occur decades after a case of chicken pox, mainly in adults over the age of 60, and those who are immunosuppressed. The reason why shingles may occur is because the virus does not completely disappear after you have chickenpox. Some virus particles remain inactive in the nerve roots next to your spinal cord. They do no harm there, and cause no symptoms. For reasons that are not clear, the virus may begin to multiply again, attach to a nerve root, causing painful lesions.

The newly available Shingles vaccine can prevent 1 shingles case over a 3 year period for every 60 to 70 patients vaccinated. The Shingles vaccine should not be given to persons < 60 years old, or those who have received the chicken pox vaccine. Post licensure studies to evaluate the safety of this vaccine are currently "under development." There is some concern that the recent increase in the outbreaks of shingles correlates with increased chicken pox vaccinations, due to less boosting of immunity by the body to the varicella virus. The chicken pox vaccination **is** effective in its prevention, but the incidence of shingles in older persons has definitely increased after the increase in chicken pox vaccinations.

Continued next week...

50 THE DECISION TO VACCINATE – Part 2

By: Tamara Glascock

December 19, 2013

The Influenza vaccine is a whole different monster, and a bit more difficult to explain. To simplify, many who receive the flu vaccine end up with the flu in some form or another. This is primarily because Influenza is a fluent virus. It changes from season to season. It is impossible to predict which strain is going to make itself known, and there are so many different strains that it is impossible to vaccinate against them all. It is also a bit smarter than us humans. It knows how to evolve and grow stronger, so even when we think we have all of our bases covered it reminds us that we don't.

Then, we have some vaccines that may be useful under certain conditions, such as the Hepatitis B vaccine. This is one that they inject as soon as your child is born. If the mother has Hepatitis B, then this vaccine could possibly be useful in stopping the baby from contracting the disease. Possibly, but not guaranteed, as the child is fed from the mother's blood in the womb and is just as likely to contract the disease in vitro or during birth. Hepatitis B is a blood-borne disease and can only be contracted through bodily fluid sharing. This includes sex, needle-sharing, unsterile tattooing, etc. Unless you are planning one of these activities for your newborn, there is no reason to have them vaccinated against the disease, and the chances of experiencing severely negative side effects are a bigger threat than them actually contracting the disease.

We also have vaccines for diptheria, tetanus, rotavirus, pertussis, polio and pneumococcal infections. While diseases like polio and pertussis (whooping cough) caused devastation throughout history, these vaccines are still questionable for several reasons. Aside from their dangerous ingredients, many of these diseases are preventable and treatable through natural means. Proper nutrition and hygiene play major roles in the prevention of these diseases. Refined sugar is a serious contributor to polio. Improper hygiene is a serious contributor to tetanus. A lack of proper vitamins and minerals are serious contributors to diptheria, rotavirus, pertussis and pneumococcal infections, as well as many other illnesses and diseases.

In areas or circumstances that don't allow one access to healthy food and fresh water, vaccines could possibly be an invaluable tool in helping to prevent many diseases. For those who live or work in unsanitary areas, vaccines may offer a viable alternative to keeping disease at bay. If existing conditions like HIV/AIDS or other immune system disorders are present, vaccines may be in order. Consult your physician and have a serious discussion on the benefits/risks.

The most effective prevention of disease comes from supplying the body with nutritious foods like fresh fruits and veggies (uncontaminated with pesticides, herbicides and GMO's), whole grains and raw nuts. These foods allow the body to obtain the vitamins and minerals necessary for the immune system to grow strong, making it capable of fighting off illness and disease of every kind. Depriving the body of things like refined sugar, processed grains and dairy products, and contaminated meat products will keep the immune system strong and healthy.

If you are serious about keeping your child and yourself free of disease and illness, spend some time at your local Farmer's Market or the produce aisle of the grocery store. Avoid boxed and canned foods that are loaded with artificial flavors, colors and preservatives. Read labels and pass on anything that contains ingredients you can't recognize or pronounce. Drink lots of water (fluoride and chlorine free, of course), eat less meat and more raw foods. Exercise. Meditate occasionally. Spend time in the sun soaking up some Vitamin D. Building a healthy immune system naturally is the best way to vaccinate yourself and your children against disease and illness.

You can learn more about Tamara's approach to natural medicine by visiting her website at tamarasherbes.com.

51 WAIT! DON'T THROW THAT CHRISTMAS TREE AWAY

December 26, 2013

As you gaze at your Christmas Tree, your first thought is unlikely to be its medicinal properties. Since 2012, research into the pharmaceutical uses of pine bark extract (PBE - sold commercially under the brand name Pycnogenol) has virtually exploded. In this article, we will explore the most impressive applications.

History

In 1535, a ship carrying a French explorer named Jacques Cartier became ice-bound in Canada. As the crew ran out of food, especially fruits and vegetables, they became ill with scurvy, due to vitamin C deficiency. Once again, the Native Americans saved the day, and showed the sailors how to make nutritious tea from tree bark. The crew members who recovered shared their story, and 400 years later, French researcher Dr. Jacques Masquelier read the account in Cartier's writings and set on a search for the miraculous tree ingredients. He was able to extract proanthocyanidins from European coastal pine tree bark, and patented the process, naming the compound Pycnogenol.

Physical Performance and Metabolic Recovery

A study published just this week in the *Journal of Sports Medicine Fitness* looked at the effect of pine bark extract on the performance of normal subjects taking the Army Physical Fitness Test, and also performance of triathletes. Among the results, participants treated with pine bark extract had improved performance and a significant decrease in cramps and post-running pain. On average, the pine-extract subjects completed the 100 minute triathlon 6 minutes faster than the control group, and both the normal subjects and triathletes treated with pine bark extract showed a faster metabolic recovery

Decongestant properties

Pine preparations have long been used as decongestants. In another study out this week, pine bark extract was used to treat allergic asthma, and relieved the symptoms by many mechanisms, including decreasing airway inflammation and decreasing mucus secretion.

Wound Healing

Several applications have been found for pine bark extract in the treatment of wounds. In one study, pine bark oil in ointment form was applied to an incision, and was found to significantly accelerate the wound healing process.

PBE also helps reduce ultraviolet radiation damage to the skin and may protect human facial skin from symptoms of photoaging. In one recent study, university researchers found "Clinically significant improvement in photodamaged skin could be achieved with regular application of pine bark extract."

Disinfectant

Pine extracts are effective against a wide range of bacteria, fungus and virus, including the influenza virus type A, and herpes simplex types 1 and 2. It will kill the causative agents of typhoid, gastroenteritis, rabies, enteric fever, cholera, several forms of meningitis, whooping cough, gonorrhea and several types of dysentery. It is very smart to add a few drops of pine oil to your cleaning products to safely disinfect your home.

A few drops can also be added to your pet's shampoo as a natural flea deterrent.

Muscle Rub/Arthritis

Besides preventing post-exercise cramping, pine oil can be used as a muscle and joint rub to ease pain and stiffness.

Nutritional Content

Pine needles **provide a good amount of vitamin A and about 5 times as much vitamin C as found in lemons.** A cup of pine needle tea can help with colds and flu. Steep a handful of washed pine needles in hot water. For a stronger tea, break the needles first.

Pine Bark Extract

To make your own, simply cut some pine branches, bark and needles included, and put them in a wide-mouth airtight jar. Cover the cuttings with grain alcohol or vodka. Shake well and store in a cool, dark place. Shake it at least once a day and start checking it after a couple of weeks. When you walk by and smell the pine smell, you will know it is ready to strain and bottle in a dark container. If you don't want to use alcohol, you can replace it with olive oil, but your tincture won't be as strong. If you are giving this as a gift, adding a sprig of clean, washed pine needles to the jar gives it that homey, homemade feel.

Please note that this is a very strong preparation, and one drop will go a long way!

Precautions

There are many more benefits, including nutritional, from both the needles and the bark of the pine tree. Unless someone has a specific allergy, pine tree products are SAFE. In fact, in 1989 I was trapped in my home for a week in South Carolina after Hurricane Hugo. Hundreds of pine trees had fallen into the reservoir, and the drinking water tasted like Christmas Trees for a long time – I never felt better!

52 ORANGE PEEL

January 2, 2014

In the category of NEVER throwing away nutritious foods, orange peel ranks at the top. There are dozens of uses for orange peel, and it provides benefits that can't be found elsewhere.

With generous amounts of Vitamin A and calcium, 1 Tbs. of orange peel also provides 14% of your vitamin C requirement, and 3% of daily dose of dietary fiber, with only 6 calories. In addition, it offers potassium, phosphorus, magnesium and some zinc as well.

Orange peel contains natural pectin, useful in making jams and jellies, and also decreases the rise in blood sugar after a meal.

Nutritional benefits aside, orange peel also contains large amounts of limonene and hesperidin, components that have huge health benefits.

Limonene

The major component in oil extracted from the orange peel, limonene has exceptional tissue healing properties. It is a potent antioxidant with anti-inflammatory effects, and in addition to its anti-cancer properties, it is effective for many other metabolic and health problems – even helping with weight management.

Anyone who has used orange oil as a cleaning agent is aware of its degreasing properties. In the body it serves as a unique fat cleanser, helping to clear cholesterol sludge, including the sludge in the gall bladder that can form stones. Another aspect of cleansing assistance is that it also helps liver detoxification enzymes, and has been proven to help hepatic steatosis (fatty liver).

Limonene helps reduce appetite and improve metabolism, making it one more nutrient to assist with healthy weight management. And of great importance, it is a superior nutrient for breast cancer prevention.

Breast Cancer Prevention

In a 2013 study published in Cancer Prevention Research, researchers recruited 43 women with newly diagnosed breast cancer electing to undergo surgical excision to take 2 grams of limonene daily for two to six weeks before surgery. Limonene was found to preferentially concentrate in the breast tissue, reaching high tissue concentration. They concluded that limonene distributed extensively to human breast tissue and reduced breast tumor cyclin D1 expression leading to cancer cell-cycle arrest and reduced cancer cell proliferation.

Because of the documented effectiveness of limonene against breast cancer, a study from the University of Arizona Cancer Center evaluated topical application of limonene to the breast as an alternative dosing strategy. They found that limonene is bio available in mammary tissue after external application of orange oil, and that this topical route of administration to the breast is safe and feasible in healthy women.

Hesperidin

Hesperidin has been studied for about 50 years. The highest concentration of hesperidin can be found in the white parts (pith) of the orange peel. Flavonoids such as hesperidin have been identified as the anti-diabetic components in a number of traditional remedies. Current studies suggest that hesperidin is beneficial for improving hyperlipidemia and hyperglycemia in type-2 diabetics by partly regulating the fatty acid and cholesterol metabolism and affecting the gene expression of glucose.

Hesperidin has a strong impact on blood cells, and is used to help treat varicose veins. In Europe, this natural ingredient is used to make Diosmin, a prescription medication used to treat venous insufficiency.

Hesperidin is also used to reduce hay fever and other allergic conditions by inhibiting the release of histamine from mast cells.

Hesperidin decreases the risk of heart disease by three major actions: improving blood flow to the heart, decreasing the ability of platelets in the blood to clot, and decreasing the level of LDL (bad cholesterol). The antioxidant and anti-inflammatory properties can also play a key role against several degenerative diseases and particularly brain diseases, including Alzheimer's.

Recipes

Dried orange peels can be ground in your coffee grinder to make a fabulous orange zest. Add it to stir-fry dishes or to cornmeal for breading fish prior to frying for enhanced flavor and nutrition.

Candied orange peel

- 2 large oranges, 1/8 inch of top and bottom cut off
- 2-1/4 cups sugar, divided
- 2 cups water

Cut peel on each orange into 4 vertical segments. Remove each segment (including white pith) in 1 piece. Cut into 1/4-inch-wide strips. If you squeeze your own orange juice, just cut strips from the peels after extracting the juice. Cook in large pot of boiling water 15 minutes; drain, rinse, and drain again.

Bring 2 cups sugar and 2 cups water to boil in saucepan over medium heat, stirring to dissolve sugar. Add peel. Return to boil. Reduce heat; simmer until peel is very soft, about 45 min. Drain.

Toss peel and 1/4 cup sugar on a plate, separating strips. Transfer peels to sheet of foil. Let stand until coating is dry, about 24 hours.

Note: add any extra sugar after coating peels back to your pot that contains the syrup. Continue to slow boil until it cooks down, and you will have a delicious orange syrup for pancakes, stir-fried dishes, etc.

Homemade candied orange slices are delicious and nutritious!

53 KALE – NEW HOPE FOR STOMACHE ULCERS

January 9, 2014

I've received a few emails from ulcer sufferers, looking for a natural cure. In addition to being painful, and sometimes embarrassing, gastric ulcers can lead to stomach cancer. Like all diseases we encounter, the cure is found in nature. In this case, that cure is kale (borecole).

Despite the common notion that ulcers are caused by stress, they are actually due to a bacteria called Helicobacter pylori, H. pylori for short, which invades the stomach lining.

Kale contains a chemical called glucosinolate isothiocyanate (ITC) that stops H. pylori in its tracks. While this chemical has anti-tumor properties, researchers have found that its only antimicrobial action targets the H. pylori organism – making it a very dedicated chemical.

Other health benefits include prevention of colon and prostate cancer. Kale contains chemicals that boost the immune system, and has been found to prevent age-related macular degeneration. Many studies have looked at the effect of kale in the diet (or absence) in relation to macular degeneration and cataracts. Kale has been consistently associated with maintaining a healthy macula in the eye, and preventing cataract formation. (Macular degeneration is the leading cause of severe vision loss in people over age 60. It occurs when the small central portion of the retina, known as the macula, deteriorates.)

Botanically, kale belongs to the cabbage family, and is close in similarity to collard greens. One cup has only 36 calories, no fat, and 20% of the recommended daily allowance of fiber. It is a richer source of many vitamins and miners that most other green leafy vegetables, and is gaining a reputation as "the new beef."

One cup of kale also provides a huge dose (1327% of the RDA) of Vitamin K, 192% of the RDA for Vitamin A, and 88% of our daily Vitamin C requirement. It is also a rich source of copper, calcium, sodium, potassium, iron, manganese, and phosphorus.

Growing Kale

You can easily grow kale in Missouri. It is an annual plant, and prefers cool climate and light frost conditions. It is grown mainly for autumn and winter harvest, because cool weather further enhances its sweet taste quality. With that said, it can tolerate temperatures as low as 20F degrees, but will start to turn bitter and become tough in temperatures over 80F degrees. The old folks will tell you that is tastes best after it has been touched by frost, but kale is a hearty and adaptable crop, ideal for Missouri gardens.

Start seeds indoors 4 to 6 weeks before the last frost by planting them in small pots filled with a mix of soil and compost. Place the seed at least ½ inch deep. Keep the soil around the seedling evenly moist throughout its growth, but allow the top layer of soil to dry between watering. Cover the pot with a plastic bag during germination, and keep it in a sunny place. You can also directly sow seeds in the garden starting 2 to 4 weeks before the last frost date or as soon as the ground can be worked in the springtime. When growing for personal use, a good rule of thumb is 3 – 4 plants per family member. You can begin harvesting the leaves 50 to 75 days from germination.

Precautions

Kale, like other members of the cabbage family, contains substances that suppress the function of the thyroid gland by interfering with iodine, and can also lead to goiters. These substances, called goitrogens, are usually no problem unless consumed raw in large amounts, or in people with iodine deficiencies. If you have a history of thyroid problems, you may want to avoid raw kale. Fortunately, cooking helps to inactivate these compounds. As a side note, everyone should be sure to purchase only iodized salt for its beneficial effects on the thyroid.

Because Kale is such an incredibly rich source of Vitamin K, eating It In large amounts may decrease the effectiveness of anticoagulant (blood thinner) medication. If you enjoy kale regularly, your physician will want to know.

Kale is also naturally high in oxalates which can interfere with calcium absorption. It is best to avoid eating a calcium-rich food at the same time as kale. People with a history of oxalate-containing kidney stones should avoid eating too much kale and other oxalate-containing greens.

Crispy Kale Chips

Ingredients

- 1 head kale, washed and thoroughly dried
- 2 tablespoons olive oil
- Sea salt, for sprinkling

Directions

Preheat the oven to 275 degrees F.

Remove the ribs from the kale and cut into 1 1/2-inch pieces. Lay on a baking sheet and toss with the olive oil and salt. Bake until crisp, turning the leaves halfway through, about 20 minutes. Serve as finger food.

Even children love Kale chips!

54 OKRA – MOST HATED VEGETABLE NO MORE!

(part 1)

January 16, 2014

Okra, a perennial plant scientifically named Abelmoschus esculentus, is also known as "lady finger," because of its long, slender pods. It is one of the most highly nutritious vegetables, is cultivated the world over, and used in classic food dishes in many countries. It is a little unusual in that the most edible part, the pod, is mucilaginous (as in slimy), kind of a put-off to many people.

Nutritional Benefits

Okra is one of the very low calorie vegetables, with only 30 calories in one cup. Okra has no cholesterol or saturated fats, but is a rich source of fiber, vitamins and minerals, making it an excellent food for dieters.

The mucilaginous part even has a benefit. It acts as a natural stool softener, relieving constipation.

One cup of okra supplies 16% of your daily fiber allowance, and 44% of Vitamin C. Okra is also rich in Vitamin A, calcium, iron, potassium, and magnesium. Perhaps most importantly, okra provides 22% of the RDA of folate – an essential vitamin during pregnancy, as it helps prevent the incidence of neural tube defects in the developing fetus.

Okra is one of the green vegetables highest in flavonoid anti-oxidants such as beta carotene, xanthin, and lutein. These compounds help prevent some forms of cancers, and are essential for vision.

Medicinal Benefits

For two decades, researchers have been looking closely at the health benefits of okra. A landmark study in 1995 found that okra in the diet reduced proteinuria (protein in the urine) and improved kidney function in patients with diabetic nephropathy. Dozens of more recent studies have replicated these findings.

Perhaps okra's most important effect on health is its powerful effect on blood sugar levels. Unlike many natural foods that lower blood sugar in Type 2 diabetics, okra appears to enhance glucose utilization and lower plasma glucose in type 1 diabetics – those that are dependent on insulin.

Researchers agree that okra extract lowers blood glucose and improves renal function in diabetics, but not HOW it does it. Okra contains a flavonoid called myricetin that has been shown repeatedly to lower blood glucose levels, but research is ongoing.

Other prominent health benefits of okra include lowering of elevated lipid profile levels to near normal in diabetic patients, and promotion of weight loss. In 2012, The Journal of Ophthalmology concluded that regular intake of okra reduced significantly the risk of blindness, cataract and glaucoma.

If you hate okra, but want to take advantage of the medicinal properties, try okra water. Take two full pods of okra, cut off both ends, and make a couple small cuts in the middle. Place in a glass of water, and let sit overnight. In the morning, remove the okra from the glass and drink the water.

In next week's column we will discuss growing and preparing okra.

55 OKRA – MOST HATED VEGETABLE NO MORE!

(part 2)

January 23, 2014

Last week we discussed the nutritional and medicinal properties of okra. In this week's column, we will look at an important drug interaction, and how to grow and prepare this misunderstood vegetable.

Precautions

A 2011 study found okra improved blood sugar control, but when taken in combination with Metformin, it resulted in a complete loss of the blood sugar lowering effect of that prescription medication. For this reason, diabetics should be careful in taking metformin with a meal that contains okra. This is not necessarily a bad thing, as okra extract is currently being studied by pharmaceutical companies in order to prepare a controlled-release form of metformin.

Preparation

In many parts of the world, the demand for okra is so high that it has to be imported. It is highly perishable because of its high moisture content, so the traditional method for preserving okra involves slicing and sun drying of the fruit until they become brittle, followed by milling into powder for further use. Since it is an important constituent of Indian food/curries, drying of okra has been practiced for centuries.

Okra oil is also a valuable commodity. Pressed from okra seeds, it is edible, with a pleasant taste and odor, and is high in oleic and linoleic acid (unsaturated fats). You can even drive your car with it, as a 2009 study found okra oil works as a biofuel.

Although the pod is the most-used part of the plant, okra leaves may also be eaten. The leaves are prepared by cooking them like beet or dandelion greens, or can be eaten raw in salads.

When the Civil War disrupted the importation of coffee in 1861, ground and roasted okra seeds were used as a caffeine-free substitute.

The fresh pods can be prepared in many ways: boiled, fried, stuffed and baked. They are a must-have ingredient in the gumbo dishes in Cajun country; and okra sliced, breaded in cornmeal and fried in a skillet has been a signature dish in the South for over 100 years.

Growing Okra

One of the easiest vegetables to grow, okra keeps on producing for months! You will have to pick it every 2 or 3 days AT LEAST. A warm season crop, okra grows best in the full sun with well-drained and manure rich soil. The plant bears numerous dark green colored pods measuring about 5-15 cm in length. It takes about 45-60 days to get ready-to-harvest fruits. Sow seeds directly in the garden, 12 – 18 inches apart, after the last frost when the soil has warmed to 60 degrees. You can typically begin harvesting your okra in July.

Okra Relleno

4 ounces pepper-jack cheese

1 pound fresh okra (4-inch-long pods)

1 cup self-rising flour

1/3 cup self-rising cornmeal

1 large egg

1/2 cup buttermilk

1/2 cup beer

Oil

1. Cut cheese into 3- x 1/4- x 1/4-inch sticks.

2. Cut a lengthwise slit in each okra pod, cutting to but not through ends; push seeds aside. Stuff pods with cheese sticks, and set aside.

3. Combine flour and cornmeal in a large bowl; make a well in center of mixture.

4. Stir together egg, buttermilk, and beer; add to dry ingredients, stirring until smooth.

Pour oil to depth of 3 inches into a Dutch oven; heat to 375°. Dip stuffed okra in batter, coating well; fry, a few at a time, in hot oil until golden. Drain on paper towels. Sprinkle with salt; serve immediately with salsa.

56 FRIENDS WITH BENEFITS – PETS AND HEALTH

January 30, 2014

Any discussion of natural cures would be incomplete without acknowledging the animals in our lives. Over the course of a 35 year career, I have personally seen the impact pets have on critically ill patients, old and young alike. I confess I have "snuck" dogs, cats and birds into the ICU, and even arranged a horse visit once (outside the patient's window). The most exotic pet visit of which I was a part involved penguins. A teenage girl's dying wish was to see the penguins at Sea World. Arrangements were made, and animal handlers brought the penguins to her bed in the ICU at UCSD Medical Center. It was quite a sight as ice water was spread on the floor for the penguins to walk through on their trek to the child's bedside.

In 2013, studies of the effects of animals on health exploded. Last August, a study out of prestigious Johns Hopkins University established that pets are good for your health. They found that in the elderly, pet ownership is associated with better self-care, improved eating, exercise, nutritional status, and better cardiac risk factors, including lower triglycerides.

Dog ownership in particular is associated with higher physical activity levels in both adults and children. In 2009, a study was conducted on 2065 children aged 9 to 10 years. Children from dog-owning families spent more time in light or moderate to vigorous physical activity and recorded higher levels of activity counts per minute than did children without dogs.

In adult studies, although only 23% of the dog owners walked their dogs 5 or more times per week, the odds of achieving sufficient physical activity and walking were 57% to 77% higher among dog owners compared with those not owning dogs. Just *owning* a dog is associated with improved physical activity and walking.

How do pets affect heart health? Study after study shows ownership of domestic pets, particularly dogs, lowers blood pressure, plasma cholesterol and triglycerides. While this is still a hot research topic, it is thought that the improved mood and emotional state of pet owners helps to decrease central and regional autonomic activity, and improve endothelial function which lowers blood pressure and reduces cardiac arrhythmias. Pet owners have calmer responses to mental stress and improved survival following myocardial infarction compared with non-pet owners. As a nurse, I can't tell you how many patients tell me they just want to get out of the hospital, and back to their dog!

Pets and Mental Health

Several studies suggest that the presence of a dog reduces aggression and agitation, as well as promoting social behavior in people with dementia. One study has shown that aquariums in dining rooms of dementia care units stimulate residents to eat more of their meals and to gain weight.

An interesting study in socially isolated people demonstrated the ability of pets to stave off the negativity caused by social rejection. In summary, pets can serve as important sources of social support, providing many positive psychological and physical benefits for their owners.

Animal-assisted therapy (AAT) is gaining popularity as part of therapy programs in residential aged care facilities. Humans and pet dogs respond to quiet interaction with a lowering of blood pressure and an increase in neurochemicals associated with relaxation and bonding. These effects may be of benefit in ameliorating behavioral and psychological symptoms of dementia.

The Myth of Pets as Disease Carriers

Animals have long been considered disease carriers, causing them to be banned from hospitals, nursing homes, and commercial establishments. As the realization of the value of pets in providing companionship and psychological support to nursing home residents becomes more evident, a lot of research was completed last year to see if there is any scientific evidence for banning pets from these areas. The answer is no.

In a 2013 study in the Journal of Environmental Health, the risk associated with pets in retail food outlets was evaluated, and found that no specific risk has been established in a clear and consistent manner.

Dogs have also been implicated as reservoirs for antibiotic-resistant bacteria. Another study investigated this possibility. The researchers reported "there is no evidence that the previously reported benefits of pet contact are compromised by the increased risk of carriage of drug-resistant staphylococci in residents associated with interaction with these animals in nursing homes. Thus, contact with pets, **always under good hygiene standards**, should be encouraged in these settings."

Therapeutic Horseback Riding

The 2013 journal of stroke rehabilitation found that therapeutic horseback riding (TR) improved the functional capacity, physical aspects and mental health of stroke patients with a positive impact on quality of life.

In another study at Western Michigan School of Medicine, published May, 2013, researchers looked at the effect of horseback riding on balance in elderly subjects with balance problems. They found that TR is a safe activity for older adults with mild to moderate balance deficits and leads to both improvements in balance and quality of life. A similar study conducted on healthy volunteers between the ages of 60 and 84 found that HR improves lower limb strength and balance in the elderly. These benefits have also been found in children with autism, cerebral palsy and Down syndrome.

Spinal Cord Injuries

Tragic numbers of veterans are returning from the Iraq/Afghanistan war with traumatic brain injuries, blast injuries, depression, traumatic amputations, and spinal cord injuries. All of these conditions may benefit from horseback riding, and therapeutic riding programs are being formed nationwide. Therapeutic riding provides physical, psychological, and psychosocial benefits to the spinal cord injured.

If you would like information on local therapeutic riding programs, contact Marie at calhorselover@yahoo.com

57 CHOCOLATE – BE SURE TO GET YOUR DAILY DOSE!   (Part 1)

February 6, 2014

History

Chocolate/cocoa has been known for its good taste and effects on health for centuries. Arriving in Europe in the 16th century from Central America, and prepared from roasted cacao seeds, chocolate has earned its reputation as the "most commonly craved food in the world." Over the years, chocolate has been considered both sinful and healthy. For decades, physicians told their patients to avoid chocolate; wrongfully assuming that it was associated with acne, cavities, obesity, high blood pressure, coronary artery disease and diabetes. As often happens, consuming chocolate has the opposite effect in all these areas, with surprising health benefits.

When the use of chocolate was introduced into Western Europe, its euphoria-causing effects were immediately evident, to the extent that the Church stated that a religious fasting would be invalidated by drinking chocolate. Meanwhile, if Europeans wanted to drink chocolate, it could only be for medicinal reasons! In Central America, cacao was a very precious substance reserved only for priests, highest government officials, military officers and great warriors. It was deemed "unsuitable" for women and children.

The Badianus Manuscript, an ancient medical text written in 1552 by the Aztecs, and discovered in the Vatican Library in 1929, outlines Mexican disease concepts and treatments. This detailed book describes the use of cocoa derivatives as nutrients or remedies for angina, constipation, tartar-related dental problems, dysentery, dyspepsia, indigestion, fatigue, gout and hemorrhoids.

Important and rare epidemiological evidence about the beneficial effects of chocolate came from studying the Kuna Indian population. The Kuna Indians live on an island off the coast of Panama, and drink homemade cocoa every day. The Indians who remain on the island have a very low rate of atherosclerosis, Type II diabetes, and high blood pressure. These benefits disappear when they move to the mainland and abandon their daily cocoa ritual.

Over the past five years, the discovery of several active compounds found in cocoa (used to make chocolate) has stimulated research on its effects in aging, oxidative stress, blood pressure regulation, atherosclerosis, and neurologic disorders.

Nutritional Benefits

During the 20th century, the concept of chocolate being good for the diet surpassed its medicinal uses, especially when it was introduced as an essential item in soldier rations. Ancel Keys (1904–2004), a University of Minnesota public health scientist, designed a lightweight, but nutritionally sound ration for the troops, called the K Ration (named after him), which originally included dry sausage, hard candy and chocolate. The K rations were consumed by millions of soldiers in World War II.

Chocolate products are made from cocoa, a dry, powdered, nonfat component product prepared from the seeds of the Theobroma cacao tree. Since cocoa was first discovered, it was considered the "drink of Gods," leading to the scientific naming of the cocoa plant in 1753 by Carl Linnaeus – Theo (God) and broma (drink). The nutritional properties of cocoa have long been recognized, with several nutritionists calling it a complete food.

Cocoa contains several active substances that affect human health:

flavonoids (antioxidants), methylxanthines (theobromine and caffeine), valeric acid, and essential minerals, including magnesium, potassium, iron and zinc. The fat found in dark chocolate is cocoa butter, which is 33% monounsaturated oleic acid. Oleic acid has a positive effect on lipid levels.

The magnesium and valeric acid in cacao relieve stress and provide a calming effect despite the presence of caffeine in chocolate. Have you ever craved a candy bar when you are under stress?

Health Benefits

Approximately 70 human studies have been carried out on cocoa products over the past 12 years, looking at a variety of possible health benefits. These studies indicate that the most significant effects involve improved endothelial function (linings of the blood vessels), lowered blood pressure, and improved cholesterol level. The effects of the active substances are much greater in dark than milk chocolate, and milk chocolate may slow down their absorption in the intestines, and counter-act the beneficial effects.

Methylxanthines are plant-produced natural products found in large amounts in chocolate. They act on adenosine receptors in the brain to enhance alertness, mood, and concentration levels. One methylxanthine, theobromine, is toxic for a variety of mammals such as dogs. In contrast, the toxicity of methylxanthines in humans is very low. The main pharmacological effects of methylxanthines include central nervous system stimulation, diuresis, cardiovascular and metabolic effects, bronchial relaxation and increased secretion of gastric acids.

The addition of theobromine to toothpastes and mouthwashes is being evaluated following an interesting study conducted on extracted human third molars that proved a consistent and remarkable protection of the enamel surface upon application of a 200 mg/L theobromine solution. Be on the lookout for chocolate toothpaste as a healthy alternative to fluoride. *Continued next week...*

58 CHOCOLATE – BE SURE TO GET YOUR DAILY DOSE!   (Part 2)

February 13, 2014

Last week we investigated the history of chocolate, and its nutritional benefits. Chocolate also has many medicinal effects, especially on the cardiovascular system. Keep in mind that the higher the cacao level in an individual chocolate product, the healthier. It is best to stick with dark, rather than milk, chocolate.

Respiratory Tract Diseases

Theobromine is able to suppress cough in both guinea-pigs and humans without the side effects displayed by other cough suppressants, such as codeine.

Scientific evidence suggests that theobromine and caffeine, both found in chocolate, improve lung function and help open the airways of asthma patients. Indeed, it has been demonstrated that patients with asthma and bronchitis may self-administer cacao/chocolate to relieve symptoms, even though they may be unaware why they are craving a candy bar or cup of hot chocolate.

Cardiovascular Diseases

Numerous studies have documented the beneficial effects of dark chocolate in cardiovascular diseases. In 2012, scientists concluded that "dark chocolate could be an effective cardiovascular preventive strategy in patients with metabolic disease."

The beneficial effects of chocolate on the heart and blood vessels occur by several different mechanisms. Chocolate is a rich source of antioxidants, which decreases the risk of hardening of the arteries. Studies in several countries have shown that dark chocolate can lower blood pressure, with one study recommending dosage - concluding "consuming dark chocolate bars for 15 days reduces systolic blood pressure in healthy subjects, as well as young and elderly persons with high blood pressure." One of the ways chocolate lowers blood pressure appears to be due to nitric oxide release that relaxes the blood vessels. Chocolate also has an aspirin-like effect on platelets – keeping them from causing blood clots.

Sleep

In a large US study involving over 5000 people, it was found that the largest contributor to sleep duration was theobromine found in chocolate. Although caffeine is also found in chocolate, the fact that cacao consumption is not linked to sleep disturbances, and actually helps people sleep *longer*, must be taken into consideration – making bedtime the best time of day to eat that piece of dark chocolate you've been saving.

Neurologic Protection

increasing data show that chocolate consumption improves brain function, as countries with more chocolate consumers apparently produce significantly more Nobel laureates, possibly through enhanced cognition. In other words, chocolate makes you smarter!

In the 2012 Cocoa, Cognition and Aging (CoCoA) study, benefits were found in cognitive function, blood pressure and insulin resistance through cocoa consumption in elderly subjects with mild cognitive impairment. Chocolate consumption improved verbal fluency, scores on the mental status exam, and on the trail making test. Insulin resistance, blood pressure, and lipid levels were also decreased in the test subjects.

Chocolate is also thought to lessen the risk of Alzheimer's and

Parkinson's. People that consume cacao/chocolate products during the middle stages of life are less prone to suffer from neurological diseases when they get older. This hypothesis fits with the main role of methylxanthines - adenosine receptor blockade that in the brain results in higher neuronal activity thereby enabling a longer life for these cells. The higher neuronal activity may be due to a regulation in the perfusion of the brain and/or an increase in cerebral oxygen consumption. Another potential mechanism for neuroprotection may be an increased cerebrospinal fluid production (although this effect may cause headaches in a small percentage of chocolate eaters.)

Flavanoids absorbed from chocolate penetrate and accumulate in the brain regions involved in learning and memory, especially the hippocampus. When my son was in grade school, he was involved in a study where students were encouraged to eat chocolate-covered raisins while taking a test – snacking on chocolate while testing resulted in higher scores.

Anti-stress Effects

There are several active components in chocolate that increase alertness. Chocolate also relieves stress by prompting serotonin production, which is a calming neurotransmitter. One study from Switzerland found that after 14 days of eating chocolate, stress parameters in adults with high anxiety profiles dropped to the level of their un-stressed counterparts.

Last But Not Least

There is a great deal of literature from the 18th Century on the medical use of cocoa and chocolate, not the least of which comes from Carl von Linné (Linnaeus), the man who gave the cacao tree its name. Linnaeus summarized chocolate's qualities as nourishment and therapeutic, adding also that it is an excellent aphrodisiac, especially when vanilla is added, confirming a tradition already existing in the Pre-Columbian culture.

59 LAVENDER – A GOOD NIGHT'S SLEEP

(Part 1)

February 20, 2014

A nursing colleague sent me an interesting study to review this week. A research study was conducted by nurses in the ICU on patient vital signs and quality of sleep. As a nurse, I can attest that helping patients get as much sleep as possible while in the hospital is one of our main objectives.

In this study of 122 patients, aromatherapy with lavender was found to lower blood pressure after 6 hours of therapy. The patients in the experimental group also reported a higher quality of sleep. Lavender aromatherapy was administered by placing 3 ml in a glass jar at the bedside from 10 pm until 6 am. The authors of the study admit that the results could be skewed as many of the ICU patients were on oxygen, with equipment like nasal cannulas that could have partially blocked the intake of the lavender oil.

The concern about the patients not being able to *smell* the oil was invalid. Lavender oil, unlike vanilla and other popular aromatherapy herbs, is also effective in patients with no sense of smell. Lavender particles in the air trigger trigeminal nerve receptors. The trigeminal nerve supplies sensation to the face, and is can be affected by certain chemicals, including lavender and capsaicin. If you've worked with hot peppers, even if you wear a mask, you quickly feel the burning effect of the capsaicin oil as particles touch the trigeminal nerve. Lavender works in a similar, friendlier way.

History

English harvesters centuries ago wore lavender sprigs under their hats to prevent sunstroke and headaches. Today, lavender essential oil is one the most widely used essential oils in aromatherapy. Many studies have demonstrated its functions in calming, assisting sleep, reducing pain and muscular spasms and improving mood. The pharmaceutical preparation of lavender is called *Silexan,* not to be confused with Silexin, another herbal preparation used to treat the prostate.

Treatment of Anxiety

Lavender oil in the form of Silexan (a capsule taken by mouth), has been authorized in Germany for the treatment of states of restlessness during anxious mood. In approving the product for use, officials overseas concluded "Since lavender oil showed no sedative effects in studies, and has no potential for drug abuse, it appears to be an effective and well tolerated alternative to benzodiazepines for amelioration of generalized anxiety."

A 2013 study published in the International Journal of Psychiatry Clinical Practice looked at the anxiety-decreasing effects of lavender. In patients diagnosed with clinical anxiety disorder treated with 80 mg of Silexan by mouth daily, a large decrease in anxiety was evident after 2 weeks. They compared the group receiving lavender to those receiving lorazepam (Ativan) a common anxiety medication. Effects of lavender were comparable to lorazepam and valium, but without the side effects of sleepiness, incoordination and addiction. There were also no withdrawal symptoms when stopping lavender, unlike what is seen with benzodiazepines.

Antidepressant effects

A 2014 study in the International Journal of Pharmacology, which I was able to review prior to publication, showed that the oral preparation of lavender (Silexan) delivered a pronounced antidepressant effect and improved general mental health and health-related quality of life, comparable to the commonly prescribed drug Paxil, without the side effects.

Another study looked at the incorporation of aromatherapy with lavender into nursing care of residents suffering from dementia, anxiety and disturbed sleep patterns. Twenty-four residents and twelve nurses from four nursing homes participated in an action research study. The use of lavender essential oil diffused nightly was perceived as an effective care modality reducing insomnia and anxiety in this patient cohort.

Basic Lavender Oil Recipe

The entire lavender plant is useful and contains the sweet, pungent oil.

1. Fill a jar with slightly crushed lavender stems, leaves and flowers.
2. Cover with extra virgin olive oil.
3. Shake jar gently every day
4. After 1 month, strain mixture and transfer oil to a clean, covered jar.
5. Put a few drops on your pillow for a restorative night's sleep

To be continued...

60 LAVENDER – A GOOD NIGHT'S SLEEP

(PART 2)

February 27, 2014

A Good Night's Sleep

Lavender has been known to improve sleep for centuries. Scientists are just now getting a handle on how it works. Lavender oil preparations have been proven time and time again to have a significant beneficial influence on quality and duration of sleep, and improved general mental and physical health, without causing any unwanted sedative or other drug specific effects.

Sleep apnea is one of the worst sleep disruptions, and current treatments involving wearing a pressurized mask at night to keep the airway open is tolerated by only a small percent of patients. To review, sleep apnea is a sleep disorder characterized by periods where an individual stops breathing several times during the night (up to hundreds of times.) This leads to a low oxygen level that causes the person to wake up frequently, and feel miserable throughout the day, with headaches, fatigue, weight gain, depression, and a host of other ill effects – caused by not getting a good night's sleep.

It has long been determined that an ideal treatment for sleep apnea would be to somehow "jump start" breathing without awakening. Different odors have been evaluated to achieve this, as odors do not arouse or awake a sleeping person. As we discussed briefly, odors can be divided into "trigeminals," so called because they activate trigeminal receptors in the face as well as smell receptors in the nose, and "pure olfactants," like vanilla, that activate smell receptors alone.

Problems with using scents such as vanilla in the sleep apnea patient arise because these individuals are generally mouth-breathers, which negates the effect of vanilla. Other trigeminal stimulants like Capsaicin are ineffective, because triggered breaths are larger following pleasant versus unpleasant odors- making lavender the perfect choice. Studies found that "spritzers" that sprayed lavender oil every 30 minutes significantly improved breathing during sleep, did not cause the person to awake, and in fact helped to maintain a deeper level of sleep. In other studies, drops of lavender placed on the pillows of immature babies raised their oxygen levels, and decreased irritability.

Cancer

Lavender is a source or perillyl alcohol which was found to prevent tumors from developing and has caused complete regression of advanced mammary tumors. It is also showing some promise against glioblastoma brain tumors.

The 2008 Journal of the National Cancer Institute reports "In human studies with advanced cancer patients not responding to treatment, lavender was found to block cell division, induce apoptosis (death of the cancer cell), and induces differentiation. The only side effect was mild nausea."

Use in Pets

In an interesting study looking at travel anxiety in dogs, lavender was sprayed in the vehicle prior to transport. It was found that dogs spent significantly more time resting and sitting and less time moving and vocalizing during the experimental condition. Researchers concluded that "Traditional treatments for travel-induced excitement in dogs may be time-consuming, expensive, or associated with adverse effects. Aromatherapy in the form of diffused lavender odor may offer a practical alternative treatment for travel-induced excitement."

Precautions

No side effects other than mild nausea or gastric distress have been associated with the use of lavender.

Lavender scones

1 tsp. chopped dried lavender buds
1 1/2 cups unbleached all-purpose flour
1/2 tsp. baking soda.
1/2 tsp. salt
1/4 cup sugar
1 cup sour cream

Preheat oven to 450 degrees F.

In a medium size bowl, mix the dry ingredients together.

Add the sour cream and stir with a large spoon until the dry ingredients are damp. (about 20 seconds)

This dough is very light. Turn onto a floured surface and knead very gently, 8 to 10 times. Roll or pat into a round shape that is 1/2 to 3/4 inches thick.
Flour your bowl scraper or spatula and cut into 4 pie shaped pieces.
Flour your spatula again and gently lift each scone onto a lightly greased cookie sheet.
Bake for 15 minutes or until golden brown.

61 AMARANTH – AN UNUSUALLY NUTRITIOUS PLANT

March 6, 2014

Amaranth grows freely throughout the Ozarks. Like many plants considered a nuisance, it is not a weed at all. Amaranth has been consumed for thousands of years by many civilizations, including the Incas, Mayans and Aztecs, where it was used as a staple food, comprising up to 80% of caloric intake. In Central America, Amaranth is used primarily in the form of tortillas and tamales made from the flour. Today amaranth can be found almost everywhere from central Canada to Argentina. This incredible plant is gaining in popularity due to ever-growing interest in nutriceutical plants - those with both medicinal and nutritional properties. Harvesting Amaranth seeds can also be profitable, as they sell for 50 cents per ounce on Amazon.

There are more than 70 species of Amaranth, with Amarantus Hybridus most common to Missouri. The tiny seeds, and leaves, to a lesser extent, have extremely high protein content; seeds have between 12 percent and 17 percent protein by weight. Though high in oils, amaranth seed is low in saturated fat and high in fiber. It is a known source of the essential amino acid lysine, which is rarely available through plant food sources. The medicinal properties of Amaranth include lowered cholesterol levels, stimulating the immune system, exerting an antitumor effect, improved liver function, blood pressure reduction, anti-anemic effect, and antioxidant activity. In addition, Amaranth is gluten-free, and can used to produce a safe flour for individuals with Celiac disease.

Use as Food

Amaranth seeds are a very nutritious and delicious replacement for many commonly used grains. Amaranth can be eaten in the place of milk-based products because of its high calcium level. It is plentiful, and easy to find growing wild in Missouri. Amaranth seeds, flowers and leaves are rich in protein, lysine, methionine, vitamins B6, C, A, and E, phosphorus, potassium, riboflavin, and folate. It also provides 82% of the daily iron requirement, 31% of the daily requirement of calcium, and 3 times the fiber of wheat flour.

When cooking Amaranth, use the tender young leaves in salads and stir-fries as you would spinach. The leaves have a nutty, tangy flavor so are best mixed with other greens. The seeds are a favorite of nutrition-conscious cooks, who like its high protein and fiber content. The seeds, which are produced in abundance, can be used as a cereal, ground into flour, popped like popcorn, toasted, or cooked with other grains. To collect the seeds, shake the tops of the older, seed-filled plants into a paper bag. When choosing amaranth plants to eat, be sure to remove any sharp spines that may be present on some varieties.

In Central America, popped amaranth grains are mixed with honey, molasses or chocolate to make a popular treat called *alegría*, meaning "joy" in Spanish.

Medicinal Uses

Cholesterol

Several studies have documented the cholesterol-lowering effects of Amaranth. In one study, cholesterol levels dropped by 50%, targeting LDL (bad) cholesterol, while not affecting HDL (good) cholesterol. Oat bran shows similar effects on cholesterol, but amaranth is better tolerated, and unlike other grains is virtually free of known allergens.

Immune System Influence

Some early research results indicate that amaranth extract enhances the immune system by directly stimulating B-lymphocytes. B-lymphocytes are hugely important in preventing disease, as they are responsible for making antibodies when we are exposed to bacteria or viruses. Antibodies are critical in destroying and removing invading organisms and toxins from our bodies.

Effect on Blood Pressure

Amaranth lowers blood pressure through its effect on the renin-angiotensin system. Sometimes the body mistakenly raises the blood pressure through this mechanism, causing it to go quite high. Amaranth blocks the angiotensin system in an effect similar to the ACE inhibitor category of drugs, like captopril.

Effect on Anemia

Several studies have found that Amaranth is an ideal cereal to treat iron-deficiency, the most common cause of anemia. Naturally high in iron, it is well tolerated, and well absorbed from the intestines.

Antitumor Potential

A protein found in amaranth has been closely studied, and was found to have an antitumor effect on 4 different cancer cell lines. The protein works by stopping cancer cells from adhering, and causing the death of malignant cells.

Popped Amaranth

After gathering amaranth seeds, pre-heat a small skillet over medium-high heat. You don't need any oil. Add 2 tablespoons of seed at a time, cover skillet, and shake back and forth briskly for about 10-15 seconds. Empty skillet and repeat process with remaining seed until you have the amount you want. The popped seeds are much smaller than popcorn, but have a satisfying crunch. They can be used in cereals, granola bars, or as a topping for ice cream and yogurt.

Amaranth grows throughout Missouri. Up to one pound of seeds can be harvested from a single plant.

62 DIATOMACEOUS EARTH

March 13, 2014

I think many of us were able to withstand the brutally cold temperatures this winter with the thought that at least the ticks and other pests would take a beating. That does not appear to be the case. Several of my friends have already found ticks, and the Japanese beetles are already arriving, way ahead of schedule!

Two years ago, my corn and beans were attacked by the Japanese beetles. I dutifully picked the bugs off twice daily, but simply couldn't keep up. Last year we broke down and dusted with Sevin, but it goes totally against my nature to use pesticides. Fortunately there is an alternative, and that alternative is diatomaceous earth (DE).

The first reported use of DE was in Germany in the 1830's. A farmer digging a well mistook the earth he displaced for limestone. After spreading the earth on his crops as fertilizer, he was amazed at the insecticide properties. Upon analysis, the white, crumbly powder was found to be diatomaceous earth.

DE is made up of diatoms, microscopic one-celled algae that are found in bodies of water. When lakes and seas dry up over centuries, the fossilized shells of the diatoms remain in copious amounts. This sediment is harvested and milled into a fine powder, and it is available at our local feed stores. Not your typical pesticide, DE contains naturally occurring silica, which acts by destroying the insect's cuticle by absorbing the protective wax layer. This results in body water loss and ultimately the insect's death by desiccation, and it is non-toxic to plants or animals if ingested. (See precautions below.)

Known as one of the most effective means of controlling Japanese beetles, DE also works by a physical, non-chemical process. Its microscopic sharp particles cut through the exoskeleton of the insect, allowing the silica to cause the insect to dry out and die. (Such sweet revenge!) It can be sprinkled liberally on your plants, or applied with a garden duster, being careful not to inhale the dust. The dust is also highly abrasive to very small organisms such as bacteria, fungus, parasites, and other insects. It can be safely applied to pets, and sprinkled on carpets, then vacuumed, to avert flea infestations.

DE comes in two types of preparations – food grade and industrial. I highly recommend the food grade, Of the 600 natural DE deposits in the US, only 4% rate as food grade by FDA standards. The other is pool grade, and is used for swimming pool filtration. These two types are similar, but Food Grade DE, which is safe for ingestion, must meet certain specifications regarding arsenic and lead content. Pool grade DE is treated with very high heat. This turns the silicon dioxide that is present in the DE into crystalline silica. Pool grade DE has crystalline silica ranging to 70 percent vs. food grade DE that has less than 1% crystalline silica, making it safe for human consumption.

Effect on Serum Cholesterol

One recent 12 week study looked at the influence of DE on blood cholesterol in 19 healthy individuals ages 35-67 with a history of elevated cholesterol. They took 250 mg of diatomaceous earth by mouth three-times daily during an 8 week observation period. By week 6, there was a 13.2% decrease in cholesterol and LDL and triglycerides were also decreased. Four weeks after intake of diatomaceous earth was stopped, serum cholesterol, low-density lipoprotein cholesterol and triglycerides still remained low, and there was also a significant increase in high-density lipoprotein (good) cholesterol.

Hair, Nails and Teeth

Our hair contains 90 micrograms of silica per gram, making it almost as rich in the element as healthy bones, containing 100 mcg. per gram. Silica helps to stimulate hair growth, and prevents cavities and preserves teeth. It also helps your nails to grow.

Detox

There are many reports of using DE to clean and detoxify the intestinal tract. DE makes its way through your system like a gentle scraper, with a purely mechanical, non-chemical action. Its gentle abrasive properties also make it a good choice for homemade toothpaste.

A Must-Have For Chickens!

The effectiveness of (DE) as a treatment against parasites and to increase feed efficiency and egg production of organically raised free-range layer hens has been heavily researched. In a 2011 study, hens fed the diet containing DE were significantly heavier, laid more eggs, and consumed more feed than hens fed the control diet. Additionally, hens consuming the DE diet laid larger eggs containing more albumen and yolk than hens consuming the control diet. In a subsequent experiment, the effectiveness of DE to treat a Northern fowl mite infestation was tested. Relative to controls, hens that were dusted with DE had reduced number of mites. The results of this study indicate DE has the potential to be an effective treatment to help control parasites and improve production of organically raised, free-range layer hens.

Precautions

Listed as GRAS (generally recognized as safe) by the FDA, food grade DE is safe to handle and consume. If you are using DE in the garden, or dusting your pet for fleas, it is a good idea to wear a mask and gloves so that you don't inhale the small particles that can cause your hands and throat to dry out. There are no side effects or known health effects of diatomaceous earth when used as a supplement. The use of pool grade DE definitely requires a mask and gloves, due to its increased potency.

63 ASPARAGUS – TIME TO MAKE YOUR BED!

Part 1

March 20, 2014

Looking for a free delicacy? From now until June, you can find wild asparagus growing throughout Missouri. Easy to identify, the wild plant looks very similar to the distinctive plant found at the grocery store. An early season vegetable, wild asparagus is perennial, and grows year after year, producing an edible plant for up to two decades. Spears, the part of the asparagus plant that are harvested, are actually immature ferns. If they are not picked, they develop into large ferns that manufacture and store energy in the plant for the next year's crop. When you locate an asparagus stand, you can either make a mental note of the location, (and keep it a secret!), or transplant the plant to a raised bed with full sunlight and room to grow. Adding fertilizer before planting will help your asparagus grow.

Nutrition

With only 32 calories per cup, asparagus is low in saturated fat, and very low in cholesterol. It is a good source of Vitamin B6, Calcium, Magnesium and Zinc, and a very good source of Vitamins A, C, E, and K, Thiamine, Riboflavin, Niacin, Folate, Iron, Phosphorus, Potassium, Copper, Manganese and Selenium. One cup of asparagus contains over 11% of the RDA of dietary fiber and almost 10% of the RDA of protein.

Therapeutic Properties of Asparagus

Effect on Cancer

Asparagus has been found to be beneficial against bladder, breast, colon, lung, prostate, ovarian and other cancers. Hepatocellular carcinoma (liver cancer) is one of the most aggressive cancers in the world, and a great deal of research is devoted to its prevention. In one recent study, asparagus components elicited significant anticancer activity by several mechanisms against hepatocellular carcinoma cells, and also enhanced the tumor-killing effects of mitomycin, a chemotherapy drug.

Anti-Inflammatory and Anti-Stress

Asparagus contains many anti-inflammatory nutrients, such as asparagus saponins and the flavonoids quercetin, rutin, laempferol and isorhamnetin, which all help to combat arthritis, asthma, and autoimmune diseases.

Asparagus has long been used in traditional medicine for improving the general state of health and for stress-related immune disorders. The effects of the methanol and aqueous extracts of the tuberous roots of the plant were examined in an experimental mouse model of stress, induced by swimming. Asparagus was found to inhibit several stress-related chemicals found in the blood stream and adrenal glands. These findings suggest that these plants may be beneficial in the management of stress and inflammatory conditions.

In humans, a preliminary and small-sized human study was conducted among healthy volunteers consuming up to 150 mg/d of asparagus stem extract daily for 7 days. The anti-stress chemical HSP70 was significantly elevated at intakes of 100 or 150 mg/day, compared to baseline levels, suggesting that asparagus stem extract might exert anti-stress effects under stressful conditions, resulting from enhancement of anti-stress chemicals.

Next week we will look at the role of asparagus in treating blood pressure, kidney stones and other diseases, hair and scalp problems, and prevention of birth defects.

Local herbalist Tamara Glascock examines a patch of wild asparagus found near her home.

64 ASPARAGUS – TIME TO MAKE YOUR BED!

Part 2

March 27, 2014

Last week we looked at the role of asparagus in treating cancer, inflammation, and elevated stress hormones. Asparagus does so much more, and as a perennial native plant that returns year after year for decades, it is the gift that keeps on giving.

Blood Pressure

One recent study looked at the role of asparagus in preventing high blood pressure. The researchers used an extract of asparagus obtained by boiling it in water. Systolic blood pressure, creatinine clearance and kidney function were all improved in the subjects that received the asparagus water. This effect was found to be due to ACE inhibitor activity, similar to that of the drug Captopril.

Kidney Stones

The amino acid asparagine found in asparagus acts as a diuretic. Retaining fluids can put you at a high risk for developing kidney stones since there is very little fluid in the urine, making it easy for tiny crystals in the urinary tract to aggregate. Ongoing scientific research has documented the role of asparagus in breaking up oxalate crystals, which form the most common kind of kidney stone. Eating asparagus can prevent these crystals from forming together in the first place. In addition, asparagus raises the urinary concentration of magnesium, which is considered as one of the inhibitors of crystal formation in the urine.

Hair and Scalp

The roots of the asparagus plant have significant antifungal activity. In combination with its anti-inflammatory properties, asparagus root extract has shown promise as an active ingredient in an anti-dandruff shampoo, and in the treatment of seborrheic dermatitis.

Diabetic Nephropathy

A major complication of diabetes, nephropathy (kidney disease) has serious consequences for the patient. A 2012 study was undertaken to investigate the effects of asparagus on early diabetic nephropathy. 100 and 250 mg/kg daily of asparagus extract was administered for 4 weeks. Asparagus extract decreased plasma glucose, creatinine, urea nitrogen, total cholesterol and triglyceride levels. Renal hypertrophy, polyuria, hyperfiltration, microalbuminuria and abnormal changes in the renal tissue as well as oxidative stress were effectively decreased by asparagus treatment.

Birth Defects

It is well known that in order for mothers to help prevent miscarriages and birth defects, they must consume sufficient levels of folate. Folate is also essential for proper cellular division. With 17% of the RDA in 1 cup, healthy servings of asparagus can prevent a folate-deficiency, which has been linked to birth defects such as spina bifida (a congenital defect in which the spinal cord is exposed through a gap in the backbone). In a fascinating recent study, fathers are not excused from taking in adequate folate. The study, which obviously can't be done on humans, revealed that offspring of mice fathers who had insufficient folate levels had a 30% increase in birth defects, such as cranio-facial and spinal deformities, compared with offspring of fathers who had adequate levels of the vitamin. The level of folate in the placenta can be up to 35% lower when the father is folate-deficient.

Diet and Digestion

Asparagus contains a carbohydrate called *Inulin* that encourages the growth of Bifidobacteria and Lactobacilli, two bacteria that boost nutrient absorption, lower the risk of allergy and colon cancer, and help prevent unfriendly bacteria from taking hold in our intestinal tract. One cup of asparagus also contains over 11% of the RDA of dietary fiber and almost 10% of the RDA of protein, stabilizing digestion, preventing constipation, and curbing overeating.

Precautions

There are a few precautions regarding asparagus. Allergies to the plant are fairly common, and usually manifest as a contact dermatitis with itchy skin rash. Also, as the plant is very high in Vitamin K which promotes blood clotting, so persons taking blood thinner should avoid eating large amounts of asparagus.

Any discussion of asparagus would not be complete without a mention of urine odor. Although it doesn't happen to everyone, asparagus has been associated with the production of a malodorous urine caused by asparagusic acid, a simple sulfur unique to asparagus. Other than being possibly embarrassing, it is completely harmless.

65 THE IMPORTANCE OF RESEARCH

April 3, 2014

Over the past year and a half, I've shown the readers scientific evidence of how nature provides for our health. Claims of medicinal benefits should never be taken at face value, and a discerning person should always validate and investigate everything they put in their body, and even the things they omit. For example, we really NEED to eat certain forms of fat, or we tend to overdose on carbohydrates.

With a Master's degree in science, I look at life as a scientist, and have been involved in several research studies. While not involving herbs or other plants, I think three of these studies would be of interest to *Nature Has a Cure* readers because of their holistic nature. This information could literally save a life. In this series, we will look at the outcomes of research on near-drownings, patient positioning, and therapeutic hypothermia.

My first research study took place in the late 1980's while I was in the graduate program at the Medical University of South Carolina. My son Sean was 2 years old at the time. One day, I was returning a video to the video store, and my now ex-husband was watching our son. When I got home, Sean wasn't in the house, and my then husband said he was outside playing. I started to panic immediately, went looking for him, and found him face down, blue, lifeless, and floating in the neighbor's pool. I jumped in the pool and began doing CPR, but got no response. My neighbor called 911 while I continued CPR. As I continued rescue breathing, I saw that Sean's stomach was distended. In my panic, I had been giving adult breaths rather than child breaths. Listening to a voice, which I know was God, I stopped everything and did the Heimlich maneuver. As I did, he regurgitated a large amount of pool water, and almost instantly, his pulse returned. He regained consciousness about an hour later in the ER, and was discharged in the morning. Many of you know him, and he is a happy, healthy young man today.

My friend did not have the same experience. The year prior her 2 year old daughter drowned in a similar manner. Despite being a nurse, and performing CPR as I did, her child died. I was enrolled in my first research class, so I determined to find out why some children survive, and some do not after drowning. I undertook a year-long analysis of every child drowning in the state of South Carolina. What I found was stunning. In the cases where the Heimlich maneuver was performed prior to rescue breathing, the child survived. If the Heimlich maneuver was not performed, the outcome was dismal.

I thought this was significant, so I wrote to Dr. Heimlich, and he wrote me back. He had been trying to change the American Heart Association protocol for treating drowning victims to no avail. They flatly refused to change their protocol, and he was very frustrated. Dr. Heimlich is now 94 years old, and the controversy continues. I'm unsure why transferring a child to the morgue is preferable to performing the Heimlich maneuver, but Dr. Heimlich has been challenged on many fronts regarding this issue.

How and why does this work? Going back to scientific principles, the answer is the ventilation/perfusion ratio. First, in about 90% of child drownings, no water goes into the lungs. Considered "dry drownings," children have a natural reflex whereby the epiglottis closes, blocking off the lungs to water. Of course, the lungs aren't getting any oxygen either. Where does that water go? The answer is, into the child's stomach. The stomach can become so distended with water, it presses on the lungs. Normally, we breathe in air, and the alveoli (little air pockets in the base of the lungs) drop off that oxygen to blood passing by in the blood vessels. This is called the ventilation (air), perfusion (blood) ratio. When the child is rescued, the epiglottis relaxes, so we can do rescue breathing, but if the blood vessels are blocked by a fluid-filled stomach, all the oxygen in the world won't get into the blood stream where it is needed. The Heimlich Maneuver rapidly empties the stomach of a drowning victim, and should be done in the face-down or side-lying position. If there is suspicion of a neck or back injury, as in a diving accident, the spine must be protected to prevent paralysis.

How long does the Heimlich Maneuver take? Approximately 4-6 seconds. Odds are, you may be in a position to aid a drowning child. Most drownings occur between the ages of 2 – 4 years old, and water and unattended children do not mix. It is hugely important to know that a child who has drowned should not be considered dead until AFTER CPR has been performed and the Heimlich maneuver has been used. Let's have a safe summer!

Next week we will look at patient position and therapeutic hypothermia.

66 THE IMPORTANCE OF RESEARCH - Part 2

April 10, 2014

Our bodies are so wondrously made, with built-in protection measures in every cell. I've always felt my most important role as a nurse was to protect the patient from any assaults, so that God could heal them. Sometimes this means making sure that the patient gets their antibiotics on time, so that dangerous bacteria don't have the chance to multiply and overwhelm the body's natural defense mechanisms. Sometimes it means keeping a comfortable, quiet environment, even for patient in a coma. Veteran Dent County nurse Joyce Leuthart knows a lot about that – a CD player in the room with favorite music playing helps the body heal. The little things can be everything to a sick person. I'll never forget the ER nurse that took care of me when my horse bucked me off, breaking my shoulder in 6 places. She knew just how to place a pad under my shoulder, instantly relieving the pain without medication.

Last week we talked about using the Heimlich Maneuver to improve the ventilation and perfusion ratio in a drowning victim, and the huge impact that can make. Following my research on drowning, I remembered back to 1979, when I was a new nurse working in the Intensive Care Unit. My senior nurses always cautioned me not to turn a dying patient on their left side, as it could hasten their demise. Unquestioning at that time, I tucked that little fact away until Graduate school, when I based my Master's thesis on the effect of patient position on oxygen levels. Interestingly enough, very little research had been done on the topic, despite the words of Hippocrates in the year 500 BC, *"It is well when the patient is found by his physician reclining upon either his right or left side, having his hands, neck and legs slightly bent, and the whole body lying in a relaxed state, for thus the most of persons of health recline. But to lie on one's back with the hands, neck and the legs extended is far less favorable."*

For my research, I followed 76 patients in the ICU. In the majority of patients, their oxygen levels rose by at least 35 points when turned on their right side. Some patients went from an oxygen level as low as 70 to as high as 248 when they were turned to their right side. Turning patients to the prone (stomach lying) position also elevated oxygen levels, but to a lesser degree. On the other hand, patients with a disease process in their right lung improved when turned to their left side. Why is this?

These dramatic changes in oxygenation can be based on the principle of ventilation perfusion. Because the right lung is larger, heavier, and has more blood vessels than the left, it can contribute more oxygen to the blood. In fact, the right lung has 3 lobes, and the left lung only has two lobes. Because of the effect of gravity, the lung in the dependent position receives more blood. Each molecule of blood is able to pick up 4 molecules of oxygen, which is then carried to the cells. Cells must have oxygen in order to heal and regenerate.

As many restorative processes happen during our sleep, many of us notice that we tend to sleep much better when lying on our right side. If the right lung is diseased, this beneficial effect is erased. These patients do much better when turned to the left side, or even prone. Keep in mind the lungs expand front to back, not side to side, so laying on one's stomach allows the lungs to more fully expand.

Sometimes the simplest things reap the greatest benefits. If you are caring for a sick family member or child, helping them into a comfortable position on their right side will not only increase the oxygen level in the body, but will lessen the workload on the heart. Over the years, I've taught my students to remember "keep the good lung down."

Next week, in the last of this 3-part series, we will discuss the role of cooling techniques in neurological injuries.

67 THE IMPORTANCE OF RESEARCH

Part 3

April 17, 2014

In the last of this 3-part series looking at research about holistic, hands-on measures that can support a person in physical distress, we are going to review the role of cooling techniques in neurological injuries.

I became interested in using cooling techniques to help critically ill patients heal in the mid 1990's. At the time, I was working in the cardio-thoracic ICU, caring for patients after open heart surgery. A common complication post-operatively was a rapid heart rate and cardiac arrhythmias as the patient rewarmed following the procedure. The standard treatment was to put the patient on a cooling blanket – a plastic sheet that had ice-water running through it. This was actually as uncomfortable as it sounds, and often had the opposite effect, as it made the patient shiver violently – raising the body temperature. With the doctor's consent and hospital approval, I developed a system of placing the intravenous lines so they ran through an ice bath, delivering cool fluids to the patient's core, rather than chilling the periphery. Not only did this lower the patient's temperature, but there was no shivering, and post-operative heart arrhythmias were controlled.

Not long after this, several researchers In Australia, Europe and Norway began investigating the role of hypothermia in treating patients who suffered a cardiac arrest outside of the hospital, a group with a normally high mortality rate. In fact, if a patient survives an out of hospital cardiac arrest, it is likely they will have significant brain damage. All the researchers found that reduction of the patient's core temperature to 33 degrees Centigrade (91.4 degrees Fahrenheit), was associated with greatly improved survival rate and neurologic function. A huge study in Norway with 459 patients concluded that keeping the body temperature less than, or equal to 100 degrees Fahrenheit was strongly associated with patient survival.

As late as 2000, the American Heart Association made no mention of induction of hypothermia to improve patient outcomes, although when they published their new guidelines in 2005, they added therapeutic hypothermia to their protocol. That turned out to be good news for Kevin Everett.

Who is Kevin Everett?

Everett was a third-year Buffalo Bills tight end, playing in the first game of the 2007 NFL season. At the beginning of the second quarter, he tackled Denver Broncos player Domenik Hixon, and their helmets crashed into each other. 26 year old Everett immediately crumpled and went to the ground. He had a spinal cord injury, and was paralyzed from the neck down. Immediately after the injury, while in the ambulance, Everett was given 2 liters of iced IV fluid in his veins. He then went into surgery at the hospital, and doctors continued to give him cold fluids overnight to keep his body temperature at 92 degrees Fahrenheit for 24 hours to counteract inflammation and fever. 15 weeks later, Kevin Everett returned to Ralph Wilson stadium, not in a wheelchair, but walking.

He will never be cleared to return to football, but he has started the Kevin Everett Foundation to assist those with spinal cord injuries, both financially and emotionally. The father of 3 children since the accident, he stays busy helping his wife raise their little girls. Head surgeon Andrew Cappuccino was quoted as saying "I will hang a good portion of my belief in this recovery on cold therapy, because we don't normally see this recovery in people with spinal cord injury."

Close to Home

Shortly after Kevin Everett's injury, my co-worker, and fellow nurse that I will call Nancy, was leaving church on a Sunday morning when she was struck by a car while crossing the street. Witnesses described her being "thrown over the car onto her head-doing a 360." Nancy was brought by paramedics to our hospital. She was unable to see, speak, or follow commands, but was very agitated. Her CT scan showed she had a huge blood clot under the dura (covering) of her brain, and her whole brain was shifted to the left. She also had a skull fracture. She was taken to surgery, and immediately placed on cooling measures. We were trialing a machine called the Cool-Gard, which continuously circulates cool IV fluids through the patient's blood, keeping the temperature low. Her temperature was kept low for 5 days, and cooling measures were stopped at that time, as she was improving. Two days later, she developed speech problems, and left sided weakness, so cooling was resumed. Two weeks after her injury, she was well enough to be transferred out of the ICU, and three months after her injury, Nancy completed her rehabilitation and was home with her family. She came back to visit our unit, complaining of being bored, and wanting to return to work. She readily remembered her coworkers and showed no signs of neurological deficit, instantly recalling numbers and dates. Six months after her injury, Nancy returned to her former position in the Neuro ICU.

How it Works

Every degree of temperature increases the work of brain cells by up to 10%. By cooling the patient down, we decrease the workload on the injured brain and neurologic tissue, allowing it to heal. Think of febrile seizures – the extra oxygen demand of the brain due to fever lowers the seizure threshhold, an effect that result in convulsions. Every parent has likely already used cooling measures, and has seen the benefit. At home cooling techniques include cold baths, or placing padded bags of ice at the groin and in the armpits. Cover the patient with a light blanket to prevent shivering. Medications to lower temperature such as aspirin or Tylenol are also effective.

Summary

Accidents happen, and medical help is not always readily available. Keep in mind the benefits of cooling measures, especially with neurologic injuries. If your child has a febrile seizure, they are not considered to have epilepsy, since epilepsy is characterized as recurrent seizures that aren't triggered by fever. Short febrile seizures have not been shown to cause brain damage, but a small percentage of children with febrile seizure (2-3%) may go on to develop epilepsy.

68 THE HIDDEN VALUE OF STINGING NETTLE

April 24, 2014

Chances are, you've encountered a stinging nettle (Urtica dioica), and now go to great lengths to avoid this wild green plant that grows virtually everywhere. The presence of nettles shows that the adjacent ground has high fertility, and is high in phosphorus. In addition to encouraging beneficial insects, nettles are wonderful as a compost activator, as they are so high in nitrogen, and also supply magnesium, sulfur and iron to the soil.

The use of stinging nettle in medicine goes back to the time of Hippocrates, who recommended the plant for no less than 61ailments. Ancient Egyptians used a tea made from the plant for arthritis pain, and Roman soldiers would hit sore leg muscles with the fresh nettle plant, increasing blood flow to the area and relieving muscle pain.

Stinging nettle is rich in vitamins and minerals. Like Sassafras, it has traditionally been used in the springtime as a tonic. Native Americans used it as a reliable food source. In rural areas in the poorer countries, its restorative powers for healing the sick are especially appreciated, as it is widely and freely available. With high levels of vitamin C and iron, nettle is a traditional remedy for scurvy and anemia. Stinging Nettle is also rich in vitamin A, potassium, manganese, and calcium. There are many reports of its use as an energy booster. At its peak, Stinging Nettle contains up to 25% protein, remarkable for a leafy green vegetable.

Medicinal Uses

Benign Prostatic Hyperplasia (BPH)

The bulk of research on medicinal uses of Stinging Nettle in the past five years has addressed its use in treating BPH (enlarged prostate). As we age, women have to contend with symptoms of menopause, while most men struggle with problems due to enlargement of the prostate that impairs urine flow, and can be quite distressing. In my experience, surgical correction of an enlarged prostate often leads to some degree of urinary incontinence.

In 2013, a 6-month study including 620 patients showed that the post-void residual (urine left in the bladder after voiding) decreased by 50%, from 73 ml to 36 ml in patients who received daily doses of Stinging Nettle. There was also a modest decrease in the size of the prostate.

Diabetes

Stinging Nettle is best known as a plant that decreases blood glucose. A study last year showed that nettles actually repair islet cells in the pancreas, responsible for producing insulin. Many plants are helpful to Type 2 diabetics, but Stinging Nettle may be the first plant to give hope to Type 1, insulin-dependent diabetics.

Precautions

Stinging nettle should be picked with gloves as it has many hollow stinging hairs on the leaves and stems which inject histamine and other chemicals, causing a stinging sensation. Stinging chemicals are easily removed by soaking the plant in water or by cooking, allowing them to be safely handled and eaten.

Stinging Nettle Pesto

- 1 cup of blanched stinging nettles
- 2 tablespoons of extra virgin olive oil
- 1 clove of fresh garlic

- ¼ cup of fresh basil - chopped
- 1 tablespoon of lemon juice
- ¾ cup of Greek yogurt
- A dash of cayenne pepper
- A pinch of Kosher salt

Blend the stinging nettles until roughly chopped inside a blender or food processor. Add all of the other ingredients and blend until smooth. Serve with pasta or as a dip.

Stinging Nettle can be substituted in recipes calling for spinach. Nettle leaves and flowers can be dried and used to make nettle tea. As a home-based business opportunity, stinging nettle root and extract sells briskly on amazon.com, bringing $6 per ounce.

Stinging Nettle grows freely throughout Missouri.

69 YARROW

May 1, 2014

Yarrow (*Achillea millefolium*) is native throughout the United States, and flourishes in Missouri. You can identify it by its flowers and unusual featherlike leaves. In fact, it is called *plumajillo* (little feather) in New Mexico and Colorado. It usually flowers in May and June, and can be found in pastures and open forests. The smell is sweet, and similar to chrysanthemums. Yarrow has been used in medicine throughout the ages. Centuries ago, yarrow was called *herbal militaris*, due to its value in slowing hemorrhage from soldier's wounds. The Latin name *achillea* originates with Achilles of Greek mythology, reported to use a yarrow poultice to treat the battle wounds of his fellow soldiers. Of course, Achilles himself ended up dying from a mortal wound to his Achilles heel.

An exceptionally good plant to have in your yard and garden, yarrow repels some noxious insects, while attracting the beneficial, predatory ones, like ladybugs, that feed on aphids. As a companion plant, yarrow can heal sick plants that are close in proximity. Yarrow is often planted to improve soil quality, and is beneficial when added to compost. Several species of birds use yarrow to line their nests to protect them from parasites.

Yarrow was a very popular vegetable used in salads and egg dishes in 17th century. High in phosphorus, potassium and calcium, but low in sodium, the fresh young leaves can be substituted for spinach. Both young and old leaves can be dried and used as a seasoning in cooking.

Medicinal Uses

Yarrow has a long history with native North Americans. The Navajo consider yarrow a "life medicine." Also used by the Plains Indians, Pawnee, Chippewa, Cherokee and Miwok tribes, yarrow leaves were chewed for toothaches, made into eardrops for earaches, boiled for steam inhalations to treat headaches, and used in a tea to reduce pain and fever and aid in sleep.

Anti-inflammatory

Yarrow has a unique property. When the flowers are distilled by steam, a bluish-tinted compound called azulene develops, not present in the original plant. Azulene has significant anti-inflammatory properties, and opens breathing passages when rubbed on the chest for colds and flu. You can also extract azulene from chamomile, but yarrow extract contains a much higher concentration. Applied topically as a poultice, the boiled leaves can decrease swelling in the tissues.

Anti-spasmodic

Active ingredients in yarrow can inhibit contractions in smooth muscle in the ileum of the small intestine, and has been proven clinically useful in eliminating intestinal spasms. It is also effective for menstrual cramps. Applied to the skin, it can help control muscle cramps.

Anxiety

Clinical studies in humans have shown anxiety-reducing effects in 21 plants to date – among them is yarrow. This is not surprising, as anecdotal evidence over the centuries has documented the effect of yarrow on anxiety level and restful sleep. The mechanism of action is thought to be through GABA, an inhibitory neurotransmitter that blocks feelings of anxiety, panic and stress, or through possible cannabinoid receptor modulation.

Hemostasis

Leaves of yarrow encourage blood clotting, so can be crushed and put in the nostril to stop nosebleeds. Crushed leaves can also be placed on wounds to slow bleeding. An external application will decrease swelling and bleeding from hemorrhoids. A poultice of the pulverized plant can be applied to burns to decrease tissue damage.

Melanin Production

Melanin is what gives color to our skin. An article released just last week found that yarrow was effective in decreasing the production of melanin, with implications for treating hyperpigmentation, and possibly melanoma. Yarrow is currently used in many cosmetics to treat age spots on the skin.

Insect Repellent

Essential oil of yarrow kills mosquito larvae. It is also an excellent insect repellant, and is easy to make. Gather 1 cup of yarrow leaves and flowers, chop them up and put them in a small Mason jar. Add enough rubbing alcohol to cover. Shake every couple of days, and strain after 3-4 weeks into a recycled spray bottle.

Precautions

Some people are naturally allergic to yarrow, and can experience severe allergic skin rashes. Prolonged use can make the skin more sensitive to sunlight, due to the blocking effects on melanin.

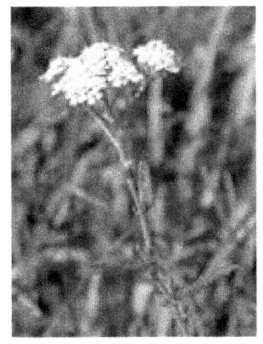

Yarrow has many medicinal uses.

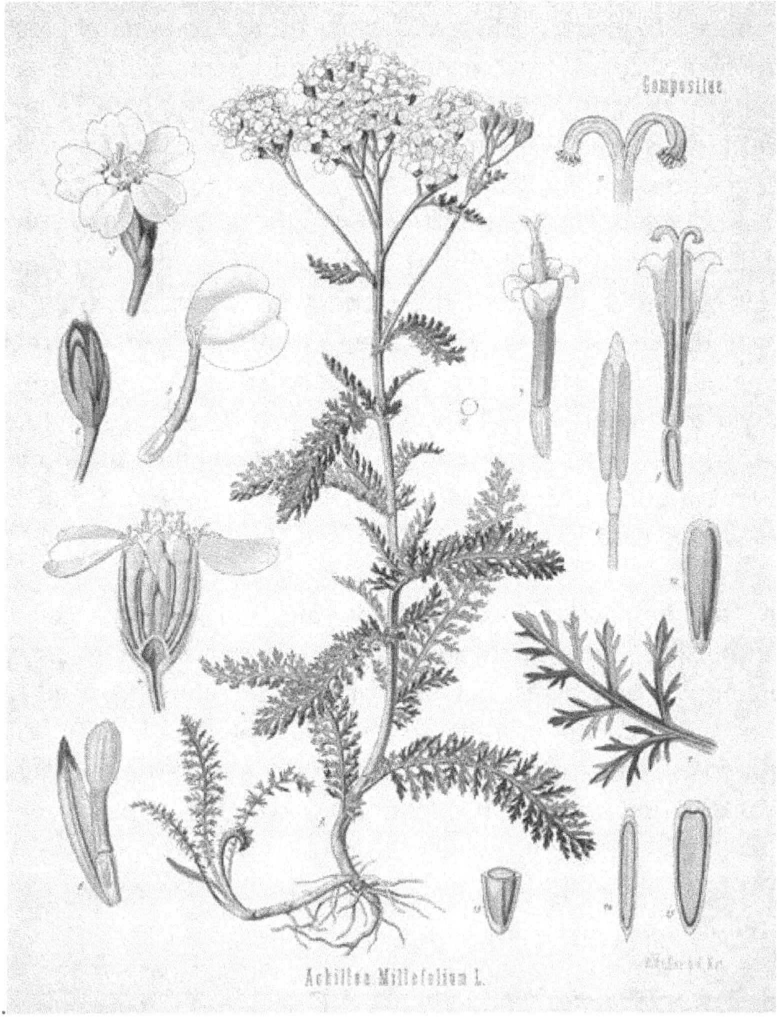
Compositae
Achillea Millefolium L.

70 THE SILVER SOLUTION

May 8, 2014

Long before the discovery of antibiotics, for over 600 years silver was the most important antimicrobial agent available. Silver has used been to treat infections and other conditions with unparalleled success. The ancient Greeks and Romans used silver to disinfect water and food supplies. During the Napoleonic wars, Russian armies used water containers lined with silver to purify drinking water obtained from rivers and streams. This practice was continued throughout WWI, and part of WWII. The first scientific description of the water cleansing effect of silver came in 1869, when Raulin found that aspergillus could not grow in silver containers. Silver was also used in ancient times to treat burns and as a wound dressing. Silver solutions were first approved for medical use by the FDA in the 1920's. Since that time, silver has established itself as an effective and well-known treatment modality for prevention of high-risk infection and in clinical wound care.

At low concentrations, silver is very safe. It kills single celled organisms, like bacteria, fungi and viruses, but is harmless to more complex organisms. Colloidal silver was commonly used to treat many infections until the discovery of Penicillin in 1928. US Army medics still carry silver dressings for use in battle, and just last week I found a sample packet of Silver solution gel in a box of band aids I purchased.

Medical Uses

Herpes Zoster (Shingles)

Herpes Zoster and the causative organism, varicella virus, is very susceptible to silver treatments. A 1986 study showed that the addition of silver sulfadiazine to cultures of varicella zoster virus completely inactivated the virus after 30 minutes exposure at body temperature. Forty-two patients with herpes zoster were treated topically with 1 percent silver sulfadiazine cream applied 4 times a day. All patients experienced complete drying of vesicles, marked reduction of redness and swelling, and striking elimination of pain and burning sensation within 24 to 72 hours. The sooner the treatment began after the onset of symptoms, the more dramatic was the response. Post herpetic neuralgia, an ongoing pain syndrome that can persist after the lesions heal, was either mild or did not occur.

Ophthalmia Neonatorum

Probably the most significant use of silver over the decades has been the treatment of Ophthalmia Neonatorum, eye infections in the newborn that can result in blindness. When I was in nurse's training in the 1970's, and doing my obstetrics rotation, it was state-mandated that all newborn infants had silver nitrate drops instilled in their eyes shortly after birth, a practice first introduced in 1884. With gonorrhea rates declining, and Chlamydia rates rising, often erythromycin is now used to treat presumed eye infections in the newborn. In a recent study of ophthalmia neonatorum at two UCLA teaching hospitals over a five-year period. 1% silver nitrate solution and 0.5% erythromycin ointment were compared. The infection rate with silver nitrate was 0.14%, and in the hospital using erythromycin, the infection rate was 0.34%, about 2 ½ times higher. The researchers concluded that silver nitrate should continue to be used as the primary protective agent.

The significant message here is that silver is safe, even in the eyes of newborns, although it can cause a chemical irritation of the eyes that resolves in a couple of days.

Prevention of Cavities

Several 2014 studies have shown that silver helps prevent streptococcus mutans, the bacteria that causes cavities. It is a fairly common occurrence to get a secondary cavity under a filling, so silver preparations are being incorporated into some resin composites used to fill teeth. Unsurprisingly, fillings containing silver were found to be a little stronger and more durable,

Similarly, artificial eyes are notorious for infection. In new research, artificial eyes containing silver were shown to have strong antibacterial activity, decreasing numbers of bacteria by 99.9% and increasing circulation in the eye socket, all of which promote the ocular health of the person wearing the artificial eye.

Strep Throat

Strep throat is very common, especially in children and teens. For those prone to frequent sore throats, consider storing your toothbrush in a small glass with silver solution overnight (directions below). Not only will your toothbrush be sterilized, but when you brush your teeth, your oral cavity will benefit from the trace amount of silver left on the toothbrush.

Precautions

There is a condition called Argyria that is associated with overuse of silver. This condition, rarely seen today, is thought to be due to impure forms of silver. A bluish skin discoloration, argyria may be related to the term "bluebloods," as the aristocracy typically used silver utensils and goblets, and were "born with a silver spoon in their mouth." Although they sometimes turned blue, Bluebloods were noted to have some immunity against the widespread plagues common in Europe in the early centuries. There are no known interactions between silver solutions and other drugs.

Using Silver At Home

Silver can be used in many ways – in a gel or wound dressing, or taken orally. There are devices on the market that use a mild current to make what is called colloidal silver, but a tried and true practice is to place a clean, new pure silver dollar in a glass of water overnight, The resulting silver hydrosol (water solution) can be ingested, gargled, applied to a wound, used as a skin wash, or even as ear drops.

71 WATERCRESS – "CURE OF CURES."

May 15, 2014

Recognizing the benefit of watercress as a healing food, Hippocrates has called this plant the "cure of cures." A man who led an exemplary life, Hippocrates served decades of jail time because of his belief that diseases had natural causes, and were not a punishment inflicted by the gods. Hippocratic medicine was based on the healing power of nature, and we are all familiar with the premise of the Hippocratic Oath, "First Do No Harm." It is thought that Hippocrates treated his early patients in a temple at Cos in Greece, on an island that boasted several springs with a plentiful supply of watercress that he used to treat his patients.

Nutritional Benefits

Popular in England, where it has been known as "poor man's bread," watercress is a staple in sandwiches. Boasting more iron than spinach, watercress is good for dieters because of its extremely low calorie content – less than 5 calories per cup. 1 cup of watercress also provides 25% of the daily Vitamin A requirement and 30% of Vitamin C.

High in sulfur, an essential mineral that promotes healthy skin, hair and nails, watercress has been used in traditional medicine, particularly in Europe for children with weak bones and soft teeth. It is also prescribed in tablet form for eczema. The Greeks saw watercress as a "wit-producing food."

Use in Medicine

Watercress has been highly studied in its role as a cancer preventative. Unlike many other plants that work to shrink tumors, watercress seems to actively disarm the carcinogens that can cause cancer in the first place. Nowhere is this more apparent than in tobacco-caused lung cancer. The American Health Foundation conducted a study to determine exactly what components of watercress provide protection from lung cancer. They found that Phenethyl isothiocyanate (PEITC), a chemical released upon chewing of watercress, protects against lung cancer caused by tobacco by breaking down and excreting the cancer causing agents before they can cause harm. In this human study, urine samples were analyzed, and in smokers taking 2 ounces of watercress three times daily, their urine had highly increased excretion of the toxic metabolites of tobacco, an effect that was seen in only 2-3 days of therapy.

Another study at the Institute of Nutrition in Jena, Germany investigated the hypothesis that watercress reduces cancer risk by "turning on" certain detoxification enzymes in the blood cells. They concluded that watercress "is able to modulate the enzymes superoxide dismutase and glutathione peroxidase in the blood" which induces detoxification. Watercress has also been shown to decrease DNA damage in the blood cells caused by toxins that can contribute to cancer risk.

An interesting study in Northern Ireland investigated the protective effects of watercress extract toward three important stages in the carcinogenic process of human colon cancer cells, namely initiation, proliferation, and metastasis (invasion). Watercress extract proved to be significantly protective against all three stages of the cancer process.

Another study compared Spinach and watercress in their antioxidant (cancer preventing) properties. While similar, watercress ranked higher than spinach in both antioxidant potential and the ability to scavenge and absorb free radicals. (A free radical is an unstable atom that wreaks havoc in the body, damaging cells and accelerating aging, causing cancer progression, and heart disease. Lots of things cause free radicals, including pollution, processed foods, cigarettes, industrial chemicals and drugs, to name a few.)

Where to find watercress

Watercress grows throughout Missouri. Luckily for us, it is most common in the Ozark counties of southern and central Missouri. A perennial plant, it is usually found around springs and spring branches, but is also found in marshes and ditches. It can be found submerged, floating, or emerging from the water. Easily transplanted and grown from cuttings, it roots at the stem nodes. Growing up to 10 inches tall, watercress blooms from April through October with white tiny flowers at the tips of the stems consisting of 4 petals.

Precautions

Watercress must be used fresh. Don't harvest leaves from polluted waters, and be sure to thoroughly wash leaves prior to eating. The juice should not be taken undiluted, as it can produce inflammation in the throat and stomach in sensitive individuals. Some doctors caution against use in pregnancy.

Preparation:

A member of the mustard family, watercress has a hot, spicy taste, without bitterness.

Watercress tea: Add one teaspoon of chopped fresh shoots to ½ cup hot water, steep for 5 minutes.

Watercress juice: Add shoots and leaves to your juicer and take 1 tsp. in milk or water, 3 times a day.

Watercress Pinwheels

1 loaf of bread or 6 inch flour tortillas
1 cup chopped watercress leaves
6 oz. Softened cream cheese
Dash of sea salt

Combine watercress, cheese and sea salt. If using bread, remove the crust. Spread ¼ cup of mixture on each tortilla or bread slice. Roll up, and wrap in foil or plastic wrap, Chill for 1-2 hours, slice pinwheels 3/8" thick.

Watercress grows along creeks and ditches throughout the Ozarks.

72 SLIPPERY ELM

May 22, 2014

Slippery Elm (Ulmus rubra), also known as Red Elm, is native to North America It is found throughout Missouri in damp woodlands and along streams. A medium tree, it grows to 65 feet in height. The leaves, seeds and twigs are a source of food for wildlife. Resistant to Dutch Elm disease, this tree with a reddish heart wood survives when other nearby elms are decimated.

Slippery Elm has been used in traditional medicine in North America for hundreds of years, and is still used to make lozenges for sore throats and coughs by several major manufacturers. Ointments made of the inner bark of slippery elm were used during the Revolutionary War to treat the wounds of soldiers, and there is some early literature claiming that George Washington's soldiers at Valley Forge survived for 12 days on porridge made from slippery elm. In 1996, a variant of the Slippery Elm tree named the *Valley Forge* was planted on the grounds of the US Capitol.

In addition to treating sore throats, the inner bark is effective for a variety of illnesses, including irritable bowel syndrome and other bowel disorders, inflammation, psoriasis, breast and prostate cancer.

How it works

The inner bark of the slippery elm provides the active ingredient used in medicine. It contains mucilage – a form of carbohydrate that turns into a slippery gel when it is mixed with water. This gel coats and soothes everything it touches, making it excellent for sore throats, irritable intestines, and skin conditions. The inner bark can be dried, ground or powdered, and Slippery Elm is available commercially in the form of tablets, capsules or lozenges. It can be used in teas, and is often combined with wild cherry bark, and sweet gum leaves for an excellent cough syrup and cold remedy. (As the reader will recall, the active ingredients in Tamiflu come from the Sweet Gum tree.)

Gastric Ulcers

In addition to providing a protective gel lining to everything it touches, some researchers speculate that slippery elm initiates the production of extra mucus in the gastrointestinal tract, an effect that can protect from ulcers due to excess acid.

Irritable Bowel Syndrome

I have noted in my practice that symptoms of Irritable Bowel Syndrome are becoming more prevalent. IBS is a disorder that can be quite uncomfortable, and I have encountered patients that are afraid to leave their home because of accidents. A 2013 study from Australia looked at the effectiveness of natural medicines in affecting bowel habits and abdominal symptoms in patients with Irritable Bowel Syndrome. They found that a formula consisting of a mixture of dried powdered slippery elm bark, lactulose, oat bran, and licorice root significantly improved both bowel habit and IBS symptoms in patients.

Psoriasis

Another distressing ailment is Psoriasis. While it is often mainly a cosmetic disorder, it can also cause severe itching, and greatly affect the quality of life in the sufferer. A recent study at the University of Hawaii looked at several forms of medical nutrition to treat psoriasis, which unfortunately has no known cure at this time. In a small study, 5 patients aged 40 - 68 years old who drank saffron tea and slippery elm water daily were studied over a 6 month period. The cases, which ranged from mild to severe, all improved on all measured outcomes over a six-month period when measured by the Psoriasis Area and

Severity Index and the Psoriasis Severity Scale.

Prostate and Breast Cancer

The majority of the studies looking at the effect of Slippery Elm involve a formulation called Essiac. Essiac has been widely used in Canada for over 70 years, and is reputed to be a Native American recipe that initially consisted of 4 plants: burdock root, Indian rhubarb, sheep sorrel and the inner bark of the slippery elm. In the 1920's an Ontario nurse named Rene Caisse made Essiac popular, claiming she obtained the recipe from a woman who was cured of breast cancer. (Note that Essiac is Caisse spelled backward.)

A study from Indiana University/Purdue University looked at the effect of Essiac tea extracts on prostate cancer tumor growth in immunosuppressed individuals. They concluded that Essiac preparations "may be able to inhibit tumor cell growth while enhancing immune response to antigenic stimulation. This may be especially valuable in immune-suppressed individuals."

In 1998, Dr.Kaegi, Director of Medical Affairs and Cancer Control of the National Cancer Institute of Canada from 1993 to 1996, published an article reviewing all of the available evidence regarding Essiac on behalf of the Canadian Breast Cancer Research Initiative and concluded that "there is some weak evidence of Essiac's effectiveness, and it is unlikely to cause serious side effects when used as directed."

Slippery Elm Lozenges

¼ cup slippery elm powder

¼ cup wild cherry bark

¼ cup sweet gum leaves (dried)

2 Tbs. local honey

Boil wild cherry bark and sweet gum leaves in 1 cup water. Pour off ¼ cup of the strained tea, and add the hot tea to the slippery elm powder with 2 Tbs. of local honey until completely dissolved. Mix the ingredients well, and roll into marble-sized balls. Roll the balls in a little slippery elm powder to coat them. Let dry for 48 hours. They will safely keep for months in a cool, dry area.

73 WAY DOWN YONDER IN THE PAW PAW PATCH

May 29, 2014

Each year, we take advantage of our local George O. White Nursery and order several seedlings. Three years ago, we planted several wild plums, and discovered a delightful surprise – there was a Paw Paw tree among the bunch, and it is already producing fruit.

The common Paw Paw (Asimina triloba) is a native fruit tree, and holds the distinction of producing the largest edible fruit indigenous to North America. The name is thought to come from the Spanish papaya, likely due to the physical similarity of the fruit, although they are actually quite different.

Recently, the cultivation of Paw Paws for fruit production has become more popular as consumers seek organic products. A native fruit with no pests, Paw Paw grows well without pesticide. Natural insecticides in the leaves, twigs, and bark of Paw Paw trees can also be used to make an organic pesticide. While most insects avoid the Paw Paw, one exception is the zebra swallowtail butterfly that *loves* the plant! The butterfly larvae feed on the leaves, and then have lifetime protection from predators, as trace amount of natural chemicals remain; making the butterfly distasteful to birds and other predators.

Nutrition

Pawpaw fruits are rich in fatty acids, the major one being octoanoate, also found in coconut oil, believed to prevent fungal infections, such as Candida, in the intestinal tract. Octoanate has also shown some benefit in patients with essential tremor.

One half cup of pawpaw fruit provides 80 calories and 1.2 grams of protein (high for a fruit), 18.8 grams of carbohydrate, 2.6 grams of fiber, and significant amounts of potassium, iron, manganese, magnesium and copper. Pawpaw can be used in most recipes in place of bananas.

Cancer Therapy

According to the Missouri Department of Conservation, Paw Paw extract has been used experimentally in cancer therapy, and has been rated 300 times more potent than Taxol, another plant extract used to treat cancer. Taxol comes from the bark of the Pacific Yew tree and is available by prescription as Paclitaxel, which is used to treat lung, ovarian, breast, head and neck cancers. Taxol is on the World Health Organization's list of Essential Medicine, detailing the most important medications needed in a basic health system. Although it is much more potent, Paw Paw hasn't reached the same distinction, but native sources for Taxol are becoming extinct, and Paw Paw itself is now endangered in NJ and threatened in NY, so cherish and plant trees before the demand increases!

The seeds have been shown to contain the chemicals asimitrin and hydroxytrilobin that have a selective toxicity against prostate and colon adenocarcinomas; that is they kill only the cancer cells, and spare the surrounding tissue. The bark of the Paw Paw tree also contains compounds shown to be useful both in fighting tumors, and as a pesticide.

An interesting 2010 study from the University of Mississippi looks at the effects of products containing Paw Paw twig extract as an alternative anticancer medication. They found that the extract destroys tumors through a complex mechanism that keeps the tumor from developing a blood supply.

The Division of Antibiotics in the Department of Drug Evaluation in Seoul, Korea looked closely at an extract from the seeds only of the Paw Paw. Using mass spectrometry, they isolated the active compounds, and found that they were effective against six human solid tumor cell lines with notable selectivity for the prostate (PC-3) and the pancreatic (MIA PaCa-2) cell lines at 10-100 times the potency of Adriamycin.

Use as Pesticide

Various parts of the Paw Paw have been extracted and used as pesticide. The small twigs yielded the most potent extract, while the stem wood and leaves were the weakest. The unripe fruits, seeds, root wood, root bark and stem bark were also potent, and generally yielded > 2% of their dry weight as an effective pesticide. The fact that the smaller diameter stems are more potent than the larger stems is important for commercial sustainability of the product as new branches can be obtained through regrowth from the parent trunk and larger branches without harming the tree.

Prestigious Purdue University found that extracts of Paw Paw were among the most potent of the 3500 species of plants screened for bioactive compounds. Researchers documented powerful cytotoxicity, in vivo antitumor, pesticidal, antimalarial, anthelmintic (wormer), antiviral, and antimicrobial effects of Paw Paw extract. In fact, commercial products made from Paw Paw extract include a shampoo, highly effective in treating infestations of head lice, fleas, and ticks; a series of pesticidal sprays, which protect host plants against a diversity of pests; and an ointment for treatment of oral herpes (HSV-1) and other skin afflictions.

Pawpaw Cookies with Black Walnuts

- ¾ c. pureed pawpaw pulp
- 1 c. all-purpose flour
- ½ tsp. baking powder
- ¼ c. butter
- ½ c. brown sugar
- 1 egg
- ½ c. black walnuts

Preheat the oven to 350° F and grease one large cookie sheet. Peel and seed fresh pawpaws and process in a food processor until fine. Sift together the flour and baking powder, and set aside. Cream the butter and sugar. Add the egg. Add the flour mixture and then add the pawpaw pulp. Chop half the nuts (reserve 16 pieces) and blend them in. Drop by teaspoonfuls onto the prepared cookie sheet and press a piece of black walnut onto the top of each cookie. Bake 12 minutes or until brown across the top. Makes about 16 cookies.

74 OIL PULLING

June 5, 2014

As everyone becomes increasingly aware of the hazards of fluoride, and it is gradually being withdrawn from the public water system, increasing numbers of people are looking into an ancient method of oral health, called oil pulling.

A procedure that involves swishing oil in the mouth for oral and generalized health benefits, oil pulling therapy with sesame oil is a form of ayurvedic medicine from India. The procedure has been found to strengthen teeth and gums, prevent tooth decay and bad breath, and prevent bleeding gums.

Oil pulling therapy can be done using edible oils like sunflower oil or sesame oil. The sesame plant (Sesamum indicum) is the most studied oil for this method of oral hygiene, with hundreds of replicated research studies documenting its effectiveness and safety. Recently, the use of coconut oil is being promoted as an oil-pulling agent, but as discussed in a previous article, last year there was a glut of coconut oil on the market, so producers were scrambling for new applications. This year, coconut oil prices are likely to go up, as exports fell 35 percent in the first two months of 2014, after typhoon Yolanda destroyed over 34 million coconut trees in the Pacific region last November.

The word "Ayurveda" is Sanskrit for "life knowledge." Originating long before the medieval period, this ancient system of Hindu traditional medicine stresses the use of plant-based medicines and treatments. While not recognized by Western medicine, ayurveda advises oil gargling to purify the entire system; as it holds that each section of the tongue is connected to different organ such as to the kidneys, lungs, liver, heart, small intestines, stomach, colon, and spine, similar to reflexology.

Sesame oil has a high concentration of polyunsaturated fatty acids and is a good source of vitamin E. Sesamin, one of the main ingredients in sesame oil has been found to inhibit the absorption of cholesterol, as well as inhibiting its production in the liver. It also act as an anti-hypertensive.

How it works

Sometimes tooth brushing is not indicated, as in cases of mouth ulcer, those with a strong gag reflex, or in the case of bleeding, fragile gums. Oil pulling can be used to clean the oral cavity in all these cases, and is 5-6 times more economical than toothpaste.

To properly perform oil pulling, take a tablespoon of sesame oil into your mouth (a teaspoon for young children), and swish it around your mouth and through your teeth for approximately 15 – 20 minutes. Unlike fluoridated toothpaste, there is no harm if you accidentally swallow some of the oil. The oil will go through a change, and turn a milky light brown. This chemical reaction occurs due to interaction with saliva, and is called saponification (soap-making). There is also the natural production of sodium hydroxide (NaOH) used in almost all whitening toothpastes. It is claimed that the swishing activates enzymes and draws toxins out of the blood. It is recommended that oil pulling be done on an empty stomach in the morning, and should be followed by rinsing your mouth with water. The 15-20 minute procedure goes by quickly, and can be accomplished during your morning shower.

Proponents of coconut oil recommend following the same procedure, substituting coconut oil and a drop or two of clove and/or tea tree essential oils for maximal antiseptic and antifungal power.

Benefits

Prevention of Cavities

Both sesame oil and coconut oil pulling have been evaluated for their effectiveness against cavities, although sesame oil has been examined more extensively. Both oils were examined microscopically after oil pulling was completed, and were found to destroy Steptococcus mutans, the bacteria that causes cavities. The presence of oral debris in the expectorated oil was considered evidence of enhanced mechanical cleansing action of the teeth and gums.

Treatment of Gingivitis

In an extensive randomized, controlled, triple-blind study of adolescent boys, the effectiveness of sesame oil pulling on plaque-induced gingivitis was compared with chlorhexidine (Peridex) mouthwash. The oil pulling therapy showed a reduction in the plaque index, modified gingival scores, and total colony count of aerobic microorganisms in the plaque of adolescents with plaque-induced gingivitis comparable with that of the potent chlorhexidine. Chlorhexidine can erode the enamel of the teeth and cause stains over time, complications not seen with oil-pulling therapy.

Halitosis (Bad breath)

A 2011 study found oil-pulling equally effective as chlorhexidene on halitosis, working by removing the organisms that cause bad breath.

Tooth Pain

Although it has not been formally studied, there are numerous anecdotal reports regarding relief of dental pain with oil pulling. I personally experienced this after my first attempt at oil pulling. The almost constant pain I had been experiencing in a pressure-sensitive rear molar was immediately relieved, an effect that appears to be permanent.

The Final Word

Although oil-pulling with sesame has been well researched, anecdotal reports of similar benefits with coconut oil are emerging. Although 20 minutes is recommended, 3-5 minutes of therapy is beneficial. It is recommended to brush your teeth after oil pulling to thoroughly remove dislodged debris from the teeth and gums, and to keep from smelling like a sesame bun! You can easily make your own fluoride-free toothpaste:

Mineralizing Tooth Paste

- 4 tbsp. Coconut Oil (in its solid state)
- 2 tbsp. Baking Soda (aluminum free)
- 1/8 tsp. stevia
- 20 drops peppermint or clove essential oil
- 1/8 tsp. magnesium (Epsom salts)

Mix all ingredients together, and store in a cool place.

75 GOLDENSEAL – NATURAL TREATMENT FOR URINARY TRACT INFECTION

June 12, 2014

I am often asked about natural cures for urinary tract infections. Cranberry juice is commonly used, but doesn't always work. Fortunately, my favorite treatment grows plentifully in Missouri – Goldenseal (Hydrastis candensis).

Goldenseal is a perennial herb in the buttercup family, native to northeastern US and southeastern Canada. It grows mostly in the Ozarks and central Missouri, and is largely absent from the western Missouri counties. It has a knotty, thick, yellow root with a purplish, hairy stem. It the summer, it produces a single fruit that looks like a large raspberry containing 10-30 seeds that can be dried and planted. Planting Goldenseal is indeed a good idea; due to its market value and many uses, it has been extensively harvested, keeping it on the verge of being an endangered plant. As one of the top five selling herbal products in the United States, growing and harvesting Goldenseal also makes financial sense for an Ozark entrepreneur. It is estimated that more than 60 million goldenseal plants are picked each year without being replaced.

When America was first colonized, Native American tribes, especially the Cherokee, had extensive knowledge of Goldenseal – both as a medicine and as a coloring agent for clothing. There is early literature from 1798 referring to the Cherokee use of goldenseal as a cancer treatment, and also as an eye wash for eye infections.

Goldenseal possesses the following medicinal properties: astringent, anticatarrhal (clears excessive secretions from the respiratory tract), anti-inflammatory, antimicrobial, laxative, and oxytocic (stimulates uterine contractions). It shows a stimulation of the immune system within 2 weeks of treatment when given to immunosuppressed patients.

Two of the active components found in Goldenseal are Berberine and Canadaline.

Berberine is a quaternary ammonium alkaloid, a type of disinfectant, with antifungal and antibacterial properties, while Canadaline is more effective against certain organisms.

Urinary Tract Infections

Together, Berberine and Canadaline, two components of Goldenseal, are potent against 6 strains of bacteria often implicated in urinary tract infections, including e.coli, staph aureaus, pseudomonas aeruginosa, streptococcus sanguis and candida albicans. Canadaline was found to be the most potent of the chemicals found in goldenseal, and is particularly effective against Candida (yeast.) Berberine has been found to have low bioavailability in general. However, it is thought that berberine concentrates in the bladder when Goldenseal is taken orally. Therefore, even though not much berberine is absorbed throughout the system, it is possible that it might reach higher concentrations in the bladder...where it is needed most.

Goldenseal is often combined with other products, such as cranberry juice, to treat urinary tract infections, providing what is essentially a punch and counter-punch. Cranberry juice immobilizes bacteria in the urinary tract and bladder, preventing them from sticking to tissue walls, making it easier to flush them out of your system, while Goldenseal actually kills the organism causing the infection.

Liver Protection after Tylenol Overdose

It is easy to reach toxic levels of Acetaminophen, often resulting in devastating effects on the liver. A 2011 study looked at what happened when Goldenseal was administered 2, 18, and 26 hours before and 6 hours after an oral overdose of Tylenol in rats. 300 mg/kg of Goldenseal protected the liver as reflected by normal liver enzymes, and even blocked the metabolism of Tylenol into its harmful components.

Hope for Diabetic Neuropathy

Berberine, one of the active components of Goldenseal was found in a recent study to lessen neurotoxicity due to high glucose levels. Diabetic neuropathy is a common and debilitating result of sustained high glucose levels. In 2013, researchers found that berberine helped to protect neurons in the diabetic from neurotoxicity and death suggesting that goldenseal be further evaluated in the treatment and prevention of diabetic complications.

Diarrhea and Gastrointestinal Infections

Berberine is effective in treating diarrhea in patients with toxic E.coli and vibrio cholera with a single oral dose of 400mg. Goldenseal is also effective against parasites like trichomonas and entamoeba At 5 mg.kg for 6 days, berberine was found to be as effective as 10 mg/kg of Flagyl for the same period when treating children with giardia.

Dosing

Adults (18 years and older)

For general use, various types of goldenseal dosing have been used, each taken by mouth three times daily, including 0.5 to 1 gram tablets or capsules, or 0.3 to 1 milliliter of liquid/fluid extract for no longer than 2 weeks. For infectious diarrhea, 100 to 200 milligrams of berberine hydrochloride taken by mouth four times daily, or a single dose of 400 milligrams taken by mouth has been studied.

Precautions

At normal doses, goldenseal is non-toxic. It can stimulate the uterus, so don't use in pregnancy. High doses can slow the heart rate, and extremely high doses can be neurotoxic. Long term use can interfere with vitamin B absorption. It should not be used by nursing mothers.

Goldenseal grows throughout the Ozarks, and is easily identified by its knotty yellow root and formation of a single red fruit filled with seeds.

76 ENGLISH PLANTAIN (Plantago laneolata)

June 19, 2014

The more I study, the more I feel there is no weed that we don't need. English Plantain, plentiful throughout Missouri, is one such weed. Introduced to North America from Eurasia approximately 200 years ago, Plantain has been incorporated into the diet of many herbivores and insects. The Plantain that grows locally is from a different family than the plantains you find in the supermarket. (The plantain that looks like a green banana is actually a vegetable, and is quite delicious when prepared.)

Excellent for first aid, the abundance of plantain assures that it is readily accessible in the outdoors. The crushed leaves applied directly to the skin can stop pain, itching and inflammation. Tea made from the dried leaves soothes indigestion, and chewing the raw leaves is a temporary cure for toothache. Many self-sufficient Ozarkians have their own recipe for Plantain salve.

In addition to first aid uses, Plantain has been studied extensively for its anti-inflammatory, immune enhancing, cancer-preventing and anti-viral properties. Its leaves and seeds have been used in almost all parts of the world for centuries as a wound healer, analgesic, antioxidant, and antibiotic.

Lung Inflammation

In 2005, researchers looked at the role of plantain extract in treating lung inflammation. Even at very small doses, the extract scavenged toxic nitrous oxide radicals in the lungs, decreasing inflammation without causing side effects. Nitrous oxide is a gas produced by inflamed lungs, especially in conditions such as asthma and chronic cough.

In another study from Germany, Plantain was used to treat infections of the upper respiratory tract. Early clinical studies showed anti-inflammatory, anti-spasmodic, and immune enhancement. The researchers recommended plantain for moderate chronic irritative cough, especially for children. In fact, a tea made from the leaves has been used for centuries to treat cough and respiratory ailments

Cancer

In 2003, extracts from seven different varieties of the Plantain plant were evaluated for cytotoxic activity against three human cancer cell lines recommended by the National Cancer Institute. The results showed that Plantago species killed cancer cells, while not damaging the normal cell. It was concluded that the plantain extracts were able to strongly inhibit the proliferation of human cancer cell lines.

Plantain has been shown to have particular promise in treating liver and breast cancer, with a 75% reduction in tumor formation in laboratory animals treated with plantain. Results from another study showed that hot water extract of Plantain possessed significant inhibitory activity on the proliferation of lymphoma and cancer cells in the bladder, bone, cervix, kidney, lung and stomach.

Anti-Malarial

Scientists are concerned because the effectiveness of anti-malarial drugs is declining at an accelerating rate, with an increase in sickness and death due to the disease. Malaria is caused by a single-celled parasite that is injected into the bloodstream of the human sufferer through the bite of the Anopheles mosquito. While we are not concerned with malaria in Missouri, in 2010 alone there were 219 million documented cases of malaria worldwide, with 1961 cases in the United States, so we are not immune to the problem. Plantain extract has been found to have antimalarial properties, while not harming the infected individual.

Wound Healing

A 2012 study looked at different preparations of plantain extract, both water and alcohol based, on wound healing in the oral cavity. Both types of plantain extract increased the formation of epithelial cells, the small buds of new tissue that fill in and heal a wound.

A different study applied ointment made from plantain to a neck injury at the base of the skull. Wound healing rates were calculated at 4, 9, 15 and 21 days after the wound occurred, and tissues samples were taken on the ninth day for analysis. Reduction of the wound area occurred earlier than expected, and on the 15th day, the wound was completely closed. A similar wound treated with typical antibiotic ointment healed much more slowly. The tissue samples taken on the ninth day showed advanced formation of new, healthy epithelial cells.

Antiviral Activity

Plantain extract has been found to be active against herpes virus, Type 1 and 2; and also against adenoviruses. It works after the infection starts, by preventing the virus from multiplying. Adenoviruses are a group of viruses that can infect the tissue linings of the respiratory tract (colds, bronchitis), eyes (pink eye), intestines, and urinary tract.

Plantain Salve

Plantain salve is easy to make and is great for many skin problems, including diaper rash. Put 1/3 cup dried plantain leaves in a glass jar, and cover with ½ cup olive oil. Cap the jar and let it sit for at least a week. Strain the herbs out of the oil by pouring through a strainer or cheesecloth. Melt ½ ounce beeswax over low heat, and stir in your infused oil. Pour the completely melted solution into a clean jar. Allow to cool, then cap the jar. Your salve will keep non-refrigerated for at least a year.

Plantain is plentiful throughout the Ozarks, and grows best in dry soil on disturbed grounds, such as yards and gardens.

77 HOME TESTING PROCEDURES

Part 1

June 26, 2014

By now, most folks seeking health through choosing nutritious, organic foods and natural medicines may be wondering if their efforts are paying off. For example, it is pretty much established in the scientific literature that having a more alkaline, as opposed to an acidic system, prevents many infections and even cancers. But how do you know if your system is acidic? Is taking apple cider vinegar even helping to correct the condition?

You can easily find the answers to these and many other questions. There are inexpensive home testing methods that provide a wealth of information. Inexpensive testing strips with 10 diagnostic parameters can be purchased locally or online. Testing strips are reliable, and *very* inexpensive. At about $12.00 for 100 strips (that's 12 cents each!), you can test your pH, leukocytes, nitrite, urobilinogen, protein, blood, specific gravity, ketones, bilirubin and glucose levels in the urine. Let's look at each of these tests in detail.

pH

pH is a measure of the acidity in a solution. The normal pH range in the urine is 4.5 to 8, with the lower number being more acid, and the high number being more alkaline. Folks trying to alkalinize their system with apple cider vinegar often see results within just 2 days of therapy. A pH test measures urine acidity. Per the National Library of Medicine, measuring pH is also a good test to see if you are at risk for kidney stones, as acidic urine is associated with xanthine, cystine, uric acid and calcium oxalate stones. There are also prescription medications such as Diamox that raise the pH.

Leukocytes

Leukocytes are white blood cells. The presence of a few leukocytes in the urine is normal, but more than a trace amount indicates a urinary tract infection. It should be noted that in the elderly, especially women, sometimes the first sign of a urinary tract infection is an unexplained fall, as the infection can interfere with equilibrium. (This was the case with Nancy Reagan when she fell in 2008.)

Nitrite

Nitrite is not normally found in the urine, but as a byproduct of harmful Gram Negative bacteria, it is another indicator of urinary tract infection, accurate 40-80% of the time. An early indicator, often nitrite will show up in the urine before symptoms of urinary tract infection are present – warranting a visit with your physician for treatment.

Urobilinogen

Urobilinogen is normally found in the urine in small amounts. A product of bilirubin, it is essentially a test of liver function, and high levels can indicate cirrhosis or hepatitis. It can also be elevated with blockage of bile flow from the gallbladder.

Protein

Protein found in the urine usually comes in the form of albumin. Healthy kidneys don't allow proteins to leak through their filters, so protein in the urine can be an early sign of kidney disease or damage, most often seen with diabetes or high blood pressure. Protein in the urine can also be due to medications, trauma, infection (common), and immune system disorders. In pregnant women, urine protein is a hallmark sign of pre-eclampsia. Diseases like multiple myeloma and amyloidosis can also cause increased production of protein in the body with a spillover into the urine.

Blood

Blood should never be found in the urine. When present, it is usually because of infection or kidney stones. Blood in the urine can be due to an enlarged prostate or prostate cancer. It can also be caused from an injury to the kidney from vigorous activity or sports. Anticoagulant medications like aspirin and heparin can also produce blood in the urine. The urine dipstick specially tests for hemoglobin in the urine. Without a test strip, urine can appear to be bloody after eating beets, a false positive known as "beeturia."

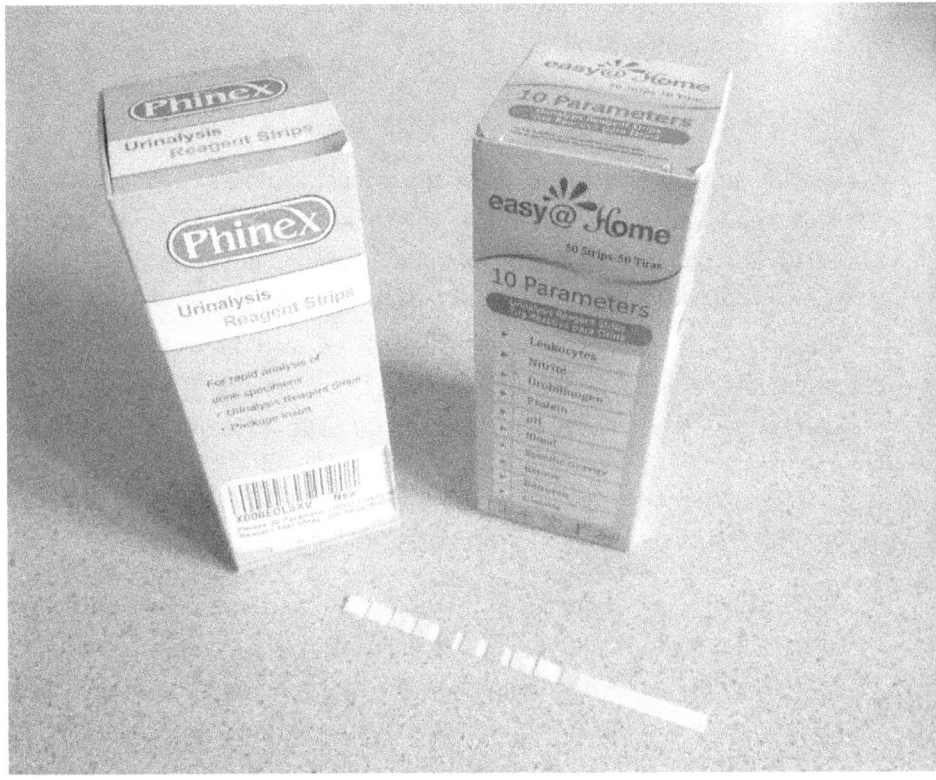

Home testing strips are very inexpensive, and provide a wealth of information.

78 HOME TESTING

Part 2

July 3, 2014

Last week we reviewed the usefulness of urine testing strips. These extremely inexpensive tools provide even more valuable diagnostic information, with tests for specific gravity, ketones, bilirubin and glucose. Keep in mind that all 10 of the tests discussed are included on one 12 cent testing strip.

Specific Gravity

Specific Gravity is a measure of the concentration of the urine, and shows how well-hydrated we are. The range is very wide, from 1.000 to 1.030, and changes with our fluid intake. Higher numbers show higher concentration. In cases of severe kidney damage, the specific gravity is fixed at 1.010. Some neurological diseases can impact the specific gravity of the urine, and it is so important that specific gravity levels are checked every two hours on neurosurgery patients in the intensive care unit.

Ketones

In the 1980's, a ketogenic diet was all the rage. Basically a modified Atkin's diet, the ketogenic diet is a high fat, medium protein, very low carbohydrate diet. With little carbohydrate in the body, the liver coverts fat into ketone bodies, which play a role in appetite suppression. Many people lost weight on the ketogenic diet before the Atkin's diet became popular. Doing a simple urine test with a dipstick would give the dieter instant feedback in the way of ketone level in the urine. A low ketone level would show that too many carbohydrates were being consumed.

With a scarcity of effective anti-obesity medications, the ketogenic diet seems to be making a comeback. A study in *Endocrinology* just published in Mar. 2014 showed a ketogenic diet induced significant weight loss within just 15 days, and at 1 year follow-up, most of the patients lost more than 10% of their initial weight with lean muscle mass preserved (meaning the weight loss was all fat.) While many epilepsy centers throughout the world use a ketogenic diet as an adjunct to treat seizures in children with varying degrees of effectiveness, that topic is beyond the scope of this article.

Bilirubin

Bilirubin is formed by the breakdown of red blood cells, and shouldn't be found in urine. (It is usually excreted in the stool.) If it is present, it means the liver is damaged, or that bile flow from the gallbladder is blocked. Even trace amount of bilirubin in the urine are significant, and require further investigation.

Glucose

Glucose should not be detected in the urine. Normally the kidneys retain and return all filtered glucose back into the bloodstream. Even small amounts are significant, and shouldn't be brushed off. Simply put, glucose is a measure of sugar in the urine, and can indicate diabetes, although there is a rare condition called renal glycosuria where glucose is released into the kidneys even though blood levels are normal. Up to half of women can have glucose in their urine at some point during their pregnancy, but it can also be an indicator of gestational diabetes.

Bleeding Time

Not a urine test, but still a test that can be performed at home is the bleeding time. There are several methods, but with the Duke method, the earlobe or fingertip is pricked with a sterile needle or lancet, after being disinfected with alcohol. The patient then wipes the blood every 30 seconds with a tissue. The test is completed when the bleeding stops, normally 2–5 minutes. You can also check your bleeding time if you accidentally cut yourself. Just time how long it takes the bleeding to stop. A very prolonged bleeding time can indicate that you are taking too much aspirin, or that your anticoagulant dosage should be adjusted, as can a very short bleeding time in patients prescribed warfarin or other anticoagulants. Several natural medications, such as Black Currant can significantly lower platelets that are important in blood clotting, and while some anticoagulation is beneficial, it can also lead to brain hemorrhage and other disastrous consequences. If you suspect your blood is not clotting properly, you should see your physician, and provide them with a full list of your medications, including natural products.

79 Combining Fun and Healthy Treats

July 10, 2014

By now, *Nature Has the Cure* Readers hopefully have quite an arsenal of dried herbs. Today we are going to talk about a unique way to prepare our own homemade vitamins, energy supplements, and natural arthritis medicine, all while having fun with our kids or grandkids.

The answer is (drumroll, please), Homemade Gummy Bears!

Yes, you can *easily* make Gummy Bears at home! While not on a vegetarian diet due to the main ingredient of glycerin, just about everyone likes gummy bears. When we make them at home, we can skip the preservatives, artificial ingredients, and processed sugars. We can also sneak in some extras – like fresh fruit, dandelion root powder, and other powdered herbs.

The Scoop on Gelatin

Gelatin contains collagen type 2, one of the components of cartilage and bones. Think of it as a more bio-available form of glucosamine/chondroitin, commonly prescribed to strengthen bones and joints. Gelatin also contains the amino acids glycine and proline, which are hard to obtain in our daily diet, as they come from parts of the animal not normally consumed today. (The old folks generally wasted no part of the animal, and their health benefitted.) It is made from boiling the tendons and ligaments of processed animals, and has no taste. There are gelatin preparations available from processed shark, and also kosher preparations made from only grass-fed cows. Gelatin is used in medicine to make artificial heart valves and as a medium for wound repair. It can be purchased at any grocery in small packets, or more economically online in bulk.

Increased Bone Density

Osteoporosis is of great concern in post-menopausal women. Women over 50 are 4 times more likely to develop this decrease in bone density as compared to men. Gelatin was given to female lab animals that had their ovaries removed to mimic menopause. Bone mineral density of the right femur (leg bone) was measured. Collagen and glucosaminoglycan were extracted from the tibial end. The study concluded that the oral intake of gelatin resulted in increased bone density, and an increase in type 1 collagen and glycosaminoglycan, making glycerin a useful supplement in treating osteoporosis.

Osteoarthritis

In a May, 2014 double-blind, placebo-controlled clinical study of the effectiveness of hydrolyzed collagen (gelatin) on patients with knee osteoarthritis, researchers found that when taken by mouth, it is absorbed and distributed to joint tissues and has analgesic and anti-inflammatory properties. They concluded that gelatin is a viable option for the management of osteoarthritis and maintenance of joint health. Other studies have found that gelatin reduces the joint pain of athletes, while keeping their joints more supple.

Skin, Hair, Nails and Weight Loss

Needed to build healthy hair, skin and nails from the inside out, gelatin contains the amino acids proline and glycine. There is also some evidence these components aid in immune function and weight regulation, and even helps to reduce wrinkles! One protocol for weight loss is as follows: stop eating at least 3 hours prior to bedtime, then take 1 tablespoon of gelatin power (in tea or water) just before going to bed.

Homemade Gummy Bears

1 cup fresh juice or (or 2/3 cup pureed fruit with 1/3 cup water)

1 Tbs. Lemon Juice

2 Tbs. Honey

3 Tbs. Unflavored gelatin.

Heat all ingredients in a small saucepan, adding gelatin last and stirring with whisk so it doesn't glob up. Heat until completely melted. Pour into silicone molds, and place in freezer to about 15 minutes. You can also use ice cube trays or candy molds. For extra health benefits, you can add dandelion root powder (my energy favorite), orange peel zest, or protein powder. Use your imagination, and have fun!

If they don't get eaten immediately, they can be stored in the refrigerator for a few weeks.

It's easy to make homemade gummy bears with local honey, kosher gelatin and fresh fruit. You can buy the silicone molds for bears (shown), worms and Swedish fish online.

80 BUTTER OR MARGARINE?

July 17, 2014

We have been deceived. Saturated fats cause heart disease, right? Actually, wrong. Dead wrong. 2014 has seen a flurry of studies showing that the change to a low fat, high carbohydrate diet has had disastrous health consequences worldwide. A long term study of 809 Japanese subjects published last month showed a significant increase in coronary heart disease in persons with the highest carbohydrate intake. Conversely, diets with the highest intake of fatty acids and total fat had the lowest risk of developing coronary disease.

Study after study has replicated these results. In March, 2014, the prestigious *Annals of Internal Medicine* succinctly concluded "Saturated Fat does not cause heart disease."

In April, 2014, another highly regarded publication, the *British Medical Journal*, in a huge systematic review of 12 studies involving 7150 participants, looked at the effects of reduced and/or modified fat diets and dietary fatty acids on all-cause mortality, cardiovascular mortality and cardiovascular events in people with established coronary heart disease. They concluded that there is "no evidence for the beneficial effects of reduced/modified fat diets in the secondary prevention of coronary heart disease."

So how did this state of affairs come about? When did saturated fat get its bad reputation? We began to distrust saturated fat in the 1950's, when Ancel Keys, a formidable scientist backed by Proctor and Gamble, did everything he could to promote unsaturated fat. In fact, Proctor and Gamble launched the American Heart Association in 1948, and subsequently put Keys on the nutritional committee. When other scientists would try to challenge his research findings, Keys would beat them down with 35 page articles in medical journals. Through the years, one researcher, Raymond Reiser, kept fighting back, and now it is a proven fact that saturated fat does not cause heart disease. In fact, all the carbohydrates we are eating in its place, likely do cause heart disease, and definitely contribute to obesity and Type 2 diabetes. The popular Mediterranean diet that we are all familiar with emerged from Key's flawed research. Dubbed "the Seven Countries Study," it included less than 100 residents from Crete, who were undergoing hardships post WWII. Contributing to the alteration in their diet was the fact the study was partially conducted during Lent. In fact, of the 22 countries available to Keys for research, he picked only the countries that would prove his hypothesis, completely skipping France, well known for its healthy people and diet rich in saturated fats.

In 1973, Reiser wrote about Ansel Keys, "one must be bold indeed to attempt to persuade large segments of the populations of the world to change their accustomed diets and to threaten important branches of agriculture and agribusiness with the results of such uncontrolled, primitive, trial and error type explorations. Surely modern science is capable of better research when so much is at stake."

But Proctor and Gamble had a hot product to sell – Crisco. Crisco was first developed as an alternative to lard in candle-making. It was produced by adding hydrogen atoms to a fatty acid chain, originally from cottonseed oil, hence the name hydrogenated oil. Hydrogenated ANYTHING is always artificial. It was not without notice that Crisco resembled lard, so Crisco was introduced as a healthy replacement. Many of us remember when Mom first switched from lard to Crisco for her pie crusts, and the resulting heaviness, loss of flakiness and after-taste from Crisco. But lard was effectively demonized, and is just now making a resurgence. As consumers become more educated, the word is out on hydrogenated fats, and Proctor and Gamble sold Crisco to another company in 2001.

-continued next week.

81 BUTTER OR MARGARINE?

Part 2

July 24, 2014

Parallel with the introduction of Crisco was the introduction of margarine. I think we all switched to *I Can't Believe It's Not Butter* at some point. This switch to a major source of trans-fatty acids parallels with the rise in irritable bowel syndrome, age related macular degeneration, heart disease, infertility and growth disorders. Traces of pesticides used on the original plant sources for vegetable oils have also found their way into margarine.

From 1996 -1969. 832 men from the long-term Framingham study were evaluated for their margarine intake. The men were followed over 21 years, and the rate of coronary heart disease rose for each increment of 1 teaspoon per day of margarine.

Other data from the Framingham study shows that women under 50 rarely get heart disease; in fact higher cholesterol levels in women are associated with longer life. Women on diets low in saturated fat increase their chance of having a heart attack, due to a decrease in their HDL (good) cholesterol.

Fat doesn't make you fat. Carbohydrates do. Carbohydrates break down into glucose, and stimulate insulin production causing us to store fat. On the other hand, saturated fats create a feeling of satiety by stimulating the release of cholecystokinin, making us feel full and satisfied, leading to a reduction in hunger and food intake. Have you ever eaten a whole bag of chips and still felt hungry? It is especially important to include some saturated fat with breakfast, such as a whole egg, cheese, or peanut butter.

There is another reason to be concerned about using liquid oils. When heated, oils create oxidation products that can lead to liver cirrhosis, heart disease and Alzheimer's. This is especially a problem with the oil is heated to a high temperature, and used over and over.

Lard, on the other hand, is very stable, even when heated to high temperatures.

The good news is we can make, or purchase our own butter and lard, supporting our local small farmers and ranchers at the same time. To make butter, buy fresh cream from a local farm, and fill a mason jar 1/3 full. Shake the jar, or have your kids shake it until the butter separates. Remove the butter from the buttermilk with a colander, and rinse it on all sides with cold water until the water runs clear. Mix in salt if you wish, and chill the butter in your refrigerator.

If you buy your butter at the store, put the used butter wrappers in a zip-lock bag in your freezer. When you need to grease a pan, use the saved wrappers. Most store bought non-stick sprays contain toxic ingredients, including propellants and silicone. I also fill a spray bottle with olive oil for some of my recipes and to season my iron skillets.

Fresh cream butter, straight from the cow. Courtesy of Dana Adams of Licking.

82 WITCH HAZEL

July 31, 2014

Witch hazel is the most widely used botanical plants on earth. Literally half a million gallons are commercially produced each year. For two generations, witch hazel has been a mainstay of the family medicine cabinet.

It should be noted that witch hazel has nothing to do with witches. In 1590, A. Harriot wrote a manuscript describing animals, plants and other notable findings in the New World, 17 years before the founding of Jamestown. When describing the territory then known as Virginia, Harriot made the following statement "Maple, and also wich-hazle, whereof the inhabitants make their bowes." Wich is an Olde English word meaning pliable or bending, a property necessary in wood used to make bows. Hazle is thought to come from the similarity of the tree to the nut-bearing shrub back in England, perhaps bringing some comfort to the homesick settlers.

Forked switches from the witch hazel shrub have long been used successfully to find water sources for digging wells, and the operator of the tree branch became known as a "water witch." How this works, and it truly does, is the subject of much debate. When I had my last well dug, the company brought out a dowser, and he located the perfect spot for the well in very short order.

Here in the Ozarks, we are blessed to have two species of witch hazel: American Witch Hazel (Hamamelis virginiana) and Ozark Witch Hazel Hamamelis vernalis. Witch hazel is a shrub that likes to grow at the base of rocky slopes and along streams. It blooms as early as January, and both the leaves and twigs can be used for medicinal preparations.

Medicinal Uses

The chief benefits of witch hazel come from its anti-inflammatory and astringent properties. It has been used to stop internal bleeding and as a treatment to reduce swelling. Called "shemba" by the Osage Indians of Missouri, they used a poultice made from witch hazel bark for ulcers, tumors and sores. There is also some evidence that the tribe used a concentrated bark extract as a liniment to keep the legs of young athletes limber. Probably the most common use of witch hazel today is as a treatment for external hemorrhoids, and it is also included in the ingredients of many shaving lotions.

New Uses

In addition to the traditional uses, researchers are finding new applications for witch hazel.

Effects on Skin

Witch hazel is excellent for your complexion. Extracts made from the leaves and bark protect the skin from sunburn and photo-aging when administered topically or taken by mouth. Witch hazel seems to exert this skin protection action through its anti-elastase (keeping skin firm) and catalase (breaking down harmful chemicals) activities with a protective effect on skin integrity against harmful effects such as ultra violet rays, making it a good toner after a day out in the sun.

A 2014 report published in *Dermatology* investigated an interesting phenomenon. It was noted that tattooed patients with a purpuric (purple lesions that occur due to bleeding under the skin) rash seemed to be immune to the rash in the area of their tattoos. When they looked into this "sparing phenomenon," they found the tattoo ink contained a witch hazel extract, concluding that witch hazel may be an effective treatment for purpuric lesions.

Anti-Viral Effects

In January, 2014 researchers looked at antiviral effects of witch hazel bark extract on both influenza A virus and the Human Papilloma virus. There are existing volumes of evidence of the effectiveness of witch hazel against the herpes simplex virus. Using extracts from witch hazel bark, researchers demonstrated antiviral activity against different viral strains, including the recently emerged H7N9. Effects against the virus were dose-dependent, and completely abolished at 24 h post infection at ≥50 µg/ml. The antiviral effect persisted at 48 and 72 h post infection. It should be noted that at the same concentrations, the bark extract had no substantial effect on measles or type 5 adenovirus (a cause of respiratory infections).

Insulin-like activity

Readers are well versed on the effectiveness of cinnamon on stabilizing blood sugar levels. While cinnamon remains the most bioactive product, it is followed by witch hazel, which comes in second. Current research evaluating effects of witch hazel extracts on insulin activity suggest a possible role in improving glucose and insulin metabolism.

Make your own!

Local plant expert Penny Clark knows a lot about witch hazel. She produces 250 gallons of aromatic witch hazel each year. She recommends this recipe for witch hazel tea: Add one ounce of witch hazel leaves to 1 quart of boiling water for a standard infusion. For more information about witch hazel, you can contact Penny at her website: www.pinenut.com.

Fresh and dried witch hazel leaves and twigs can be used in a variety of topical preparations and teas.

84 MAKING HERBAL PRODUCTS

Tamera Glascock

August 7, 2014

Preparing herbs to use in their medicinal capacity is an interesting business. There are so many different herbs, and so many ways to prepare them, that it can seem a bit overwhelming at first. Fortunately, it doesn't have to be complicated and it doesn't require any special equipment or work area.

Before you dive in to making your own herbal remedies, it is vitally important that you are knowledgeable concerning the herbs you are working with. Some herbs have their active constituents in the root, some in the leaf, some in the flower, and some allow the use of the entire plant. Some plants may have incredible healing properties in the leaf or flower, but the roots or berries are deadly. Knowing which part of the plant is safe, as well as the best method of preparing it, can mean the difference between healing and harming.

Start by deciding if you will be using the herb fresh or dried. Fresh is always best, as fresh herbs will retain the most beneficial properties. Drying herbs is a wonderful way to preserve them for use later on, but a freshly-harvested herb will always be far more potent than dried. However, if it is the middle of winter and you are in serious need of some burdock root, dried may be your only choice. That's okay. Pull out that dried burdock root from last fall and give thanks that you had some on hand!

The best time of year to harvest each of the herbs depends on a couple different factors. There are a few exceptions, but a good rule of thumb is this: harvest aerial parts (stems, leaves, flowers and seeds) when they are visibly ready - usually late Spring through early Autumn. When you see the flowers blooming, use a sharp knife or scissors to harvest the part you need. To get the most out of your freshly-harvested plant, lightly macerate the plant material immediately before you use it. This will help break up the cell walls and let the plant release more of its healing properties, faster.

Herbs that are harvested for their leaves and/or stems are most simply tied into bundles and hung to dry. You don't want your bundle to be any larger than 1" around. This will allow good air flow so the plants are less likely to mold.

Seeds can be harvested as soon as they appear, but it is usually best to leave them on the plant until they are almost ready to fall off on their own. The easiest method to use when collecting the seeds is to place the seed pod or blossom in a brown paper bag with holes punched in the sides to allow air to circulate. Give the bag a light shake every day.

Roots should be harvested early in the Spring before the plant is blooming, or in the Fall after the blooms have died off. Once a plant blooms, all of its energy goes into making the flowers and leaves so the roots contain much smaller amounts of the active medicinal properties. To dry roots, rinse all dirt from the roots (a toothbrush is handy for getting in between the bends of folds that most roots have), pat the root dry, cut it into small pieces, then lay it out in a single layer on a screen or any other flat surface. Cutting the root into pieces is not a necessity, but it makes it easier to work with once they are dried. A screen is the best drying option because it allows air to flow around the root as it dries, whereas using a cookie sheet will require a daily stirring of the root to prevent mold and mildew. Since most roots contain a good amount of moisture, they are exceptionally prone to growing mold if they aren't provided with the proper amount of air circulation.

All herbs should be dried out of direct sunlight. The perfect temperature is between 60-70 degrees with plenty of airflow and low humidity. Once dry, place herbs in airtight containers, preferably glass, and store them in a cool, dark spot until you are ready to use them.

Continued next week...

84 MAKING HERBAL PRODUCTS (Part 2)

By: Tamara Glascock

August 14, 2014

In last week's article, we discussed harvesting herbs for later use. So, you have gathered all of your herbs and are itching to make something with them, right? Now, it is time to decide which method of preparation is best for your situation.

There are many ways to use your herbs once they have been harvested. Cook with them, add them to salads, drink them in teas, make salves, poultices, tinctures, elixirs...the list is long! My two favorite methods, and the ones I most often use, are herbal teas and salves.

Herbal Teas

Herbal teas are the most versatile, efficient delivery method, and are beneficial for all ailments. To prepare an herbal tea you need 1 cup of distilled water and 1tablespoon of herb/herb blend. Place the water in a stainless steel or glass pot on medium heat. You want it very hot, but not boiling.

Place your herbs in a tea ball or cheesecloth and drop it in your water. Let it steep for at least 10-15 minutes to allow the herbs time to release their healing properties. You can add honey to help sweeten up your tea or cover the flavor of herbs that aren't always so tasty.

Salves

If you are feeling more adventurous, herbal salves are a wonderful way to preserve the healing properties of herbs. They are simple to make, but require a bit more time and finesse. To prepare an herbal salve you need half cup oils/butters, 3-4 tablespoons of powdered herbs and 1-3 ounces of beeswax. I know the ingredient amounts seem a little sketchy, but the nature of salves is a bit fickle and will change from batch to batch.

For the beginner, olive oil is great choice of oil for a salve, as are coconut, sesame or sunflower oils. Butters that work well are shea butter or cocoa butter. You can add as many oils as you like, but make sure you do a bit of research and see which oils' properties are best for your situation. I suggest starting with a simple olive oil salve.

To make your salve, place your herbs in a glass, heat-proof container like a Pyrex measuring cup, and then pour your olive oil over them, stirring until all of the herbs are completely saturated. There should be a couple inches of oil over the top of your herbs at this point. Place your herbs/oil container in a small pan of water on the stove and gently heat them on a very low setting. The length of time you let them simmer this way is up to you. A minimum of 3 hours is best, but I often let them go for 9-24 hours, especially if my herb blend contains barks or roots.

When you are satisfied that they are finished, remove them from the heat and strain the herbs through cheesecloth. You will likely have bits of herb that get through your straining process. That is fine and won't affect the final product, but if it bothers you, re-strain your oil. Add other oils/butters and your beeswax to the infused oil and return it to heat. Beeswax has a much higher melting point than the oils and butters, so you will need to bump your heat up just a bit, but not too high. You don't want to cook out all those herbal benefits you spent so many hours collecting! Start by adding 1 oz of beeswax and stir gently until the beeswax is completely melted. Remove from heat and let it cool.

You will need to wait until the mixture cools and hardens before you know if you are finished. You can place it in the fridge for a few minutes to speed up this process. If your salve reached the consistency that you like, you are done. Put it in a jar, label it and store it in a dark, cool place for up to 3 years. If you aren't happy with the consistency, place it back on the heat and add more beeswax. Repeat this process until you have the texture and thickness you want. If you want to add essential oils, wait until you have found the perfect consistency and then heat the salve just enough to soften it, add your oils, stir well and let it harden back up.

Tamara Glascock is a local herbalist from Edgar Springs.

For more information on natural products, visit her website at tamarasherbes.com.

85 CHICKEN SOUP, INFLUENZA, AND THE COMMON COLD

August 21, 2014

I hate wasting food. Mom always threw away the cut off ends of carrots, broccoli stalks, onions, celery, etc. I learned early on that most of these "left-over ends" could be planted, growing a new vegetable, or of course, used in the compost pile. A few years ago, I got a great tip from an old-timer. Now I save my little scraps of vegetables in a zip lock bag in the freezer, and put them in my homemade broth as I cook down my chicken carcass. As flu season officially starts in 6 weeks, this is a good time to stock up on home-made chicken broth.

It is part of our American tradition to eat chicken soup when we are sick. As good friends, we take chicken soup to our ill neighbors. In the Jewish culture, chicken soup is referred to as "Jewish Penicillin." How has the chicken soup tradition come about? Is it really beneficial? Let's take a look.

In the year 2000, an absolute flurry of articles about the benefits of chicken soup were published in the prestigious *Chest* journal. Researchers were particularly interested in the mechanism by which chicken soup seems to be a trusted remedy for symptomatic upper respiratory infections. In order to evaluate how chicken soup "works," researchers from Nebraska Medical Center used a traditional chicken soup recipe entitled "Grandma's Soup," credited in the research article as coming from a personal letter written in 1970 to one of the researchers. (See the actual recipe used in the study below). What the researchers found was that chicken soup significantly stops neutrophil migration in a concentration –dependent manner. In other words, the more concentrated the soup, the stronger the effect. (Neutrophils are a type of white blood cell that are deployed in the case of infection and are the main component of pus. They are largely responsible for the immune response that accompanies a cold or the flu, with sneezing, runny nose, watery eyes, etc.) Although chicken soup was not found to be *cytotoxic,* (killing the causative organisms), the researchers concluded that "chicken soup could result in the mitigation of symptomatic upper respiratory tract infections."

In a subsequent study from Delaware published just last year, researchers did find that chicken soup actually killed troublesome viruses, going so far as to call it "A Panacea for tomorrow for various flu ailments." This is important because there are several forms of flu virus, and the flu virus has a unique ability to change its surface structure, allowing it to escape recognition by the body's immune system and causing illness. Most cases of influenza occur within a 6- to 8-week period during winter and spring. Epidemics occur when there are minor changes in the nature of the virus so that more people within a community are susceptible. Influenza A is more likely to cause epidemics. Obviously it would be impossible for a vaccine to keep up with the ever-changing flu virus, Carnosine, one of the major components of chicken soup, allows a correction within the cell of nitric oxide release, one of the important factors of natural immunity, working by stopping the virus from replication through its effect on viral RNA. (Infants in the neonatal ICU are given Nitric Oxide to improve lung oxygenation). The authors conclude that chicken soup preparations "have promise in the control and prevention of influenza A (H1N1) virus infection, cough, and cold."

The Official "Grandma's soup" recipe (C. Fleischer; personal communication; 1970).

- 1 5- to 6-lb stewing hen or baking chicken;

- 1 package of chicken wings;

- 3 large onions;

- 1 large sweet potato;

- 3 parsnips;

- 2 turnips;

- 11 to 12 large carrots;

- 5 to 6 celery stems;

- 1 bunch of parsley; and

- salt and pepper to taste.

Clean the chicken, put it in a large pot, and cover it with cold water. Bring the water to a boil. Add the chicken wings, onions, sweet potato, parsnips, turnips, and carrots. Boil about 1.5 h. Remove fat from the surface as it accumulates. Add the parsley and celery. Cook the mixture about 45 min longer. Remove the chicken. The chicken is not used further for the soup. (The meat makes excellent chicken dumplings.) Put the vegetables in a food processor until they are chopped fine or pass through a strainer. Salt and pepper to taste. (Note: this soup freezes well.)

86 BURDOCK ROOT – MORE PROOF OF GOD'S INFINITE DESIGN

August 28, 2014

"Yesterday I walked through a twice ploughed, black earth fallow field. As far as the eye could see, there was nothing but black earth - not one green blade of grass, and there on the edge of the dusty grey road there grew a bush of burdock...black from dust, but still alive and red in the centre... It asserts life to the end." Leo Tolstoy (from his journal in July 1896)

Burdock is a noble plant, after drawing the admiration of Tolstoy in the 1800's, its greatest accomplishment was yet to come in 1941. While on a hunting trip with his dog, Georges de Mestral, an engineer, became intrigued at how the burrs from the burdock plant adhered so perfectly to his clothes and his dog's fur. When he got home, he looked at the burrs and saw that they had little tiny hooks, perfectly made for catching on to fabrics, which have tiny loops. He invented the prototype for Velcro (composed of the word Velour for the fabric side and Crochet for the hook side) Velcro really took off when NASA adopted it for storing equipment along the walls of the spacecraft.

Burdock (Arcticum lappa) is a biennial plant, taking two years to complete its life cycle. It is found in pastures and other rural areas with animal or human activity. It is also known as cocklebur. The root of the place has been used for centuries for medicinal purposes. It contains a high level of nutrients, and is a staple in many Japanese diets. While generally the root is used, the stalk and leaves are also edible. 1 cup of burdock root has 110 calories, 2.6 grams of protein, significant amounts of B6, folate, magnesium, phosphorus, potassium, calcium and manganese. You can buy burdock root online, where it sells for $1.00 per ounce.

Medicinal Uses

Lowering Blood Sugar

In a 2014 study from France, researchers used an extract from burdock in vitro (in the test tube) and in vivo (in animals) where it was found to improve glucose uptake into the muscle cells, and stabilize blood sugar by decreasing the release of glucose from the cells. There was no effect seen on insulin secretion. The researchers concluded that burdock root works to prevent elevated blood sugar.

Burn and Wound Treatment

In March, 2014, the Journal of Holistic Nursing published a fascinating report. The study looked at pain associated with dressing changes, associated infection, and healing times of burn-injured Amish in central Ohio using an herbal therapy consisting of Amish burn ointment and burdock leaves. (Amish burn ointment contains honey, lanolin, olive oil, wheat germ oil, marshmallow root, aloe vera gel, wormwood, comfrey root, white oak bark, lobelia inflata, vegetable glycerin, bees wax, and myrrh.) The dressing changes caused minimal or no pain; none of the burns became infected, and healing times averaged less than 14 days. The trauma of dressing changes was virtually nonexistent.

The study was replicated by a different set of researchers from the Shriner's Hospital in Cincinnati, Ohio and was published last month. In this study, they looked at the germ killing properties of an Amish burn ointment and burdock leaf dressing. They found no growth of organisms with use of the combination. They cautioned that for very severe burns, a laboratory developed product similar to Amish burn cream was harmful to new tissue cells at high concentrations.

In anecdotal reports from the Amish themselves, applying the Burdock leaf over the burned area after the ointment is applied seems to instantly lessen the pain. Also, when the dressing is removed, the old, necrotic skin seems to cling to the burdock leaf – essentially debriding the wound. There are also case reports of pain relief by applying the burdock leaf to any painful area.

Weight Management

In recent Asian studies, Burdock root has been shown to reduce body weight in animal subjects. This is an area still under investigation.

Scalp and Hair

Oil made from the burdock root is called bur oil. It is used as a scalp therapy to prevent hair loss and dandruff. Active ingredients, including fatty acids and phytosterols in the root also boost hair growth and health.

Cancer Benefits

Arctigenin is a biologically active agent extracted from the seeds of the Burdock plant that provides anticancer activity against a variety of human cancers. It works by stopping the reproduction and metastasis of cancer cells. Recent studies have shown beneficial effects on ovarian, breast and lung cancer. Cancer cells are specifically susceptive to the effects of this extract from the burdock plant, leaving normal cells intact.

How to Prepare

Burdock root is a staple in the Japanese diet, and tastes like a cross between artichoke and celery. It can be stir fried in peanut oil with ginger, carrots and other vegetables added. The root can also be chopped, and added to soups, spaghetti sauce, or stir-fried rice. It can be pickled, using your favorite recipe, but should be parboiled for 2 minutes first so that it is not tough.

Burdock is plentiful throughout Missouri, and is useful as both a food and medicinal plant.

87 BLACK MUSTARD

September 4, 2014

Many think that Jesus was referring to Black Mustard (plentiful here in Missouri) when he taught the parable written in Matthew 13:31-32:

"The kingdom of heaven is like a mustard seed, which a man took and planted in his field. Though it is the smallest of all seeds, yet when it grows, it is the largest of garden plants and becomes a tree, so that the birds come and perch in its branches."

Also known as Brassica Nigra, Black Mustard is often considered a weed, as it has established itself on its own after "escaping cultivation." Today, many heirloom seed companies have it available. Even if one considers it a weed, it is friendly, as it is an annual, usually grows only in disturbed soil, and doesn't displace native plants. In the Europe and the Middle East, Black Mustard has been cultivated for at least 2000 years.

In keeping with its biblical history, the black mustard plant has small yellow flowers, with the 4 petals making a cross, approximately 1/3 inch wide. It blooms between April and November, so now it the time to locate a patch. It can grow as high as 2 to 8 feet tall, and a good place to look is along roadsides. The mustard plant is a source of food for honey bees, and imparts its own flavor to the honey.

Black Mustard used to be the mainstay for adding the flavor to table mustard, until it was replaced by brown mustard, which is more efficiently harvested, in the 1950's. There are about 40 different species of mustard plant, but Black Mustard is the most robust. The flavorful seeds are used in Indian curries, and can be ground and prepared as table mustard. Black Mustard seeds have a great deal of fatty oil (including omega 3 fatty acids), often used as cooking oil in India. The seeds can be added to hot cooking oil, where they pop like popcorn, imparting a nutty flavor to the oil. The seeds can also be sprouted for use on salads, and the leaves of the mustard plant are also edible.

In Europe, ground black mustard seeds are commonly mixed with honey as a cough suppressant. In Eastern Canada, *mouche de moutarde* was used to treat respiratory infections around the turn of the century. Translated as "mustard plaster," it was made by mixing ground mustard seeds with flour and water, and creating a poultice with the paste. This "plaster" was then put on the chest or the back and left until the person felt a stinging sensation.

A mustard plaster is still used today in many parts of the world to treat conditions such as pneumonia, pleurisy, arthritis, and lower back pain. In addition, mustard seeds also have antiviral, antimicrobial, antifungal, and anti-inflammatory properties.

Cancer

In a 2012 study from the University of Heidelberg Cancer Research Center, mustard seed oils were recognized as natural antibiotics, antiviral drugs and antimycotics (stopping fungus). One of the oils found in mustard seed is sulforaphane, which targets the most malignant cancer stem cells, cells that are not affected by conventional cancer treatments. Based on these results, the first prospective clinical studies with cancer patients and sulforaphane have now been initiated in the United States.

Kidney Disease

Another recent study looked at the protective effect of Black Mustard leaves on the kidneys exposed to toxins. In animal studies, they found that doses of 200 and 400 mg. per kilogram of body weight protected both the liver and kidney tissues of the test subjects when they were administered strong toxins.

Pityriasis Versicolor

Often obscure plants offer hope for sufferers of rare disease. This is true in the case of purslane for oral lichen planus. Pityriasis Veriscolor (PV) is another fairly obscure disease. It is a fungal disease of the skin that causes patches to flake and drop off, obviously a very distressing disease that usually occurs in teenagers. It is very hard to treat, but in a 2012 study, forty-six patients with PV were allocated to test and control groups. In the test group, a topical application of black mustard was applied to the lesions, while in the control group, the standard treatment of sodium thiosulphate lotion was applied for duration of 1 month. The severity of the disease and effectiveness of treatment were compared and analyzed. The preparation made with Black Mustard was found superior to the standard treatment, with the benefit of no unpleasant side effects.

Carrot Salad with Black Mustard

1 lb carrot, roughly shredded
1 tablespoon peanut oil
1/2 tablespoon black mustard seeds
1/2 tablespoon cumin seed
1 green chili pepper, chopped
1 teaspoon brown sugar
1/2 teaspoon salt
1/4 teaspoon turmeric
2 tablespoons lime juice

Shred carrots and place in a bowl, set aside. Heat oil in a skillet on medium heat until hot. Pour in mustard and cumin seeds. Be careful, they are like popcorn – so cover the pot. As soon as the popping stops and they become fragrant, remove skillet from stove. Add sugar, salt, chili pepper and turmeric, stirring until you get a smooth paste. Cool about 5 minutes. Stir warm spice paste into carrots, add lime juice and mix well. Chill for about 30 minutes before serving, then mix well again and serve.

88 ROSE OF SHARON

September 11, 2014

The beautiful bushes used to landscape yards throughout Missouri are commonly called Rose of Sharon in the United States, and Rose Mallow in England. Native to Asia, the plant is actually *Hibiscus syriacus*, mistakenly named for Syria, previously thought to be where it originated. Its fragrant blossom is the national flower of South Korea, where it is called mugunghwa, meaning "eternity" or "inexhaustible abundance."

An important plant, well known since the year 1611 when the name Rose of Sharon first appeared in the King James version of the Bible, for centuries the leaves have been used in herbal teas, and the delicious flowers are added to salads. High in carotene, thiamine, and Vitamins E and C, Rose of Sharon is a good addition to any diet. It is very easy to propagate with cuttings, and some homeowners complain that it produces unwelcome new shoots without any assistance.

Although it is very hardy, environmentalists use Rose of Sharon as kind of a canary in the coal mine to monitor for effects caused by changes in the ozone layer. A healthy Rose of Sharon plant indicates that all is well in the local growing area, but visible injury can predict failure of nearby field vegetation.

Medicinal Uses

While the flowers and leaves are an excellent food source, scientists are looking to the root bark of Hibiscus syriacus in the treatment of illness, including anti-cancer therapies. 4 previously unknown and 12 known pharmacologically active compounds have been isolated from the root bark. Human lung cancer cells were exposed to the root bark extract and "Significantly reduced cell viability was observed," leading researchers involved with this 2014 study to conclude that "H. syriacus L. may warrant further investigation for potential as anticancer therapies."

Fungal Infections

There is a long history of the Hibiscus syriacus root being used for treatment of fungal diseases such as tinea pedis (athlete's foot). When this anti-fungal was investigated in the lab, and compared with current anti-fungal agents, it was found to have four times higher antifungal activity.

Anti-aging

Rose of Sharon has been found to have anti-oxidant and anti-aging properties via its effect on human neutrophil elastase. Elastase has been implicated in contributing to the changes in the lung with empysema, and also attacks proteins in the skin causing loss of elasticity. In addition to eating the flowers, a beautiful, fragrant Rose of Sharon water can be made by pouring hot water over gathered petals of the plant, allowing it to steep for 30 minutes, then straining the solution. The Rose of Sharon water can then be applied to the skin like a toner, or consumed as a tea.

Blood Pressure

While multiple studies have documented the beneficial effects of another type of hibiscus on lowering blood pressure, specifically *Hybiscus sabdariffa,* no studies to date have been published using Rose of Sharon, although there are positive anecdotal reports

Cough and Phlegm

Rose of Sharon's flowers contain mucilage, a gooey medicinal compound made of polysaccharides. This component can ease cough and sore throat, aid in removing respiratory secretions, and relieve pain from menstrual cramps and urinary tract infections.

Stuffed Rose of Sharon

20 Rose of Sharon whole flowers

20 Rose of Sharon petals (coarsely chopped)

1 cup cottage cheese

½ cup yogurt

Your favorite herbs and spices

1. Remove pistils and stamens from the whole flowers and set aside.
2. Process cottage cheese in blender until smooth
3. Stir in yogurt and chopped flower petals, reserving 2 tablespoons for garnish.
4. Add herbs and seasonings – chopped green onion, fresh basil, thyme and oregano work well.
5. Spoon the dip into the center of the whole flower
6. Garnish with chopped petals
7. Cover and refrigerate overnight.

The beautiful flowers of the Rose of Sharon are actually hibiscus blossoms.

89 DITTANY - AKA WILD OREGANO

"Why send to Europe's bloody shores For plants which grow by our own doors?"

-- 1830 Shaker
Herb Catalog

September 18, 2014

I made what may be a life-changing discovery last week that I want to share with my readers. I was out on a nature walk, looking for wild Missouri ginseng, when I looked down and saw a clump of wild flowers with small purple petals. The plant just *looked* important, so I pinched off a clump of flowers, rolled them between my fingers, and released the unmistakable aroma of oregano! I have written before on the incredible powers of wild Mediterranean oregano, even though it isn't a local plant, just because it is crucial to keep on hand to ward off most viral illnesses. The problem with Mediterranean oregano is that is expensive, and since it isn't available locally, continued supply is questionable.

I posted pictures of the plant I found with the experts – the Missouri Native Plant Society, and it was identified promptly as Cunila origanoides, also known locally as Dittany. The Latin name for home grown Dittany shows that it is, indeed, a member of the oregano family. Native throughout the southeast US, Dittany, also known as wild oregano, is in the mint family. A perennial, it returns year after year and flowers July through November. It is easily overlooked, but makes itself known when you brush against it, making the air smell like pizza.

The leaves and flowers of Cunila originoides have a long history of medicinal use in the United States, and were offered in the Shaker herb catalogs from 1830 to 1880 (see below). Cunila oil, the essential oil produced from the plant, has historically been used as a stimulant and tonic on the nervous system. The leaves and flowers can also be used to replace traditional oregano in sauces, giving a more robust flavor. The Cherokee used the leaves to make tea, which has been shown to effectively treat headaches, colds and fevers. (Pregnant women should limit their intake, as dittany can induce menstruation.)

Recently, wild oregano has proven to be a very effective antiviral agent. Specifically, it has shown antiviral effects against HSV-1 (herpes simplex virus type 1), HSV-2 (herpes simplex virus type 2), poliovirus, and VSV (vesicular stomatitis virus). Make a note of this, as the current localized epidemic of enterovirus D68 is from the same family as the poliovirus. One recent study did show poor effectiveness against the common adenovirus, which usually causes respiratory symptoms.

Just like the Mediterranean oregano used in commercial Oil of Oregano, Dittany also contains the active component carvacrol and thymol. Carvacrol is a natural phenol that inhibits the growth of several bacterial strains. Thymol is an active ingredient in many mouthwashes and is a powerful fungicide. It has also been found to decrease bacterial resistance to antibiotics, working together with the antibiotic to make them more effective.

Frost Flowers

Along with only a handful of other plants, Dittany produces "frost flowers." A Frost flower occurs when thin layers of ice push out from the stems of certain long stemmed plants. These thin layers of ice form into exquisite patterns with curls that resemble flower petals. They seem to be most plentiful early in the morning after a hard freeze, following a warm day. They usually last until noon, before melting in the sun. Frost flowers are a rare delight, and we are fortunate that conditions in the Ozarks seem to be perfect for their formation.

The Shakers

Because the Shakers are arguably the first folks to turn medicinal plants into an industry, they deserve a small mention. An off-shoot of the Quaker community, the Shakers were social pioneers, inventors, wonderful craftsmen, and extremely successful gardeners. In the mid-1800's, they developed several successful businesses, the most notable of which was their extensive line of medical herb products. Those of us who enjoy a simple lifestyle have much to thank the Shakers for. Shaker furniture is unique in its durability and functionality, and they did much to advance the use of medicinal plants.

Today the Shakers are almost extinct, along with their way of life. At its most robust, the Shaker movement lasted more than two centuries and included nearly 17,000 people in several states. Incredibly, there are only seven Shakers living today, in a small community in Maine. Despite their remarkable gardening skills, they neglected to grow many children, as the most devout in the congregation eschewed marriage and remained celibate.

Wild Oregano, also known as Dittany, is plentiful in the Ozarks

The exquisite formations of frost flowers can be found where wild oregano grows, even after it goes dormant.

90 BE A POKE SALAD ANNIE

September 25, 2014

Those of us at a certain age remember the Elvis song"Poke Salad Annie." Many of us ate Poke Salad growing up, as it was a favorite of our grandparents. Somehow, poke has disappeared from the menu, and many younger folks may not even recognize that huge plant with dark purple berries that seems to grow up in obscure, or not so obscure, areas.

The name poke salad is actually a misnomer. The correct term is "Poke Salet," salet being the German word for salad, and German settlers in the Ozarks very likely brought the plant with them. Native Americans called the plant "pocon," so the name poke salad is an interesting derivation of both German and Native American linguistics, two cultures that greatly appreciated the plant.

Contributing to the decline in pokeweed's popularity is the fact it has been listed as poisonous in some herbal guides. Pokeweed is quite edible, and has been for centuries, but requires a little extra attention. The stalks and the leaves make delicious greens in early May, or later in the year if plucked as new growth. The young shoots and leaves are boiled in 2 changes of water, and taste like asparagus. No new plants can grow in my horse lot, because as soon as it emerges, my horses eat it down to the ground. I suspect they are also eating new growth on larger plants, due to the tell-tale purple dye the berries leave behind. The berries have been used in the past as food coloring, including adding the color to port wine. They aren't very tasty (except to the birds), and the seeds are considered poisonous, so avoid the berries.

When making your first batch of poke salad, it is recommended that you have an old-timer show you the ropes.

Childhood Leukemia

In a 1997 study from the Hughes Institute in Minnesota, researchers revealed a possible cure for Childhood Leukemia could be found in the common Pokeweed. In studies performed on mice, and then primates, animals treated with what they termed "pokeweed antiviral protein" had a marked-increase in leukemia-free survival without any side effects. Much earlier, in 1961, researchers Seibel et al. conducted a study using B43 PAP (pokeweed antiviral protein) in newly diagnosed children with the higher risk Acute Lymphocytic Leukemia. Without explanation, they withdrew pokeweed from the study, and subsequently published studies recommending stronger doses of chemotherapy. Draw your own conclusions on that one.

A more recent 2009 study from York University in Toronto, Ontario looked at effective anti-retroviral treatment option for the human T-cell leukemia virus I (HTLV-I - the causative agent of adult T-cell leukemia and the neurological disorder HTLV-I-associated myelopathy/tropical spastic paraparesis.) They also found an anti-viral protein in Pokeweed that was actually effective against a number of viruses, that works by preventing replication of the viruses, but not toxic to the cell, like most chemotherapy.

Arthritis

Use of pokeweed as an arthritis treatment goes back to the Native Americans. In the Smoky Mountains where my grandmother lived her whole life, it was widely used to treat "the rheumatism."

Immune stimulant

Pokeweed works well as an antiviral, inhibiting the replication of influenza, HSV-1, upper respiratory viruses and poliovirus. In immune suppressed persons, it stimulates B and T lymphocytes to divide and multiply, leading to a healthier immune system. Pokeweed is so efficient at stimulating B and T cell that it is a standard reagent used in laboratory studies to study the immune response in certain diseases.

Emetic

Sometimes our children eat or drink something they shouldn't, and it is necessary to induce vomiting. Poke berries have long been valued as an emetic, and are usually readily available. One documented usage is an infusion of 1 tbsp. of the cut berries in a pint of water. The infusion is taken in one tablespoon doses until vomiting occurs. Remember the seeds are considered poisonous, so remove them from the berries before starting. Of course, you should also see your physician immediately for further treatment.

Preparation

Cooking Pokeweed requires a little care. It is recommended not to eat the plant raw. Poke root and leaves should be boiled twice in two batches of salted water. Draining and off and discarding the first batch of water, then boiling and rinsing it again at which time it can be eaten. In Louisiana kitchens, the stems are cut into rounds and fried like okra. Once the stem starts turning bright red, it is no longer edible.

Poke Cakes (courtesy Anara Brinmere)

After cooking the young poke leaves and discarding water, make a cornmeal batter. Use coarse cornmeal, an egg and just enough water to make a batter, not too runny. Add salt or your favorite seasonings and garlic powder. Fry like fritters. Best if not fried too fast.

91 WHEELBARROW SALAD – DON'T FORGET THE GROUND CHERRIES!

October 2, 2014

As I was musing about this week's column, I walked by my wheelbarrow that holds mulch used for bedding plants. To my surprise, my wheelbarrow was full of salad fixins! Growing wild were healthy purslane plants, physalis and finger millet. We've talked about purslane before (my favorite) and will save finger millet (the famine food) for another column. This week is dedicated to a member of the physalis species, ground cherries.

To those not familiar with ground cherries, you can use this information to amaze your children and grandchildren. Usually found on the edge of the woods, in the middle of pastures, or in this case, in my wheelbarrow, physalis looks like a little Chinese lantern. When you open the papery husk, inside you will find a single fruit, the "ground cherry," that looks a lot like a tomatillo, to which it is closely related. A member of the nightshade family, Missouri boasts 13 *Physalis* species, all of which have the paper husk around the berry and grow scattered throughout the state.

If you're like me, the term "nightshade" is a little off-putting, but the nightshade family also includes tomatoes and potatoes, eggplant and bell peppers. So just as with those vegetables, you wouldn't eat the leaves, stems, or even the fruit before it is ripe. Ground cherry is closely related to tomatillo; they are in the same genus, and both have edible berries covered by a papery husk. If you ever order the steak tacos at Cozumel, they are served with a tomatillo sauce, yum!

Native Americans loved the fruit of the physalis plant. The small, encased berries start out green and turn yellow when ripe. You can use them for jams, jellies, salsas, or just eat them raw. Several sources say not to eat the green berries, but although they are tart, I have found them very flavorful and have had no ill effects. Ground cherries are rich in potassium, magnesium, calcium vitamin C and beta-carotene.

The physalis plant is important to the bees, who like to visit the flowers. Livestock instinctively avoid the leaves and stems, as they are toxic to them. The plant is spread by the birds and some other animals that eat and disperse the seeds.

Male Fertility

In a 2014 study from Cairo, Egypt, the fruit of the Physalis peruviana plant was used in a study looking at agents that could provide a mechanism against reproductive toxicity affecting the testes in male rodents. They found that 2 ml/kg of body weight of physalis juice helped maintain normal serum levels of testosterone, luteinizing hormone, and follicle-stimulating hormone, and concluded that physalis may have a therapeutic role in free radical-mediated diseases and infertility in males.

Neurotoxicity

In a 2014 study from the Asturias Institute of Biotechnology in Spain, researchers looked at the role of physalis in preventing neurotoxicity. Test animals were injected with cadmium, a highly toxic metal found in cigarette smoke. Cadmium affects the brain by decreasing levels of dopamine and serotonin in the cerebellum, hippocampus and cerebral cortex. In the test animals pretreated with physalis, brain chemistry remained near normal levels.

Melanoma

Another study published this year looked at the effect of physalis on melanoma. The authors first reviewed the use of physalis for the treatment of sore throat, hepatitis, eczema and tumors in China. They found in their research that physalis induces apoptosis (shrinkage) in human melanoma cells.

Liver Toxicity

The liver is the main site in the body for intense metabolism and excretion. A number of chemicals and drugs which are used routinely cause liver damage. Researchers treated test animals having high levels of liver enzymes with the whole ripe fruit of the physalis plant. Animals fed various preparations of physalis showed significant lowering effect in the elevated levels of serum markers like ALAT, ASAT, ALP, LDH, creatinine, urea and bilirubin indicating protection against hepatic (liver) cell damage.

Kidney Damage

Another recent study looked at the effect of physalis extract on test animals receiving cisplatin injection. Cisplatin is a chemotherapy drug that is very hard on the kidneys. Pre-treatment with physalis resulted in a significant reduction in serum creatinine, urea, blood urea nitrogen, and increases in total protein, albumin, and total globulin compared to the control group. Higher levels of albumin in the blood are associated with better nutrition, and physalis seems to bind with serum protein, with implications for further study on its role in maintaining adequate nutrition.

Ground Cherry Jam

(from Cooks.com)

3 c. ripe ground cherries
1/4 c. lemon juice (or Real Lemon)
1/2 c. water
1 pkg. Sure-Jel
3 c. sugar

To a quart saucepan, add ground cherries, lemon, water, and Sure-Jel. Bring cherries to a boil and mash them. Be sure they are all mashed so they'll absorb the sugar. Add sugar. Boil according to directions on Sure-Jel package. This will make 3 medium jars of jam.

The Physalis plant gives us the remarkable ground cherry, encased in a Chinese Lantern.

92 PUMPKIN TIME! (CURCUBITA PEPO)

October 9, 2014

It's that time of year, and gardens and roadside stands are full of pumpkins. I laugh at the excitement of my granddaughter when she just *sees* a pumpkin, and realize that I get a little excited, too,

For many years, I have to admit that I threw away the pumpkin innards. That changed in the mid 1990's. Working the 12 hour overnight shift in the hospital, several of us got hungry. There was no food to be had. The cafeteria was closed. Then we noticed the pumpkin decorations at the nurses' station. In what was probably an act of vandalism (thank goodness the statute of limitations is up), we promptly procured the seeds, and toasted them in a small toaster oven in the break room. I will always remember that as the best meal I ever had.

Since that time, pumpkins have been more about nutrition than decoration in my mind. The nutritional value of pumpkins is astounding. With only 49 calories per cup, you also get 282% of your vitamin A requirement, 20% of the daily Vitamin C requirement, 1.5 grams of protein, 563 mg of potassium and miniscule amounts of sodium. Vitamin A is important because it boosts the immune system in several ways. It helps maintain healthy skin and lining of internal organs, preventing harmful viruses or bacteria from entering. Vitamin A also encourages the production of both white and red blood cells, and prevents the growth of cancer cells in the body. Maybe even more important is the effect Vitamin A has on eyesight. Vitamin A contains a compound called *Retinol* that binds with the protein Opsin to form Rhodopsin used in the rod cells in the eye. Our rod cells are what help us to see in low light conditions. Everyone has experienced the effect of Rhodopsin. When you enter a dark movie theater, you can initially see nothing, but in about a minute or two, your vision is restored, and you can then find your seat.

Pumpkins also have several other applications in maintaining health, including prostate health in men, controlling blood sugar levels in diabetics, and improving bladder function. Pumpkin seeds provide the active ingredients for these pharmacologic functions.

Enlarged Prostate

Dozens of studies have looked at the effect of pumpkin seeds on enlarged prostate. Over half of men over age 50 have an enlarged prostate, so this is a huge problem. Although not recognized in the US, a proprietary medication made with pumpkin seed oil is available over the counter in Europe. A large study published last month in *Urology International* looked at the effect of pumpkin seed in men with urinary tract problems due to enlarged prostate. A total of 1,431 men (50-80 years) with enlarged prostate were randomly assigned to either pumpkin seed extract (500 mg grams twice daily) or placebo (sugar pill). The study ran for 12 months, and documented a significant decrease in prostate enlargement in the subjects receiving pumpkin seed extract.

Another 2014 study compared pumpkin seed oil and prazosin, a prescription drug used to treat enlarged prostate. Researchers found that pumpkin seed extract was as effective as the prescription medication, with no side effects.

Blood Sugar Control

Pumpkin seeds have long been used in South America for blood sugar control. Since the first of this year, multiple studies have been published looking at how this occurs. While there is some discussion whether the normalization of blood sugar is due to an enzyme system, or certain chemicals found in pumpkin seeds, it is agreed that pumpkin seeds "possess hypoglycemic properties and could assist in maintaining glycemic control," especially in type 2 diabetics after eating a meal.

Improving Bladder Function

Pumpkin seed oil has been shown to be useful for the treatment of nocturia (getting up at night to void.) It is documented that the Cherokee tribe gave pumpkin seeds to children as a treatment for bed-wetting. In a 2014 study from Japan, subjects were given 10 grams of pumpkin seed oil daily for 12 weeks. Bladder function was assessed at 6 and 12 weeks with the OABSS (overactive bladder symptom score), which showed that pumpkin seed oil significantly reduces symptoms of overactive bladder.

Preserving Pumpkins

By the end of October, pumpkin growers are going to have their hands full. It has been heralded far and wide that you cannot can pumpkin, mostly due to the density. While it is true that pureed pumpkin is likely not a candidate for home canning, I have canned pumpkin with the following method for several years, with great success. I often add canned pumpkin to my zucchini bread, making it a little moister and sweeter, and even more nutritious. Here is the method I use:

Wash your pumpkin, cut it in half, and scrape the insides (saving the seeds for toasting). Cut the pumpkin (including rind) into quarters, and cook until soft. I do this by steaming it on the stove top for 20 – 30 minutes, but it can also be microwaved for 10 minutes. You should now be able to easily peel off the outer pumpkin skin. Being careful not to mash it, cut the pumpkin into 1 inch chunks. Fill your sterilized jars with the pumpkin chunks and the cooking liquid you saved. Add enough extra boiling water so there is one inch headspace. Pressure cook the pumpkin at 11 lbs. pressure for 55 minutes (pints) and 90 minutes (quarts).

93 HOPS – MORE THAN BEER

October 16, 2014

I get lots of emails and facebook messages, and I read them all and respond to as many as possible. Lately, there has been a great interest in Hops and bitters.

With the unlikely name *Humulus lupulus*, the common hop grows throughout Missouri, with the exception of the bootheel. Hops are the fruit of the plant, and are commonly used in making beer, but were popular in baked products prior to the advent of yeast. Easy to grow, the strobilies (flower clusters) are usually picked in the fall. Only the female plant produces the flower used for medicines and brewing. Male and female flowers grow on different plants, with the male plant only useful for pollination. Attractive to butterflies, flowers of the common hop give off a pine-like scent. Golden colored *Lupulin* gives the bitter flavor considered to be an acquired taste in beer, and hop acids also act as a preservative, and strongly inhibit the growth of several types of bacteria.

Lupulin is the main active ingredient in the common hop, It is contained in the grainy powder on the see-through flower parts. It is regarded as a cure for anxiety and insomnia, and there are reports of hop-pickers falling asleep in the fields. Hops have also been studied in the treatment of ADHD, although their use is not recommended in children. Hop flowers also contain phyto-estrogens that are similar to estrogen, and can be used to treat cramps and uterine disorders. Other uses include anti-tumor properties, and treatment of tuberculosis and bladder infections.

Anxiety and Sleep

Hops have been approved by the German equivalent of the FDA in the treatment of anxiety, restlessness, and insomnia. Hop oil contains several compounds that produce a central sedative effect. A 2013 study compared hop extract favorably with Ambien for the treatment of primary insomnia.

A 2012 study with nurses working rotating or night shifts found a significant increase in sleep quality after the nurses drank non-alcoholic beer with supper (which still contains hops), as compared to the control group who did not consume any beer.

Other studies found that non-alcoholic beer decreased nocturnal activity, i.e. tossing and turning, further improving the quality of sleep.

Anti-inflammatory

Multiple studies have documented the effects of hop extract on inflammation. The anti-inflammatory effect seems to target the affected area, with no systemic affects as seen with traditional anti-inflammatory drugs.

One 2012 study looked at hop water extract in treating allergic rhinitis, nasal inflammation due to allergies, and found it to have "potent preventative properties."

A 2006 study found that hop extract worked like a Cox-2 selective inhibitor (example: Celebrex) in decreasing the inflammatory pain of arthritis.

Anti-Tumor

Hops may help fight cancer. A 2012 study showed the anti-tumor effect of hops on human liver cancer cells, keeping them from replicating. A compound called *linolool* found in hops works with chemotherapeutic agents to increase their effects while reducing adverse effects. In a review of 50 current research studies, hops seem to exert the best anti-cancer effects against liver and colon cancer. With breast cancer, results are mixed, and seem to be dose dependent. The estrogen-like activity of hops may help explain their lack of potential in treating breast cancer, as many breast cancers feed off estrogen.

Anti-infection and Anti-viral

A 2005 study showed that xanthohumol and other chemicals found in hops protect against bacteria, funguses, viruses, and malarial protozoa. Hops inhibit the growth of staphylococcus aureus and streptococcus mutans, Antiviral activity has been shown against the Epstein-Barr virus, cytalomegalovirus, herpes simplex type 1 and 2 and HIV-1.

Menopause symptoms

Hops contain estrogen-like chemicals that help with discomforts associated with menopause. A daily intake of hop extract has a positive effect on hot flashes and other symptoms associated with menopause.

Acne

Hops contain seven naturally derived components effective against the bacteria that cause severe acne – acne vulgaris. An added benefit is the anti-oxidant effect that protects the skin, and keeps it from scarring. Several popular brands now include hops in their anti-acne creams and lotions.

Bitters

Hops are very bitter, to the extent that hop extract is named "bitters." We have a bitter receptor on our tongue, and there is a reason for that. Bitter foods trigger the gallbladder and liver to release bile, helping to digest our food, and keeping it flowing smoothly along the digestive tract. When our biliary system doesn't work correctly, we can have indigestion, gas problems, acid reflux, and poor nutrient absorption. Unfortunately, most diets today pretty much exclude bitter foods and drink. Bitters were first formulated by a 16th century physician named Paracelsus who used them for a variety of illnesses. You can easily make your own! 15 – 30 drops of bitter before eating is helpful for digestive problems.

Take 2 parts of hop flowers, 1 part burdock root or other bitter herb, 1 part peppermint and put the crushed dried herbs in a mason jar. Fill jar with enough apple cider vinegar to cover the herbs, cap with a tight lid, and let the herbs steep for about 4 weeks, shaking the jar at least every couple of days. After about a month, strain the solution and store in a dark glass container. No refrigeration needed.

You can also make Hop Tea by steeping one to two teaspoons of hop flowers in a cup of boiled water for 5-10 minutes.

94 ALL ABOUT THE GRAPE

October 23, 2014

I often think that here in the Ozarks we are living in the middle of a modern day Mesopotamia. Like the ancient ground, we also live in a "Land of Rivers," giving us very fertile ground (albeit a bit rocky). My theory can be backed up by the fact that there are at least 7 species of wild grapes in Missouri.

Our native wild grapes are smaller than the cultivated variety, and are all highly edible. Wild grapes are sweeter as the growing season progresses, and are harvested between September and November. The leaves of the grape plant are also edible, and prominently featured in Mediterranean diets. The popular Greek dish *dolmades* is made with grape leaves.

Watch out for moonseed that can mimic a grape. Moonseed has one seed contained within the fruit that looks like a crescent moon – it may be poisonous, so beware. The seeds of the wild grape are round or look like a tear drop.

Many cultivated varieties of grape have been developed to remove the seeds. This is unfortunate, because several medicinal qualities of grape come from the seed itself. The berry of the wild grape contains over 10 healthful compounds, one of which is Melatonin, a chemical that helps maintain sleep/wake cycles and is currently being studied for its role in maintaining blood vessel integrity in Ebola patients. Another is Resveratrol.

While different grapes vary in their nutrient content, the darker grapes contain more nutrients. On average, per 3.5 ounces of grapes, you get the following: Protein 5 gm, 76 Calories, Potassium 167 mg, Magnesium 7 mg, Vit. C 6 mg, Fiber 3 gm, and Resveratrol 1170 mcg. 1 cup of raw grape leaves provides 13 calories, supplies 77% of the daily Vitamin A requirement, plus small amounts of Vit. C, Iron and Calcium along with 120 mg of Omega-3 fatty acids.

Anti-Aging

Resveratrol is found in the skin and seed of wild grapes, and is the "antibiotic" that some plants make when they're under attack. Whether it's disease or fungus, resveratrol helps the plant fight it. A study from Harvard University documented the efficacy of resveratrol as an anti-aging agent. Resveratrol stimulated production of SIRT1 in the body, a serum that speeds up the energy production centers in the mitochondria of our cells, helping not only to block diseases, but to delay the effects of aging. Resveratrol also encourages the expression of 3 separate genes related to longevity.

Blood sugar control

Grapes are a low glycemic index food, with an index ranging between 43 and 53. Compare that with watermelon that has a glycemic index in the range of 70-75, and grapes are a much better choice for diabetic patients.

Heart Health

Grapes are a super-food when it comes to the heart. Grapes are associated with normalization of high blood pressure, improvement in cholesterol levels, stabilization of blood vessel walls, decreased inflammation (Grapes block Cox-1 and Cox-2 inflammatory enzymes), and increased blood levels of glutathione, one of the most important anti-oxidants in the body.

Cognitive effects

Grape extract prevents the accumulation of beta-amyloid protein in the brain (the main component of the plaque found in the brains of Alzheimer's patients), and also decreases inflammation. We are all aware of the adverse effects aluminum can have on our cognitive functioning. Aluminum can be absorbed through deodorants, cookware, or even in the general environment. In a March, 2014 study published in Neurotoxicology, the researchers found that grape extract provided protection to the brain when exposed to aluminum, and further, grape extract was associated with "significant improvement in the short-term memory, cognition, anxiety, locomotion and muscular activity." An interesting, but unexpected finding was that exposure to aluminum increased serum glucose levels.

Dolmades

12 grape leaves, washed and soaked in water overnight.
1 lb. Ground round, lightly browned.
Salt and pepper to taste
1 Tbs. minced fresh parsley
½ cup raw rice or tabouli mix
1 small onion finely chopped
1 garlic clove, finely chopped.
20 oz. Chicken broth
2 lemons
2 eggs

Rinse and dry the grape leaves. In a large bowl, mix the ground beef, seasonings, onion, garlic and rice. Lay each grape leaf with the stem up, and put 1 Tbs. of the mixture near the stem. Fold stem up over the meat mixture, then fold one side over meat, then the top, and then the other side of the leaf. You can secure your stuffed grape leaf with a toothpick if necessary. Place the stuffed leaves in a 1 gallon pot. Cover with chicken broth, then bring to boil for 2 minutes. Turn heat down and simmer for about 30 minutes. Remove about 2 cups of the broth, and let it cool for 5-10 minutes, Beat the eggs until frothy, and add fresh lemon juice. Gradually add in the warm broth while continuing to beat the eggs. Once fully mixed, add the broth/egg mixture to the pot on the stove. Cover pot and turn heat off, let stand 10 minutes before serving.

95 SMARTWEED – PUT SOME PEPPER IN YOUR LIFE

October 30, 2014

Common in Missouri, Smartweed, a member of the buckwheat family, is found in moist areas and along pond dams. Unlike buckwheat, you would never use it to make flour, but it is great for adding a little spice to your meal at deer camp, and can be used fresh or dried as a pepper replacement. It has been used in food flavoring since prehistoric times, and anecdotal reports say the white flowering plants have the best flavor. An annual plant, it can grow to 3 feet tall. It flowers between July and September, with blossoms on spikes at the end of the stems, beginning green, then turning white or pink in color as they mature.

Although considered a weed to some, Smartweed is beneficial to habitat and as a food source for aquatic waterfowl, songbirds, quail, doves, and small mammals. Smartweed acts to hold soil and purify the water on lake and pond dams. Submerged portions of the plant provide habitat for tiny invertebrates that are a food source for fish, amphibians and reptiles, and the seeds are heavily consumed by birds and small mammals.

Likely named Smartweed not because it makes you more intelligent, but because your mouth will smart if you take too big a bite, Smartweed has been compared to a jalapeno pepper. It has also been used as an inexpensive replacement for wasabi in Japanese cooking. The leaves, stems and seeds are edible, raw or cooked. The leaves contain 7.5% protein, 1.9% fat, 8% carbohydrate, and also contain the active ingredient *rutin*. The raw seeds are used as a pepper substitute, and sprouted seeds are used as a garnish on salads – popular in Japan.

There are several species of Smartweed in Missouri, but *Polygonum hydropiper* (mild water pepper) has a long history of medicinal uses, thanks to the Native Americans and current research. Smart weed is mentioned frequently in folk lore, and placing the plant on the floor of a room was said to rid it of fleas. There are reports of cholera victims being wrapped in sheets soaked in water in which Smartweed was boiled. With an effect similar to capsaicin, Smartweed has also been added to bath water to help with arthritis pain.

Smartweed is used mostly for its astringent properties. It is useful in treating bleeding, skin problems, hemorrhoids and diarrhea. It contains several active compounds - Rutin helps to strengthen fragile capillaries. A poultice made from the plant can be used to treat swollen and inflamed areas. Other beneficial effects of Rutin include decreasing platelet clumping and decreasing capillary permeability, making the blood thinner - improving circulation and preventing blood clots, helping to prevent heart attack and stroke. Rutin is also an antioxidant.

Smartweed also contains a chemical known as *emodin* that is effective in regulating bowel motility. A 2012 study looking at the anti-inflammatory properties of Smartweed extract found that it decreased inflammation via several pathways and concluded that Smartweed has a "major ethno-pharmacological role as an anti-gastritis remedy." Emodin is also being studied as a potential agent that could reduce the impact of Type 2 diabetes by limiting the effects of glucocorticoids and improving insulin resistance. Pharmacological studies have demonstrated that emodin exhibits anti-cancer effects on several human cancers, including human pancreatic cancer. In a 2013 study, Smartweed showed cytotoxicity against human mammary carcinoma, human colon carcinoma, human hepatocellular carcinoma, human prostate carcinoma and human erythroleukaemia cells.

Emodin found in Smartweed is also shown to block cytomegalovirus infections as well as herpes simplex. Research is currently being performed in this area

Precautions

A 1972 study in Reproduction Journal showed that extract from Smartweed impaired fertility in animal studies, preventing implantation of the embryo through changes in the lining of the uterus. In some areas in India, Smartweed is used extensively as a contraceptive agent.

Smartweed is plentiful in Missouri, found in moist areas and along pond dams.

96 MICROWAVE OVENS

November 6, 2014

As an early adopter of technology, I used to be a big fan of microwave ovens. I first became concerned in the late 1980's when I was pregnant. I was standing next to the microwave in the nurses' lounge, warming up my lunch, when I felt a strangle tingle in my abdomen and some violent fetal movement. I quickly moved away from the microwave, and although I have since used them, I became accustomed to quickly leaving the room after pushing the start button.

When my 10 year old microwave died a natural death a few years ago, I decided not to replace it. It was a little scary, but being of a certain age, I knew it was indeed possible to live without it, and my mind went back 40 years, remembering how my mother cooked, warmed up leftovers, and popped popcorn without a device in her kitchen that used microwave radiation.

Suspicion and rumors abound in regard to microwaves. Some true, and some are just urban legends. The valid facts concern effects on some areas of health, and also effects on nutrient value of foods. Microwaves are part of the electromagnetic spectrum, and emit radiation ranging in frequency from 300 million cycles per second (300 MHz) to 300 billion cycles per second (300 GHz), which correspond to a wavelength range of 1 m down to 1 mm. This non-ionizing electromagnetic radiation is absorbed at the molecular level and manifests as changes in vibrational energy of the molecules which creates heat. If the microwave is well-shielded, this should hypothetically not create a problem, unless there is damage with the door hinges, latch or seals allowing the microwave oven to leak. Leakage happens often, and the FDA web site has the following warning "don't stand directly against an oven (and don't allow children to do this) for long periods of time while it is operating."

Microwave Ovens and Cataracts

The lens of the eye is particularly sensitive to intense heat, and exposure to high levels of microwave radiation can cause cataracts. Microwaves have repeatedly been shown to cause lens opacity in experimental animals exposed to microwave radiation for single or repeated exposures. There have also been reports of microwave-induced cataracts in humans. Microwaves are so efficient at inducing cataracts that they are used to create cataracts in pig eyes for cataract training purposes.

Effects on Male Fertility

Likewise, the testes are very sensitive to changes in temperature. Accidental exposure to high levels of microwave energy can alter or kill sperm, producing temporary sterility. A 2014 animal study found that microwave radiation induced a significant decrease in sperm count and sperm viability along with the decrease in seminiferous tubule diameter and degeneration of seminiferous tubules. There was also a decrease in plasma testosterone levels. As there are multiple sources of microwave radiation in the environment that may be unavoidable (like cell phones and wi-fi), it makes sense to limit an extra source via microwave in our home.

Oral cancers

Cancer can be considered an outcome of the interaction between genetic factors and environmental exposures. We can't change our genes, but we can modify our environment. Microwave cooking has been found to increase the risk of oral cancer, including salivary gland tumors, because of the formation of heterocyclic amines formed with microwave radiation of food. Heterocyclic amines are potent mutagenic and carcinogenic compounds formed during heat processing of foods high in protein, like fish, beef and poultry.

Migration of toxic chemicals into foods

A just published 2014 study looked at migration of chemicals from tableware into foods during the microwave process. This study looked at melamine dishes. In case you didn't know, melamine contains large amount of formaldehyde. Heating food for just 1-2 minutes allows a significant transfer of formaldehyde from melamine cookware into food. Volatile compounds released from plastics, such as Styrofoam, can also migrate into food. Another method of potentially hazardous migration includes absorption of potentially toxic chemicals from the non-stick inner coating of the microwave popcorn bag.

Sterilization

There has recently been promotion of the use of a microwave to sterilize your kitchen sponge. The problem with this, other than unnecessary use of radiation, is the fact that in order to fully disinfect a sponge, it would have to be heated in the microwave so long that the sponge material itself would deteriorate. Thanks to the scientists that study these things, we know that soaking a sponge in white vinegar is a very effective, inexpensive sterilization method. Soaking toothbrushes overnight in vinegar also kills bacteria commonly found on them.

Living Without a Microwave

Yes, there is life after getting rid of your microwave oven! For quick warm-ups, a toaster oven is ideal, and a whole dinner with a variety of leftovers can easily be warmed up in a cake pan. I purchased a whirly-top type popcorn maker, and have perfect, fresh popcorn in about 2 minutes on the stove top. Many things, like mashed potatoes, can be warmed in a sauce dish on the stove top, with a few drops of water or milk added. The best way to retain nutrients is through steaming. As we have gotten out of the habit of the instant cooking offered by a microwave oven, we are now doing more outdoor cooking, on an open flame in a fire pit, and working on building an outdoor wood oven.

97 SPEARMINT (MENTHA SPICATA)

Part 1

November 13, 2014

Spearmint is a plant native to Europe and Asia that thrives well in North America, and has become an invasive species in the Great Lakes region. It gets its name from the leaf tips that resemble spears. I consider it an indoor/outdoor plant here in the Ozarks, because it grows like crazy outdoors in the summer, and continues to provide aromatic leaves when I bring it into the house during the winter months. It is an incredibly hardy perennial, and is a natural air freshener in any room in which it is kept.

Spearmint is valuable for its oil, produced from the leaves which can be used whole or chopped, fresh, dried, or frozen. Ground spearmint imparts a fresh flavor to toothpaste, and also helps prevent cavities. Spearmint sprays have been used to control pests and can be added to cleaning agents for disinfection. In aromatherapy, spearmint is known for its ability to relieve anxiety and lift mood, and it acts as a mild stimulant. It can also bring on a sweat and break a fever

Medicinal Properties

Hirsutism

Spearmint belongs to a group of drugs called anti-androgens. Reducing the activity of androgen hormones in the body is helpful in polycystic ovarian syndrome, acne, enlarged prostate and cancer of the prostate and hirsutism (excessive and unwanted hair growth).

In one study of 21 hirsute women, 12 with polycystic ovarian syndrome, and 9 with idiopathic (no known cause) hirsutism, the subjects drank a cup of tea steeped in spearmint twice a day for 5 days prior to ovulation. There was a significant decrease in free testosterone and increase in luteinizing hormone, follicle stimulating hormone and estrogen, hormonal corrections that can reverse excessive hair growth in women.

Osteoarthritis

A double-blind study published in July, 2014 looked at the effect of spearmint tea on persons with medically diagnosed osteoarthritis of the knee. 62 participants were followed, with pain, quality of life, and physical function scores assessed at baseline and week 16. Scores for stiffness and physical disability significantly decreased from week 0 to 16. Knee pain was relieved in a dose-dependent manner (tea with the highest concentration of spearmint provided the greatest pain relief.)

Seizures

A 2103 study looked at the effect of pre-treatment with spearmint essential oils on the frequency and severity of seizures induced in mice with a chemical agent. All groups of mice treated with the spearmint oil showed reduced activity and stability after the administration of the oil, and reduced severity of seizures (ranging from simple twitches to complete seizures).
There is also anecdotal evidence that spearmint tea can reduce the incidence of non-epileptic seizures, those not associated with abnormal electrical activity in the brain.

Antimicrobial

Another study looked at the effect of essential oil of spearmint on the proliferation of Helicobacter pylori, Salmonella enteritidis, Escherichia coli, and Staphylococcus aureus, both methicillin sensitive and methicillin resistant. The essential oils inhibited the proliferation of each strain in liquid culture in a dose-dependent manner and also exhibited bactericidal activity. The researchers concluded that spearmint oil may be useful as an antibacterial agent for stopping the growth of several types of pathogens. Its antimicrobial and whitening effect makes it a popular additive to toothpaste.

Next week we will discuss how to process Spearmint, and other valuable health properties, including its role in memory.

98 SPEARMINT

Part 2

November 20, 2014

Last week we looked at some of the well-documented medicinal properties of spearmint. There is a flurry of new medical research looking into more applications for this herb and its effect on memory, mood, and even addictive behavior.

Substance Abuse

The use of herbs in the treatment of substance abuse is a relatively new phenomenon. Spearmint has been used in the treatment of recovering addicts, specifically helping with cravings.

Memory

It is unclear if chewing spearmint-flavored gum improves memory; evidence is mixed. One study with spearmint chewing gum during a learning exercise showed no change, but a follow-up study showed it was beneficial. I don't believe in gum containing artificial sweeteners (and all of them do, except Fruit Stripe), as they usually contain the toxic aspartame, but I wrap a spearmint leaf in a stick of Fruit-Stripe gum, and chew it that way when I need a little mental boost.

In 2013 Prof. Susan Farr, from Saint Louis University School of Medicine in Missouri, presented her early findings regarding the effect of Spearmint on memory at the Neuroscience 2013 conference. Using new antioxidant-based extracts made from spearmint, Prof. Farr tested the effects on mice with age-associated cognitive decline. When evaluating memory and learning in 3 tested behaviors, spearmint extract compound improved memory in two of the behavioral tests. She also found that spearmint reduced oxidative stress in the part of the mice brain that controls learning and memory. Rosemary showed similar benefits.

Spearmint was used in a recent study looking at potential decline in the olfactory sense (smell) as we age. Functional MRI was used – a form of MRI that lights up when different areas of the brain are activated. After sniffing spearmint, both young and old subjects showed significant activation in major olfactory brain structures, including the primary olfactory cortex, entorhinal cortex, hippocampus and parahippocampal cortex, thalamus, hypothalamus, orbitofrontal cortex, and insular cortex and its extension into the inferior lateral frontal region, although the older persons had lower activation volume and intensity. The conclusion can be drawn that smelling spearmint puts your brain through a pretty good workout!

Irritable bowel

Spearmint can be helpful for digestive issues and to calm the stomach. These properties, and also its tooth whitening ingredients, have ensured the continued manufacture of spearmint gum.

The herbal remedy Carmint (made from spearmint, lemon balm, and coriander extracts) plus loperamide or psyllium depending on the type of IBS, has shown promise as a treatment for irritable bowel syndrome with abdominal pain and bloating. Additional studies testing spearmint alone have also been conducted. To treat a stomach ache, it is suggested to drink mint tea, prepared by adding one tablespoon of fresh mint leaves to hot water. Spearmint tea has not been shown to be effective in the treatment of GERD (gastrointestinal reflux disease).

Precautions

Spearmint appears to be safe in healthy individuals when consumed in amounts normally found in food or beverages. Based on available research, it appears that spearmint is well tolerated in recommended doses up to 500 milligrams daily or taken as a tea twice daily for 30 days. In rare cases, spearmint may cause an allergic response.

Traditionally, spearmint tea is often recommended to relieve nausea and morning sickness in pregnant women. Due to the hormonal effects, it should be used sparingly for this purpose.

Preparation of Spearmint

Spearmint leaves can be used dry or fresh. There has been a great deal of research on the best processing method to preserve the active ingredients in spearmint leaves. Oven-drying at 113 °F and air-drying at room air were the methods that produced the best results. An increase in monoterpenes was observed in all of the dried samples. Freeze-drying results in substantial losses of active ingredients. From a sensory standpoint, drying the leaves brings about an increase in minty odor.

To treat dandruff, it is suggested to mix a sprig of spearmint and rosemary in eight ounces of cider vinegar, let it sit for one week, and then apply to the scalp after shampooing.

99 UNWRAP THE BENEFITS OF CRANBERRIES

November 27, 2013

Cranberries (Vaccinium macrocarpon) are native to North America, and found at higher altitudes in the Eastern US, as far south as North Carolina. They are distinct from every other fruit, as they are rich in A-type proanthocyanidins (PACs), unlike any other berry. PACs possess antimicrobial, anti-adhesion, antioxidant, and anti-inflammatory properties. Their unique composition makes them the single best fruit for urinary health, and their effect on heart health is becoming increasingly evident. Cranberries usually are not eaten fresh, mainly due to their tartness, but once you taste a fresh cranberry salsa (recipe below), you won't look at canned cranberries in the same way.

Nutritional Content

A very low calorie food, cranberries have only 51 calories per cup and provide 20% of the daily fiber requirement. Rich in Vitamin C, one cup provides 24% of the RDA. Naturally cholesterol-free, cranberries are also a good source of vitamins A, E, and manganese.

Medicinal Uses

Urinary Tract Infections

Urinary tract infections (UTI's) are common in women of all ages, and in young children, especially girls. In a randomized, double-blind study of women in a nursing home; patients drank 10 ounces of artificially sweetened cranberry juice daily for 6 months. After one month, the presence of bacteria in the urine was significantly lowered for the patients drinking the juice.

In another case report, a 66 year old woman with chronic pyelonephritis not responding to antibiotics was treated with 6 ounces of cranberry juice twice a daily. Her infection was almost completely cleared after 9 months, and she didn't need treatment again for 2.5 years.

In addition to killing bacteria, the A-type PACs keep E-coli bacteria from sticking to the walls of the urinary tract, washing them out of the body with urination. (E-coli is the most common organism causing urinary tract infection.)

Elevated cholesterol

There is strong experimental evidence that cranberries have favorable effects on blood pressure, glucose metabolism, lipoprotein profiles, oxidative stress, inflammation, and endothelial (blood vessel lining) function.

Animal and human studies suggest that consumption of cranberries lowers LDL (bad) cholesterol and increases HDL (good) cholesterol. Favorable effects of cranberry juice on blood lipids have also been demonstrated in other populations, including in obese men, patients with diabetes, and patients with elevated triglycerides.

Oral Health

The role of cranberries in treating gum disease is coming to light in the past 2 years. Once again, the PACs bountiful in cranberries are shown to be effective in the prevention and management of periodontitis, an inflammatory bacterial disease that affects the tissues that support the teeth.

Possible mechanisms of action of cranberry PACs include the inhibition of bacteria and enzymes that break down tissues in the mouth. Cranberry also has an anti-inflammatory effect on gum tissue. Cranberry components are potential anti-cavity agents since they inhibit acid production and attachment with biofilm formation by Streptococcus mutans, the bacteria that causes cavities.

As in protection of the urinary tract, the "non-sticking" qualities of cranberry extract also keeps bacteria from lodging on the teeth long enough to cause cavities. Components of cranberries reduce tumor necrosis factor, and also increase phagocytosis (gobbling up and getting rid of) P. gingivalis in the mouth.

Eye Health

There are early reports that cranberries significantly improve symptoms of cataract, macular degeneration and diabetic retinopathy. Getting back to the unique property of "non-stickiness" that cranberries possess, they are also being used in contact lens solution to prevent a bacterial biofilm from forming on contact lenses. Once again, cranberries make bacterial slide right off.

Cranberry Salsa

1 bag cranberries
1 cup sugar
1 cup orange juice

In sauce pan, boil above ingredients gently for about 10 minutes until you hear cranberries "pop." Add chopped green onions and/or chopped cilantro to taste. Great served with tortilla chips or as a side dish.

100 VERTIGO – CORRECT IT AT HOME

December 4, 2014

About two weeks ago, a reader contacted me on Facebook. She was having horrible bouts of dizziness with nausea, and was having trouble even sitting up. In neurology, a common complaint we see in the office is positional vertigo. People with vertigo feel as though they are actually spinning or moving, or that the room is spinning around them. Vertigo can be peripheral or central. Peripheral vertigo is the most common cause of dizziness, and is due to a problem in the part of the inner ear that controls balance. Think of the inner ear like a gyroscope. Inner ear structures, the vestibular labyrinth or semicircular canals, help us maintain our sense of position. Vertigo can also be central, due to a problem with the brain or systemic causes, such as multiple sclerosis, migraine, stroke or tumors.

Benign paroxysmal positional vertigo (BPPV) is a very common cause of peripheral vertigo, and is characterized by brief recurrent episodes of dizziness triggered by changes in position, such as rolling over in bed, and is worse when turning to the affected ear. BPPV is believed to be due to displaced otoconia, small calcium particles that are usually attached to a membrane in the ear. Due to trauma to the ear, infection, aging (average age 49 years), or for no known cause, the otoliths can break loose and collect in any of the semicircular canals of the ear. Movement of the head causes these otoliths to inappropriately trigger the receptors in the semicircular canals and send false signals to the brain, causing vertigo.

Symptoms of BPPV usually resolve spontaneously within 1–2 weeks, but may persist for up to several months. Forty-four percent of BPPV patients experience a single episode of dizziness while 56% are recurrent. Attacks tend to occur in clusters and symptoms may recur, following periods of apparent remission. The main symptom is a sensation that you or the room is moving or spinning. The spinning sensation may cause nausea and vomiting. Other symptoms can include dizziness, hearing loss in the affected ear, loss of balance, and ringing in the ears. Although rare, it is possible to have BPPV in both ears

In the doctor's office, BPPV can be diagnosed with a bedside test called the Dix-Hallpike maneuver. To help resolve your symptoms, your health care provider may then perform the Epley maneuver in order to clear the particles from the canal of the affected ear (see below). Repeated physical maneuvers during a single treatment session seem to be clinically superior to a single maneuver. Patients who fail to respond to a single treatment session or with frequent recurrences of BPPV are often sent home with instructions to perform a "self-treatment" maneuver.

Precautions:

Although the Epley maneuver can be safely performed at home, the cause of any brain disorder causing vertigo should be identified and treated by a licensed neurologist as there could be significant pathology of the cerebellum or brainstem.

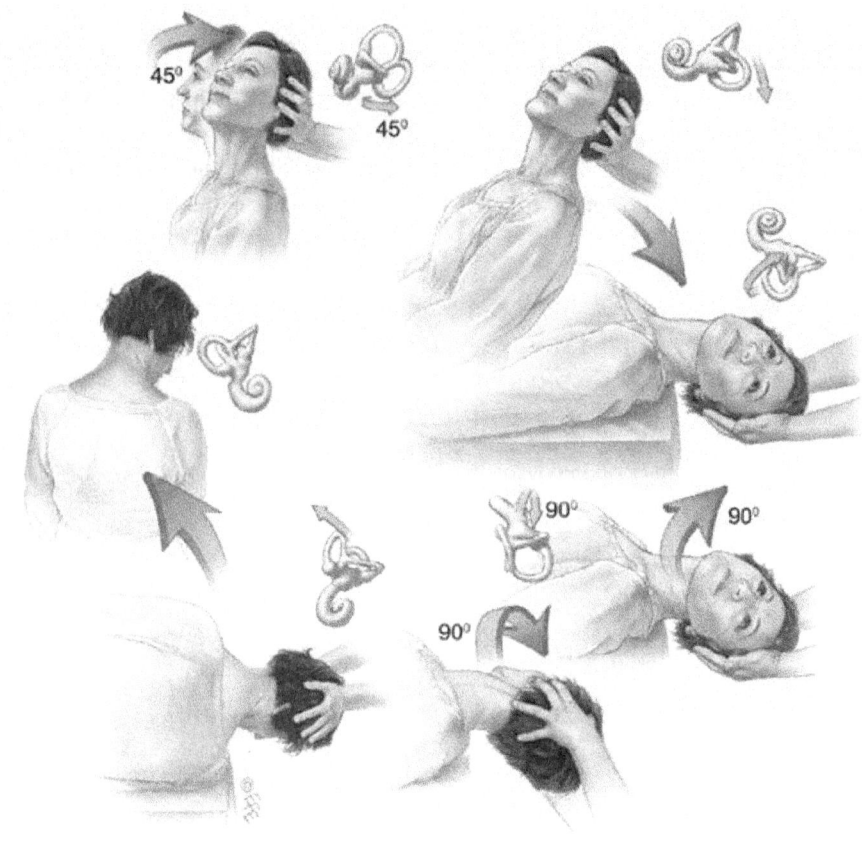

The Epley Maneuver. Courtesy of Australian Family Physician. January/February 2013

1. Sit upright in bed. Rotate your head horizontally approx. 45 degrees toward the ear causing your symptoms. Hold the position for one minute.
2. Keeping your head and neck at a 45 degree angle and gently lie down on your back. Maintain this position for one minute. You may feel briefly dizzy, which is normal.
3. While still laying flat on your back slowly rotate your head towards your good ear as far as possible or approximately

90 degrees. Maintain this position for one minute. This position may again provoke either transient dizziness or vertigo.

4. With your head still rotated towards your good ear slowly roll your entire body on to your "good side". Keep your head and neck fixed as much as possible. If done properly you should be able to stare down at the floor. Maintain this position for one minute.

5. To complete the Epley maneuver return to a sitting position with your head up but flexed forward approximately 45 degrees. Maintain this position for one minute.

6. Three complete cycles should be performed prior to going to bed.

ABOUT THE AUTHOR

Marie Lasater is a Masters prepared Registered Nurse with certifications in both Neuroscience and Critical Care. Throughout her career, she has been interested in holistic healing, and natural approaches to patient care. She has dozens of peer-reviewed articles in medical journals.

www.ingramcontent.com/pod-product-compliance
Lightning Source LLC
Chambersburg PA
CBHW060448290526
45791CB00001B/22